D1548702

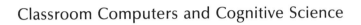

Classroom Computers and Cognitive Science

THE EDUCATIONAL TECHNOLOGY SERIES

Edited by

Harold F. O'Neil, Jr.

U.S. Army Research Institute for
the Behavioral and Social Sciences
Alexandria, Virginia

Harold F. O'Neil, Jr. (Ed.) Learning Strategies

Harold F. O'Neil, Jr. (Ed.) Issues in Instructional Systems Development

Harold F. O'Neil, Jr. (Ed.) Procedures for Instructional Systems
Development

Harold F. O'Neil, Jr. and Charles D. Spielberger (Eds.) Cognitive and
Affective Learning Strategies

Jane Close Conoley (Ed.) Consultation in Schools: Theory, Research,
Procedures

Harold F. O'Neil, Jr. (Ed.) Computer-Based Instruction:
A State-of-the-Art Assessment

Gary D. Borich and Ron P. Jemelka. Programs and Systems:
An Evaluation Perspective

Gale H. Roid and Thomas M. Haladyna. A Technology for
Test-Item Writing

Robert S. Logan. Instructional Systems Development: An International
View of Theory and Practice

Alex Cherry Wilkinson (Ed.) Classroom Computers and
Cognitive Science

Classroom Computers and Cognitive Science

Edited by

ALEX CHERRY WILKINSON

Department of Psychology
University of Wisconsin
Madison, Wisconsin

1983

ACADEMIC PRESS
A Subsidiary of Harcourt Brace Jovanovich, Publishers
New York   London
Paris   San Diego   San Francisco   São Paulo   Sydney   Tokyo   Toronto

This book is based upon work supported by the National Institute of Education under Grant No. NIE–G–81–0009. Any opinions, findings, and conclusions or recommendations expressed in this publication are those of the authors and do not necessarily reflect the views of the Institute or the Department of Education.

ACADEMIC PRESS, INC.
111 Fifth Avenue, New York, New York 10003

United Kingdom Edition published by
ACADEMIC PRESS, INC. (LONDON) LTD.
24/28 Oval Road, London NW1 7DX

Library of Congress Cataloging in Publication Data

Main entry under title:

Classroom computers and cognitive science.

(Educational technology series)
Includes bibliographical references and index.
1. Computer-assisted instruction--Congresses.
2. Individualized instruction--Congresses.
I. Wilkinson, Alex Cherry. II. Series.
LB1028.5.C525 1983   370'.28'5   83-8741
ISBN 0-12-752070-8

PRINTED IN THE UNITED STATES OF AMERICA

83 84 85 86   9 8 7 6 5 4 3 2 1

Contents

84-3505

7. Teaching Vocabulary-Building Skills: A Contextual Approach
Robert J. Sternberg, Janet S. Powell, and Daniel B. Kaye

8. Reading, Vocabulary, and Writing: Implications for Computer-Based Instruction
Charles A. Perfetti

III. COURSEWARE FOR CLASSROOMS   165

9. A Rationale for Computer-Based Reading Instruction
Alan M. Lesgold

Contributors

Numbers in parentheses indicate the pages on which the authors' contributions begin.

Marianne Amarel[1] (15), Educational Testing Service, Princeton, New Jersey 08540

Marcia J. Boruta (219), Laboratory of Comparative Human Cognition, University of California, San Diego, La Jolla, California 92093

Robin S. Chapman (95), Department of Communicative Disorders, University of Wisconsin, Madison, Wisconsin 53706

Christine Dollaghan (95), Department of Communication Sciences and Disorders, University of Montana, Missoula, Montana 59812

T. R. G. Green (71), MRC/SSRC Social and Applied Psychology Unit, University of Sheffield, Sheffield, S10 2TN England

Daniel B. Kaye[2] (121), Department of Psychology, University of California, Los Angeles, Los Angeles, California 90024

O. T. Kenworthy (95), Department of Communicative Disorders, University of Wisconsin, Madison, Wisconsin 53706

Jill H. Larkin (53), Psychology Department, Carnegie–Mellon University, Pittsburgh, Pennsylvania 15213

Alan M. Lesgold (167), Learning Research and Development Center, University of Pittsburgh, Pittsburgh, Pennsylvania 15260

[1]Present address: School of Education, Stanford University, Stanford, California 94305.
[2]Present address: Psychology Department, Yale University, New Haven, Connecticut 06520.

James A. Levin (219), Laboratory of Comparative Human Cognition, University of California, San Diego, La Jolla, California 92093

Jon F. Miller (95), Department of Communicative Disorders, University of Wisconsin, Madison, Wisconsin 53706

Janice Patterson (3), Wisconsin Center for Education Research, University of Wisconsin, Madison, Wisconsin 53706

Charles A. Perfetti (145), Learning Research and Development Center, University of Pittsburgh, Pittsburgh, Pennsylvania 15260

Janet S. Powell (121), Psychology Department, Yale University, New Haven, Connecticut 06520

Andee Rubin (201), Bolt Beranek and Newman Inc., Cambridge, Massachusetts 02238

Robert J. Sternberg (121), Psychology Department, Yale University, New Haven, Connecticut 06520

Mary T. Vasconcellos (219), Laboratory of Comparative Human Cognition, University of California, San Diego, La Jolla, California 92093

Richard L. Venezky (31), Educational Studies, University of Delaware, Newark, Delaware 19711

Alex Cherry Wilkinson (3, 183), Psychology Department, University of Wisconsin, Madison, Wisconsin 53706

Preface

The classroom computer will come of age in the 1980s. There will be more computers in a greater variety of size and sophistication and more diverse courseware than even the most optimistic proponents of computerized instruction might have predicted a decade earlier. Recognizing this development, the Wisconsin Center for Education Research, under the auspices of its primary funding agency, the National Institute of Education, commissioned an interdisciplinary volume on prospects for classroom computers. Work on the volume began in November 1981 at a conference attended by an invited group of cognitive scientists that included educators, computer scientists, psychologists, and linguists. This book is the culmination of that work.

This book is intended for educational researchers, cognitive scientists, and those who develop courseware for classroom computers. Accordingly, the book has three major parts. Part I introduces the book as a whole; topics include a discussion of the history of computerized instruction, the methods of evaluating computer courseware, and analyses of the role of the computer in the social milieu of the classroom. Part II presents perspectives from cognitive science. It contains scholarly analyses of how a computer may represent a student's knowledge of scientific concepts, of language and vocabulary, and of reading and writing. Part III deals with courseware for classrooms. In this concluding part, the authors discuss how computer courseware can be designed so as to incorporate principles from cognitive science; examples of existing programs and actual classroom activities are included. To aid the reader in integrating the interdisciplinary topics of the book, each of the three parts begins with a brief overview that describes the chapters in the part and explains the connecting theme.

Many people contributed time, work, and ideas to the book, although their names do not appear as authors of any chapter. Ramsay Selden, Larry Frase, Joel Levin, Pat Dickson, and Marshall Smith all contributed ideas; John Wende, Chuck Bilow, Bob Cavey, Pat Klitzke, Karen Hauptly, Bob Cattoi, and Debbie Stewart generously provided technical assistance. Special thanks go to Lois Opalewski for her administrative assistance, and to Berland Meyer, DuWayne Kleinschmidt, and Robert Patton for revealing realistic problems and exciting accomplishments by using computers in their own classrooms.

PART I

Perspectives from Education

The chapters in this section place the computer squarely in the context of the classroom. First comes a chapter by Alex Cherry Wilkinson and Janice Patterson that serves a dual purpose. It provides an integrative overview of the book as a whole. At the same time, it defines issues at the meeting point of theory in cognitive science and educational practice in classrooms; the issues are ones that need attention if the gap between theory and practice is to be bridged effectively. The next chapter is by Marianne Amarel. It raises the important question of how the computer is to be integrated into the social fabric of the classroom. The sobering point is made that the social organization of the classroom is likely to be a potent determinant of the educational outcome of computer courseware, more potent in fact than the technical adequacy of the courseware itself. The final chapter in the section is by Richard Venezky. He discusses both the history of computerized instruction and attempts to evaluate its efficacy.

Two broad themes emerge from these chapters. The first theme is that computer courseware does not stand or fall on its own merits. Rather, its utility depends on the manner in which it is integrated into the classroom setting and harmonized with general instructional objectives. The second theme is that an important objective for educational technology is to develop courseware that is sufficiently compact to be used on small computers, yet sufficiently powerful to incorporate a sophisticated cognitive model of what students know and how they learn.

1

Issues at the Interface of Theory and Practice*

Alex Cherry Wilkinson
Janice Patterson

OVERVIEW

As computers become smaller, more powerful, and more readily available in schools, there are new sources of tension between practice and theory. First, there is no consensus on what the major goals of instructional computing ought to be. Indeed, the potential uses of computers in schools and classrooms are so numerous that there is a pressing need for well-specified criteria to set priorities. Different choices are undoubtedly appropriate in different settings, but there is no unifying theory that captures the impor-

*Preparation of this chapter was supported by grant NIE-G-81-0009 from the National Institute of Education. Any opinions, findings, conclusions, and recommendations in the chapter are the authors' and do not necessarily reflect the views of the Institute or the Department of Education. Requests for reprinted should be sent to Alex Cherry Wilkinson, Psychology Department, University of Wisconsin, 1202 West Johnson Street, Madison, WI 53706.

tant criteria for making the choices. Second, considerable progress has been made recently in cognitive science—a field of study at the intersection of linguistics, artificial intelligence, and psychology—but the ideas and findings of this new field have been slow to find their way into the courseware actually available for use on classroom computers.

With the two problems come two vexing questions. How can a decision be made to use computer technology to serve a particular instructional goal when the rationale for differentiating among competing goals is vague? And how can instructional software be evaluated effectively when its likely effects on a student's learning have yet to be clearly articulated by cognitive science? These dilemmas are both likely to persist unresolved for some time. We do not propose to solve them here. Rather, the purpose of our chapter is to delineate each problem and thereby, we hope, to sharpen the insights of educators, researchers, and courseware developers who must somehow make their own peace with the troublesome questions.

Having no definitive answers to offer, we set our sights on a more modest goal. Our aim is to define certain critical issues that need resolution if the gap between theory in cognitive science and practice in instructional computing is to be narrowed. We discuss several issues that merit the attention of both educators and cognitive scientists. In discussing each issue, we explain why it lies at the interface of theory and practice, discuss how scientists and practitioners alike may benefit from giving the issue their careful consideration, and tell how the issue is examined in other chapters of this volume.

DEFINING COMPUTER LITERACY

It is becoming commonplace to assert that schools should make children of the information age computer-literate. The concept of computer literacy is vague, however. Consequently, the first decision confronting a school as it embarks on a program of computerized instruction is a question with cognitive implications. What kind of computer literacy do we want students to attain?

Definitions of computer literacy vary greatly. Some argue forcefully for teaching children, even very young ones, to program computers. The argument is that learning to program inspires logical reasoning and creativity. It is often summarized with the admonition that people should control computers, not be controlled by them. As Papert (1981, p. 89) explains it, "In teaching the computer how to think, children embark on an exploration about how they themselves think." Leuhrmann (1981), too, views the computer as a tool for teaching children how to think. He argues that with "hands-on" access to a computer, students learn new ways to analyze and solve problems. In this mode, the computer does not deliver instructions. Rather, according to Leuhrmann, it is a tool for children to use in experimenting with how to probe problems and seek solutions.

Others argue, with equal force, that universal literacy in programming is unnecessary and may be infeasible. The alternative objective is to implement a program of computer-assisted or computer-managed instruction (CAI or CMI). In CAI, the computer tells the child what to do by giving instructions, tests, and feedback; in CMI, it keeps extensive records that allow the teacher to monitor the student's performance (see Baker, 1981, and Malone, Suppes, Macken, & Zanotti, 1979, for overviews). The computer is often seen as a delivery system in CAI and CMI, not as an intelligent tutor. Its purpose is to present a packaged curriculum efficiently, not to provide instruction in a subject that is unique to the computer. The student and teacher learn no more about the computer than they know about stereo systems, tape recorders, or television sets. They can operate the machine but are not expected to know how it works or how to program it. The argument for this view of computer literacy might be summarized by an analogy: Teachers and students let experts write textbooks and design technologically sophisticated instructional media, such as educational films; they should leave computer programming to experts, too.

Between the extremes of literacy as knowledge of programming and literacy as experience with CAI, there are many compromises. Are there criteria for deciding where the compromise should be made? The answer, we think, turns in part on theoretical considerations. It is important, for theoretical reasons, to consider cognitive consequences for students who receive CAI or instruction in programming.

If computer literacy is taken to mean successful involvement in CAI, the intended consequences may be no different from those for a comparable curriculum taught without a computer. In the coming years, however, there is likely to be an increase in what some have called intelligent CAI (ICAI). Venezky (this volume), Larkin (this volume), and Sleeman and Brown (1979), among others, have argued for ICAI. What distinguishes ICAI from CAI, primarily, is that ICAI aims beyond the ordinary goals of giving information, presenting tests, and keeping records; it also constructs a model of what the student knows. In so doing, it is better able to tailor instruction to correct specific deficiencies and can better advise the teacher about what the student knows or does not know. A program offering ICAI can, in theory, be cognitively more sophisticated than most text-based curricula. Such a program's capability for cognitive diagnosis is thus an important evaluative criterion for both the programmer who creates it and the educator who adopts it.

If, in contrast, computer literacy is taken to mean knowing how to program, then it would be informative to know how programming is learned, what languages are best or easiest to learn, and what knowledge a student acquires by learning to program. Green (this volume) discusses these important questions and explains why none of them is currently satisfactorily answered. His analysis provides a conceptual framework that can guide the cognitive scientist in efforts to understand the psychology of programming. It also offers a sobering perspective for the practitioner who might otherwise accept, without critical analysis, the injunction that students ought to become programmers.

Actually, to know what children can or should learn by becoming programmers, we need to go a step beyond analyzing programming languages. As Chapman, Dollaghan, Kenworthy, and Miller (this volume) explain, children themselves can tell us much about how they learn to use a language. By examining how children use verbs of motion in spoken language, by investigating how parents might teach these verbs, and by exploring how a computer might do the teaching, Chapman and her colleagues provide an integrative discussion of what might be considered the simplest sort of programming language. Their purpose is to design an interactive system that allows very young children and the handicapped to make simple responses so as to converse with the computer about verbs that express motion.

To be sure, there is a great gap separating, on the one hand, the simple dialogue between computer and child that Chapman and her colleagues envision and, on the other hand, the powerful programming concepts analyzed by Green. The gap needs to be bridged in the long run, however, if we are to devise effective means of introducing children to programming. Chapman et al. and Green begin to show how the bridge might be built.

Apart from the cognitive consequences of how computer literacy is defined, there are practical considerations. The cognitive goals of a computer curriculum can affect what type of computer a school decides to buy, how many it buys, and where it puts them. We turn to these questions in the next section, where we argue that they should be of concern not only for educators, but for courseware developers as well.

SELECTING AND DISTRIBUTING THE HARDWARE

When a school decides to buy a computer, the most influential consideration, without question, is cost. And cost sets limits on quantity. Schools selecting the most expensive machinery will ordinarily have a small number of computers or terminals and are unlikely to have one in each classroom. These schools may decide to use computers for CAI on specialized topics or for teaching programming to a selective group of students. In contrast, schools that choose the least expensive microcomputers may buy enough of them to have one accessible to virtually every student, but the instructional uses of the machines are likely to be limited to some simple educational games and a rudimentary introduction to programming.

Clearly, there is a trade-off between the number and power of the computers purchased with a fixed budget. Similarly, there is a trade-off between how many students can be taught and how sophisticated is the curriculum they receive. The financial aspect of these trade-offs is easy enough to compute; the educational aspect is not. Pragmatically, some sensible advice regarding selection of hardware is that a school should purchase a computer with an established body of users in the local area, should buy from a local dealer who will provide service, and should avoid accessories other than a printer. More important, however, in the long run, is the manner in which choice of hardware affects classroom activities and students' learning.

If given a choice, almost any cognitive scientist working on the development of computerized courseware would choose a machine by criteria very different from those of the budget-conscious educator. The preference of the courseware developer would likely be for a machine that has ample on-line memory, generous off-line storage, and ready access to well-structured programming languages such as Pascal. These capabilities are not available on the inexpensive microcomputers that are likely to be most appealing for use in schools. Ironically, this conflict between the preferences of educators and courseware developers may be irrelevant in light of a more fundamental issue.

As Amarel (this volume) eloquently explains, the real effect of making a computer part of the curriculum may depend less on the machine itself than on how it functions within the social environment of the classroom. Included among the important features of this environment are how students' access to the computer is scheduled, whether students work alone on the computer or in small groups, how the curriculum of the computer is integrated with the broader curriculum, and how the teacher organizes, monitors, and supplements the students' interaction with the computer. Some of these factors bear on the type of machine. For example, Levin, Boruta, and Vasconcellos (this volume) describe a newsletter project in an elementary classroom that worked well with a small group of students collaborating on a portable microcomputer. This project would have not been feasible on the least-costly microcomputers currently available, and might have proven unworkable on an immobile terminal situated outside the students' own classroom in a separate laboratory for computerized instruction.

There is a lesson here for both courseware developers and educators. Put simply, neither the cost of the computer (which is likely to be the factor of greatest concern to the educator) nor the power of the computer (which is likely to be foremost in the mind of the courseware developer) should be considered in isolation from the manner in which the computer is to be woven into the social fabric of the classroom. Thus we turn next to the special role of the classroom's leading figure: the teacher.

THE TRAINING OF TEACHERS

Early CAI programs were designed with an expectation that the traditional preeminence of didactic instruction would be supplanted by a new allegiance to individualized, student-paced learning. In Bunderson's (1981, p. 95) words, the new ethic of individualized learning was expected to be so appealing that it would gradually but systematically "alter the culture of the school." Exactly the opposite happened; CAI programs withered in neglect unless they were adapted to the teacher-centered culture of the classroom.

To be usable in classrooms, computerized courseware must first be accessible to teachers, who will decide whether to use it and how to make it fit their own instructional goals. There is considerable interest in computerized courseware among today's teachers, but the interest is often coupled with lack of experience. For example, in 1981, a survey by the Minnesota Educational Computing Consortium (MECC) revealed that 80% of the teachers surveyed felt a need to be trained in instructional computing. Clearly, in-service training of teachers is vital to the success of instructional computing. Three rather different methods of training have all had a measure of success.

One method has been used by MECC since 1974. It is a statewide program in which a team of instructors visits schools, holds workshops, teaches demonstration classes, and gives informational lectures. In one year, the MECC team presents 200 workshops, 20 classes, and 400 lectures, and visits some 700 different schools (Rawitsch, 1981). The strength of this program is that an experienced team can provide more consistent and more systematic training, and can reach more teachers than would be possible with separate in-service programs organized locally.

A second method that has proven effective is to begin by identifying a small number of teachers who are interested in computers and have used them in their own classrooms. If given suitable facilities and some release time, these teachers can serve as expert consultants to their fellow teachers, thereby propagating ripples of interest and activity. We know of teachers in Wisconsin who were so vibrant and enthusiastic that they generated not ripples, but waves.

Finally, teachers have effectively learned about computers from their students. Gass (1981), for example, reported that teachers in Ridgewood, New Jersey, found students to be valuable tutors on topics that ranged from teaching about hardware to developing software. Watt (1982) reported similar observations in a study of the programming language LOGO.

Interestingly, all three of these methods involve having the novice teacher learn from an expert who is also an insider. The insider may be the representative of a network specifically created by teachers and school administrators to coordinate instructional computing statewide, a fellow teacher from a nearby school, or a student. The important point is that the teacher's tutor has two qualifications: knowledge of computers and firsthand experience as a participant in education at a grade level close to that of the teacher. Teachers and students learn best from an expert whose interest in computers is anchored in the classroom.

To some degree, a well-designed program of computerized courseware is its own tutorial for the user, whether teacher or student. The chapters in this volume by Lesgold, by Rubin, and by Wilkinson offer a variety of examples of tutorial devices incorporated into software. Although these devices may genuinely ease the novice's task of learning, there can be no pretense that they obviate the need for human instruction. The expert insider is indispensible.

The necessity of the expert insider raises questions of mutual interest for those who do research in cognitive science and for their counterparts in educational research. An active area of research in cognitive science concerns the ways in which the expert's knowledge differs from the novice's (Chi, Feltovich, & Glaser, 1981; Larkin, McDermott, Simon, & Simon, 1980). In educational research, studies of peer tutoring (Allen, 1976; Allen & Feldman, 1973; Bierman & Furman, 1981; Gartner, Kohler, & Reissman, 1971; Rosen, Powell, & Schubot, 1977) are pertinent if the expert and novice are both students. One example of research on this general topic would be to study differences in the investigative strategies adopted by novice and expert students as they attempt to debug their programs or to learn how to operate packaged courseware. Another example would be to study how exchange of information between novice and expert normally takes place and how the exchange may be optimized. In the present volume, Levin and his colleagues present some preliminary evidence on strategies of using a text-editing program for students with varying amounts of expertise. More research of this sort is needed, and we hope that the chapters of this volume will give prospective investigators some guidance.

ASSESSING COGNITIVE OUTCOMES

Once a program of computerized instruction has been launched, it is natural to ask what results it has produced. The problem of evaluating computerized courseware is thorny indeed. Venezky (this volume) gives a scholarly review of research evaluating CAI, and he discusses various levels of complexity at which evaluative research may be undertaken. His chapter also introduces a theme that is echoed elsewhere in the book.

The theme introduced by Venezky concerns the value—and the difficulty —of constructing a cognitive model of the student. Efforts to construct such models appear in the chapters by Larkin, who examines students' knowledge of physics and chemistry; by Sternberg, Powell, and Kaye, who analyze knowledge of vocabulary; and by Perfetti, who considers verbal abilities that students use in the domains of reading, writing, and vocabulary.

It is readily apparent from reading these chapters that the problem of evaluating cognitive outcomes is a persistent source of tension between cognitive science and educational practice. It is also apparent, however, that the tension is healthy. The rich and detailed models of human cognition that are the objective of cognitive science can improve the quality of instruction. Evidence that supports this assertion appears throughout the volume. At the same time, the needs of educators argue strongly for the pragmatic value of usable courseware, and they push program developers to provide courseware with visible outcomes.

For cognitive scientists, the ultimate reward may be a cognitive model sufficiently powerful both to simulate the skill of an expert and to recognize the causes of error in a novice. For many teachers and parents, the most convincing testimonial to the value of computerized courseware may be the child who visibly and proudly holds in hand a printout showing the outcome of a successful interaction with the computer. We do not mean to denigrate parents, teachers, or, for that matter, printouts. On the contrary, one of the provocative insights from the last decade of courseware development is that a properly designed display, appearing on the computer's screen or on a printout, can capture a powerful idea that is cognitively complex, yet visually compact, and which seductively beckons its viewer to analyze it more deeply (Lawler, 1982). We shall return to this concept at the end of our chapter.

EPILOGUE AND RECOMMENDATIONS

We close by reviewing the issues that we identified as crucial for merging theory and practice. As we review each issue, we reframe it with a recommendation.

First, both the purchasers and the developers of software need to clarify the meaning of computer literacy. Between the extremes of literacy as knowing a programming language and literacy as being able to respond to packaged courseware, there is a compromise that we find commendable. In Poler's (1982, p. 50) words, "Instead of a blind faith in the utility of one kind of computer literacy for all students, educators ought to see what computers can do for particular disciplines, and tailor courses to the likely student uses of computers." In tailoring courses, the emphasis should be on using the computer as a tool, not on understanding its architecture as a machine. Thus, the computer is for some a tool for composition and text editing, for others an intelligent calculator, and for still others a device for constructing graphic displays.

Emphasizing that the computer is a tool suggests a resolution of our second issue, which concerns how the computer is integrated into the classroom. Like any tool, the computer should be available when needed but otherwise should be in the background, and it should be accessible both to individuals and to small groups. As Fields and Paris (1981, p. 67) observed, "there is a definite trend toward the development of smaller, stand-alone...systems that may be used, or even owned by individual students." The reasons for this trend include, according to Fields and Paris, lower costs of development for more compact courseware and consumer preference for courseware that is "personal, controllable, ownable, and physically available" (p. 67). We would add that the characteristics most appealing to consumers are precisely the ones that make the computer usable as a tool.

Our third issue concerns the training of teachers, who will surely play a pivotal role in the adoption and use of courseware. A few teachers may become experts in using computers and writing programs for them; most, we suspect, will be informed novices who are satisfied to be familiar only with certain uses of the computer that fit well within the curriculum of their own classrooms. They will seek consultation with an expert insider when and if the need arises. Because teachers themselves may not become computer experts, it is important that courseware be designed to be accessible to the informed novice. Cognitive scientists, for their part, would be well advised to study the knowledge that an informed novice has and the way in which such knowledge is most readily acquired.

Finally, there is the issue of assessing cognitive outcomes. Given our preference for using the computer as a small, portable, and personalized tool, we also prefer compact representation of cognitive outcomes. Courseware constructed with a sophisticated cognitive model of the student is a commendable goal. To expect teachers and parents to appreciate the model in all its richness and detail, however, seems unrealistic. Instead, we need powerful ideas that capture the essence of the model and make it visible in a simple display or printout. Finding such powerful ideas offers a hope and a challenge for reconciling the aspirations of cognitive science with the needs of education. It is the task of cognitive science to devise models of knowledge that represent the complexity of human learning, yet can be summarized cogently in ways that appeal to teachers, parents, and students. It is the task of education to promote the development of courseware that finds a balance between being anchored in a sound model of cognition and being readily usable in classrooms.

ACKNOWLEDGMENTS

We owe much to DuWayne Kleinschmidt, Berland Meyer, and Robert Patton. As pioneers among teachers using computers in their classrooms in Wisconsin, they were to us a valuable source of practical experience and an inspiration to many of their fellow teachers.

REFERENCES

Allen, V. (Ed.) *Children as teachers: Theory and research on tutoring.* New York: Academic Press, 1976.

Allen, V., & Feldman, R. Learning through tutoring: Low achieving children as tutors. *Journal of Educational Psychology,* 1973, *42,* 1–5.

Baker, F. Computer-managed instruction: A context for computer-based instruction. In H. F. O'Neil, Jr. (Ed.), *Computer-based instruction: A state-of-the art assessment.* New York: Academic Press, 1981.

Bierman, K. L., & Furman, W. Effects of role and assignment rationale on attitudes formed during peer tutoring. *Journal of Educational Psychology,* 1981, *73,* 33–40.

Bunderson, V. C. Courseware. In H. F. O'Neil, Jr. (Ed.), *Computer-based instruction: A state-of-the-art assessment.* New York: Academic Press, 1981.

Chi, M. T. H., Feltovich, P. J., & Glaser, R. Categorization and representation of physics problems by experts and novices. *Cognitive Science*, 1981, *5*, 121–152.

Fields, C., & Paris, J. Hardware-software. In H. F. O'Neil, Jr. (Ed.), *Computer-based instruction: A state-of-the-art assessment*. New York: Academic Press, 1981.

Gartner, A., Kohler, M. C., & Riessman, F. *Children teach children: Learning by teaching*. New York: Harper & Row, 1971.

Gass, S. Using computer-wise students...wisely. *Electronic Learning*, 1981, *1*, 26–27.

Larkin, J. H., McDermott, J., Simon, D. P., & Simon, H. A. Expert and novice performance in solving physics problems. *Science*, 1980, *208*, 1335–1342.

Lawler, R. W. Designing computer-based microworlds. *Byte*, 1982, *7*(8), 138–160.

Leuhrmann, A. Planning for computer education—problems and opportunities for administrators. *Bulletin of the National Association of Secondary School Principals*, 1981, *65*, 62–69.

Malone, T. W., Suppes, P., Macken, E., & Zanotti, M. Projecting student trajectories in a computer-assisted instruction curriculum. *Journal of Educational Psychology*, 1979, *71*, 74–84.

Papert, S. In: "The classroom computers." *Newsweek*, March 9, 1981, pp. 88–91.

Poler, E. M. Computer literacy: Different strokes for different folks. *New York Times*, Summer Survey of Education, August 22, 1982, p. 50.

Rawitsch, D. C. An inside look at inservice. *Classroom Computer News*, 1981, *2*(1), 16–17.

Rosen, S., Powell, E. R., & Schubot, D. B. Peer-tutoring outcome as influenced by the equity and type of role assignment. *Journal of Educational Psychology*, 1977, *69*, 244–252.

Sleeman, D. H., & Brown, J. S. (Eds.). Special issue on intelligent tutoring systems. *International Journal of Man-Machine Studies*, 1979, *11*(1).

Watt, D. Logo in the schools. *Byte*, 1982, *7*(8), 116–134.

2

The Classroom: An Instructional Setting for Teachers, Students, and the Computer*

Marianne Amarel

INTRODUCTION

There are at least two ways computers can contribute to the educational enterprise: as aids to learning and instruction in the classroom, and as protean tools in research on human cognition. In this chapter, I emphasize the classroom and the role that computers may play in that setting. This is not the dominant perspective of the chapters contained between these covers. Rather, in this rich sampler of computer applications to learning, teaching, and to understanding cognitive processes and skills, the boundaries of the instructional environment have been quite closely drawn: The focus is on the interactions of learners and computer programs. As a consequence, the influence of the larger setting, which may be a classroom, generally has remained a peripheral concern.

I shall elaborate on the implications of this selective view, but would like first to preview my own orientation to the uses of computers in the class-

*Requests for reprints should be sent to Marianne Amarel, Educational Testing Service, Rosedale Road, Princeton, NJ 08541.

15

room. In this discussion, I hew to the literal referent of *classroom,* eschewing such metaphors as "the world as classroom," however suggestive they may be. In fact, I center on the elementary class, the educational setting most familiar to me, and a place that affords a clear view of the impact of computer-aided learning. I begin by describing some common features of elementary classrooms, highlighting those most salient to the adoption of new curricular resources. Next, I draw on my own experience with evaluating an elaborate demonstration of computer based instruction to illustrate some of the effects of introducing computers into classrooms. Last, I consider selected instructional issues raised by contemporary views of cognition, using this discussion as an opportunity to express some misgivings about the present state and conduct of primary education, with or without the aid of computers. In this concluding section, I refer to trends in public education and attempt to assess the potential of computers for fostering or countering these trends.

THE INFLUENCE OF RESEARCH SETTINGS

The tenuousness of the classroom connection in this volume speaks to more than a trifling misalignment between title and content. It suggests that the efforts of recent years to close the gap between research and practice in education opened a new fissure, one I will stutteringly call the research–research gap. The crack appeared when investigators began to turn attention to the classroom in the hope that disciplined inquiry into its phenomena would yield double dividends—gains in the general understanding of learning and teaching, and a better grasp of their particular manifestation in schools. The best of this work identified structures and practices common to classrooms and elucidated some of the constraints and opportunities inherent in that environment (Barr & Dreeben, 1978; Doyle, 1978; Kounin, 1970). Large-scale correlational studies of specific teacher behaviors and student achievement were also undertaken in search of stable relationships that would lead to the identification of effective instructional patterns (Evertson, Anderson, Anderson & Brophy, 1980; Good, In press; Good & Brophy, 1975). Research on the cognitive processes of individual learners was rarely undertaken in the classroom, even though such currently fashionable variables as time-on-task and engaged-time stand in fact in proxy for students' cognitive efforts. Studies of mental events continued to be conducted in the more traditional laboratory settings; work on cognitive variables that mediate between instructional stimuli and learning (Rohwrer, 1972; Rothkopf, 1976), the influence of previous knowledge structures on new learning (Anderson, 1977), and the role of memory organization on encoding and retrieving knowledge (Rumelhart & Ortony, 1977) were some of the targets of inquiry.

The broadening of research perspectives brought about a more realistic understanding of the complexity of classroom learning, along with a less-welcome bonus: Research conducted in schools diverged from the work going on in more controlled and controllable settings, and further fragmented a weakly integrated field. This development should have been anticipated, as the choice of a particular research setting both reflects and shapes the questions studied, predisposing, at the same time, the class of answers that will result (Shulman, 1981). The benefits, even the necessity, of taking multiple routes to understanding educational phenomena are not at issue; the integration of knowledge derived from the multiple research traditions, however, is a challenge yet to be met. The relationship between instructional events and the students' cognitive activities that mediate learning is not well enough understood to guide teachers' decisions, nor are the effects of different classroom organizations sufficiently clear to determine the design of these settings. Yet, the development of pedagogically sound and classroom-friendly computer instruction is contingent on such understandings—the technology per se does not benefit education. Computer technology may, however, facilitate the synthesis of knowledge drawn from diverse research traditions. It can also provide better access to learners' mental activities through the capacity to elicit and record responses to finely tuned instructional events. Some recent work uses computer technology to make translucent the thought processes of students learning subtraction, or solving algebra problems (Brown and Burton, 1978, Sleeman, 1982). Confined though it is to specific problem domains, and not directly translatable into teaching strategies, the work suggests powerful instructional applications. In this volume, Wilkinson, Lesgold, and Perfetti, among others, speak to future prospects made feasible by the technology. Similarly, Venezky's higher level evaluation models pivot on just such capacities.

As the future beckons with appealing promises, the present use of computers in classrooms easily slips out of focus. To blur the line between the possible and the available, to mistake sophisticated technology for sophisticated instruction, and to assume productive outcomes when students communicate with computers is all too tempting. I will try to resist such blandishments and will look around before looking ahead.

Little of what follows is uniquely pertinent to computer-based instruction. From the vantage point of the classroom, the germane questions concern the compatibility of novel educational resources with classroom ecology, rather than the adaptability of that setting to the dictates of the innovation.

THE CLASSROOM

This last observation prefigures the portrayal of classrooms, for a remarkable stability of basic features is one of their noteworthy aspects. These durable organizational forms have absorbed successive and diverse innovations by molding them to their prevailing contours. Whether classrooms are seen as highly successful adaptations, or as prematurely fossilized structures, curriculum developers will at their own peril underestimate their hardiness.

Common Features

What then are the salient features of the perdurable classroom? Above all else, a classroom is a communal setting, one in which the collectivity of individuals who come together at the beginning of the school year soon evolves into a working social group. A set of rules, mutual obligations and responsibilities, differentiated roles and functions, and even status distinctions, develop. The evolution and mode of operation of this community is guided and constrained by what have been called *frame factors* (Dahllöf, 1971), factors that lie outside the control of a single teacher or student. The system of rules, values, and practices characterizing classrooms is influenced both by physical frame factors, such as the location and spatial arrangement of the room, and by administrative factors, such as schedules, testing requirements, and the way students are classified and grouped. These by-no-means-trivial constraints, however, still leave varying degrees of discretion in the hands of each teacher.

Such conditions bring about classrooms that, despite forces promoting uniformity, are not true replicas of one another. Common dimensions are realized in somewhat different ways. The distinctness of each classroom is not solely a result of the teacher's latitude; it arises out of another characteristic of classrooms—the diversity of their inhabitants. Students bring varying abilities, competencies, interests, styles of learning, levels of motivation, expectations, and previous experience to the business of schooling. Of necessity, then, classrooms are interactive settings, where teachers, in transaction with the qualities of their students, bring to life instructional environments wherein the aims and practices of education are construed and realized in a unique way.

The Aims of Instruction

I backed into the heart of the matter—the purpose and goals of classroom instruction—by design, for while the aims of schooling largely determine the character of the classroom, these aims defy enumeration or specification. They are, in fact, best described as a series of dilemmas that force choices between sets of positive values and actions, where the optimal realization of one may conflict with the optimal realization of the other. A commonplace example is the tension between inculcating students with the values, customs, and received knowledge of the prevailing culture, and enabling them to rethink and reshape the traditional norms and forms of that culture in response to changing conditions. Equally pervasive, particularly in the education of young children, is the dual objective of conveying academic subject matter and of cultivating personal and social qualities desirable in the society.

In addition to such endemic dilemmas, many more context-specific contentions remain to be resolved at the classroom level. All teachers confront the choice of helping students acquire particular skills and bodies of knowledge efficiently, and of supporting self-directed, independent efforts that trade short-term results for more slowly developing competencies. At the same time, teachers need to balance the claims of individual students against each other and, more difficult perhaps, the claims of individuals against the demands entailed in maintaining a functioning community.

I want to be sure that my depiction of the classroom as a working social system is not mistaken for sentimentality. A working social system does not necessarily work for the benefit of all its participants, nor does the image imply any particular mode of organization or value orientation. A social system may be cooperative or competitive, exploitative or egalitarian. It is simply a group of people who, voluntarily or by coercion, abide by a set of rules and engage in a set of activities that have a measure of continuity. The kind of community any classroom becomes thus depends on the way the enduring dilemmas are resolved by the group.

COMPUTERS IN THE CLASSROOM

Introducing computers into the classroom gives substance to many of the dilemmas inherent in educational praxis. The additional resource enriches the class at the same time that it creates scarcity, requiring the teacher to develop an allocation strategy. Several judgments are entailed in such a plan for orderly and equitable access. The teacher needs to weigh the value of time spent in other classroom activities and to assess the differential benefits to individual students. Equally important, the optimal distribution of the teachers' own time and attention in supporting the students' engagement

with the computer has to be considered. Whether these decisions are carefully deliberated, or are reached by default, the students' educational experiences will have been affected.

A National Survey

A useful context for a closer look at the impact of computers on classroom life is some recent information about the scope and nature of computer facilities in the nation's schools. From a survey conducted by the
National Center of Educational Statistics (Goor, Melmed, & Ferris, 1981)
of a national sample of public school districts, a picture of fairly broad,
but extremely shallow, penetration emerges. Although about half of the
school districts report having at least one microcomputer (micro), only 3%
of the districts have 20 or more micros available for instructional use.
Translated into availability to schools in the "have" districts, less than 3%
of primary schools and less than 1% of secondary schools have 20 or more
terminals or micros for student use. The most frequently reported use of
on-line instruction is in computer literacy courses, which typically provide
some familiarity with a programming language. Remedial and compensa-
tory education, on the one hand, and providing additional challenge for
high-achieving students, on the other, round out the types of student activities reported. As of 1981, then, CAI (computer-aided instruction) was
not used to deliver main-line instruction or even to provide a significant
addition to traditional curricular offerings, and it was least used by the
middle range of students. It is not surprising to learn, then, that computers
in the classroom are atypical; often they are placed in resource rooms or
single-purpose computer rooms. All in all, CAI offerings in public schools
have an ad hoc quality at present, and they represent an activity that is
relatively free of the burgeoning regulations besetting school programs
(Sheingold, 1981).

A Case of Classroom Implementation

The project that will serve to exemplify some of the persistent motifs in
that special case of curricular innovation, CAI, is the PLATO Elementary
Mathematics and Reading Demonstration. This effort brought about a
hundred technically sophisticated interactive terminals to more than forty
classrooms and upward of a thousand students in the course of two school
years (CERL, 1977). It represents the single most extensive installation of

CAI in primary classrooms, and though the demonstration occurred during the mid-1970s, its illustrative value still remains intact.

By far the most significant finding of the elaborate evaluation that accompanied the demonstration (Swinton, Amarel, & Morgan, 1978) was the powerful effect the teachers had on both the course and the outcome of the implementation. The contributions of the computerized curricula to student achievement (reading for Grades 1 and 2, mathematics for Grades 4 and 6) were masked by the teacher effects, thus contesting the persistent myth of CAI's imperviousness to situational influence. The impact of the courseware was moderated not by mystifying or elusive factors, but by the teachers' decisions about such commonplace problems as the schedules that controlled access to the terminals, the integration of the computerized lessons with ongoing instruction, and the allocation of their own time to various classroom activities.

Time Allocation

A most straightforward, yet central, variation between classrooms—student time on the terminal—provides a dramatic illustration of the teachers' influence. The official strategy devised by the program developers for allocating time on the terminals called for uniform allocations: half an hour daily for the older students receiving the math lessons, fifteen minutes a day for the primary grades on the reading lessons. The individual lessons were, in fact, centrally controlled, an arrangement accepted by the volunteer teachers, who agreed to provide a hospitable environment for the PLATO terminals. It was surprising, then, to find that at the end of the second year, when the system was reasonably stabilized, the on-line year-end summaries indicated large differences in the time students spent on the terminal. In the math classes, mean student time ranged from 10 to 68 hours, whereas in the reading classes average times ranged from 7 to 20 hours per student. Student use, in fact, reflected the solutions evolved in the classrooms to the basic problems posed by the terminals: (1) how to distribute a limited resource, given 4–6 terminals per class, and (2) how to trade off with other instructional activities, given the finite school day.

Various management strategies were observed in the classrooms. In a few rooms, the school day was in fact extended, arrangements having been made for students to work on the terminals before and after school hours. More commonly, students were scheduled throughout the day, or restricted to specified portions of the school day. However, the ultimate difference in the amount of time students spent working through the courseware was less a function of the formal arrangements than of the way they were monitored and enforced. In this regard, the teachers needed to reconsider not only the students' use of class time but their own as well because PLATO siphoned off teacher time in several ways. Equipment maintenance and troubleshooting fell on the teachers, particularly during the first year of the project, when frequent malfunctions interfered with the reliable delivery of lessons. Schedules and classroom routines were disrupted, requiring the reshuffling of student assignments. Even under normalized conditions, it took time to ensure that children took their turn at the terminal or that they did not overstay their slot. In each classroom there were enthusiasts who would have monopolized the terminals, and a few who were reluctant users of the resource.

As might be expected, teachers differed in the amount of time they were willing to devote to managing CAI. Teachers also differed in their conceptions of optimal patterns of utilization. Understanding the range of teacher attitudes and values is critical to anticipating implementation effects. Before discussing some of the insights we gained about the links between teachers' pedagogical constructs and classroom decisions, I consider another implementation variable sensitive to teacher influence: integrating the computer courseware with classroom instruction.

Curriculum Integration

Two main mechanisms were available to teachers for linking the two curricular strands in the room: to relate the PLATO lessons to ongoing instruction, or to adjust classroom activities so as to mesh with the courseware. Either approach required logistical as well as complex pedagogical solutions. The logistical problems concerned the teachers' ability to time their own presentations so that they coincided with the content offered on-line. The pedagogical issues related to judgments about instructional compatibility. The feasibility of integrating the curricula thus depended on the degree to which the courseware and classroom instruction were uniform across students. If either was individualized so that students worked with varied content or were at different points in a sequenced curriculum, integration either was not possible or had to be accomplished on an individual basis.

A set of intricate issues concerned the compatibility of pedagogical values embedded in the courseware with the instructional precepts espoused by the teachers. The introduction and explication of new concepts, the problem-solving strategies and algorithms presented, the sequencing of lessons, and the particular forms of drill and practice used all embodied instructional precepts. In toto or in part, they may or may not have represented the teachers' own approaches and methods. This aspect of the PLATO implementation was further complicated by differences in pedagogical approach that characterized the reading and mathematics courseware, and still further by distinctions between the four strands that constituted the mathematics program. The reading lessons were relatively consistent, having been based on a task analysis of beginning reading skills that were then hierarchically ordered to form a linear string of lessons. The mathematics program had grown out of an instructional philosophy that may be loosely characterized as an inquiry method: the lessons were not austerely didactic, but guided the students toward problem-solving strategies and the consideration of alternative solutions to similar problems. Practice lessons tended to have a game format. This general orientation notwithstanding, each of the math strands bore the imprint of the teams that developed them.

The Teachers' Influence

The teachers who aspired to relate the computerized lessons to ongoing instruction were faced with a sequence of moves: they needed enough familiarity with the lessons to be able to discern the specific content, the particular methods, and the general instructional approach they embedded; to assess the compatibility of the lessons with their personal instructional practices and values; and, finally, to decide on a posture toward the two sources of curriculum now available to the students. This last set of decisions formed the basis for implementing PLATO in the classroom.

The varied patterns of implementation that emerged in the classrooms were not idiosyncratic, yet the bases for specific modes of implementation were difficult to disentangle. It became apparent early on that teachers who exercized relatively greater control over curricular decisions exerted greater control over the use of the terminals. The direction of the control, however, whether used to promote or to restrict access to the PLATO lessons, proved independent of the degree of centralized decision making. The ultimate fate of the computerized curriculum depended on such factors as the teachers' assessment of the quality and value of the lessons relative to their own instruction, on the amount of disruption they were willing to tolerate, and on the firmness with which they held to their customary teaching practices. Consequently, the PLATO demonstration did not represent a single educational experience but a collection of experiences that varied across classrooms in their acceptance, intensity, isolation from or integration with the prevailing curriculum, and interaction with teacher coverage and style. This thin description can only suggest the more thickly documented effects of decisions regarding the use and deployment of CAI in the classroom (Amarel & Swinton, 1976). Their consequences ripple across classroom routines well beyond the relatively closed system of student–computer interactions. Even decisions that appear trivial at first glance reveal complex underpinnings when broader concerns are brought to bear on them. Such simple tasks as scheduling students on-line become problematic in the light of equity considerations: computer jocks are familiar figures on the computer landscape, and the lesser involvement of girls with instructional technology has been noted repeatedly. Relegating academic underachievers to drill and practice programs while encouraging successful students to take an exploratory stance toward computers represents another common pattern (Sheingold, 1981). Any effort to address or redress such pervasive inequities confronts the teacher with yet another set of dilemmas. The dilemmas need to be resolved in real-life classrooms which, I have tried to show, are dynamic, and to some extent unique settings, likely to resist formula solutions. Stripping away the broader context when studying educational encounters does permit understandings to emerge that are otherwise masked by the white noise of natural settings but, in designing educational encounters, that context must be anticipated, if not restored.

TRENDS IN PUBLIC EDUCATION

The most consequential issue of all—the nature and value of computer-based instruction—has been broached only indirectly so far. The PLATO courseware is not an apt foil for such a discussion, as it represents but one possible instructional application, that is, the delivery of relatively traditional curricular content. The computer is also used to familiarize students with this ubiquitous technology, often in the form of computer literacy courses. A less prevalent mode, yet one with great potential, is illustrated by Levin, Boruta, and Vasconcellos (this volume). They show the computer serving as an open-ended tool for classroom activities and projects that combine traditional and novel instructional opportunities in an imaginative and apparently effective manner.

The mixed character of present and projected courseware inhibits general pronouncements about worth, quality, or educational effectiveness. I will therefore approach this issue by way of an overview of some general trends in public-school instruction.

Changes in the Teacher's Role

At least three related currents are certain to intersect with any sizable growth of instructional technology: (1) the proliferation of highly prescriptive curricular programs and materials, (2) the increasingly detailed specification of instructional objectives, and (3) the expansion of standardized accountability procedures as the primary method for assessing student progress. The design of curricula, the setting of objectives, and the evaluation of achievement are taking place at some distance from the classroom, accomplished by subject-matter specialists, publishers, and district or state administrators. Necessarily, and perhaps intentionally, these trends curtail the exercise of teachers' judgments and diminish their decision-making responsibilities. Planning, designing, and evaluating educative experiences, activities considered integral to the teaching role, are passing from the teachers' domain to that of administrators who formulate these decisions in positions well removed from the place where teaching and learning occur. Some view these changes as an attempt to undermine the already fragile professional status of the teacher, to be designed to "de-skill" the classroom teacher in order to mechanize and thereby gain firmer control over the conduct of education (Apple, 1982). The interests and ideologies that fuel these trends may be disputed, but their direction is generally acknowledged.

The transformation of the teacher into an educational functionary does not bode well for public education. Paradoxically, the prescribed objectives, the mandated materials, and the external evaluations only serve to emphasize the centrality of the teacher in the instructional process. For however they may be classified or homogeneously grouped, the students in any classroom remain a diverse lot, who, like all other human beings, are purposeful agents in their own right. They actively select, order, and interpret experiences, so as to make sense of the world, and they will continue to respond differentially to uniform instruction. It thus remains the function of the teacher to negotiate the territory between individual differences and educational aims.

The view emerging from cognitive science does not support restricting the teacher's role in this task. On the contrary, the problems of instruction become more complex, as differences among learners expand beyond abilities and competencies to include individual ways of organizing, retaining, and retrieving information—processes that interact with learning.

A View from Cognitive Science

Calfee (1981) provides a framework for deriving what the critical instructional functions may be in light of the reconceptualized view of cognition. The purpose of schooling, he holds, is

> to create a set of mental structures that parallel the various curriculum programs, both those that are named (literacy, mathematics, science, physical education) and those that are implicit (self-discipline, responsibility, courtesy, competitiveness). Thus, students who have been taught to read become the possessors of a complex "frame" . . . which will provide them a culturally designed and sanctioned tool for handling a set of tasks that are important for the society and for the individual. (p. 33)

The "frames" constitute the stable structures of the public knowledge of the culture and are thus immune to the influence of teachers. Teachers can, however, play a critical part in enabling students to acquire and use these structures. Investigations of the acquisition of complex systems of knowledge suggest that learners must organize elements of that knowledge into internally coherent, and functionally interelated groupings. These infrastructures, a single one of which may encompass a disciplinary domain, are presumed to be less stable and more variable across individuals than are the larger frames. Each individual constructs what are probably unique configurations, but yet have enough common features to make public communication possible. The nature and efficacy of these mental organizations are certain to be influenced by instruction, either for the benefit or to the detriment of the student. It appears plausible that for supportive instruction to occur, teachers must possess two kinds of knowledge: (1) They need to have mastered the domain well enough to understand its internal organizers, even to perceive alternate ways of relating its basic elements; to do, in fact, what Hawkins (1974) called "unpacking the curriculum" so as to offer students a choice of entry points and to empower them to construct and reconstruct their own conceptual maps. (2) Even more difficult perhaps, teachers must, in the words of Yue-zheng (200 B.C.), a disciple of Confucius, "know students' minds" to have an awareness of the student's understandings and characteristic patterns of learning and perceiving. To some extent, all teachers do some of these things. Few, of course, are intellectually, perceptually, emotionally, and morally well enough educated and motivated to reach optimal levels of teaching. I seem to be talking about human teachers, but of course, each curriculum guide, each text, and each computer-based instructional program embeds a teacher. The beliefs, values, knowledge, and responsive capacity of these teachers provide the basis for assessing the value of any instructional resource. I do not mean to suggest that each program, each course, has to enfold all these capacities. There may well be, as Lesgold and Perfetti (this volume) suggest, a need for well-designed opportunities to practice and drill. If they are to be used in an educationally responsible way, such opportunities must be made available in a context in which the education of the student, not just the acquisition of a skill, is the aim of instruction.

A CONCEPTION OF TEACHING

I can do no better than to conclude with two passages from Maxine Greene (1981) speaking first in the voice of the philosopher, then in the voice of the teacher, exemplifying what the philosopher envisions.

> Teaching involves a triadic and not a dyadic relationship. Most simply, this means that to teach is to teach something to somebody not simply to instruct in subject matter or to engage with a child. If any person teaches, there must be something he/she teaches and someone he/she teaches to . . . . To be a good teacher means not only to *know* a good deal about what one is teaching but to *care* about what one is teaching as well as those to whom one is teaching it.

The triadic relationship Greene describes was compressed by Hawkins (1974) into the modified Buberian phrase, "I, Thou, and It." Greene brings the principle to life in her own teaching:

> When I taught a Shakespeare play, for instance, or Melville's *Moby Dick,* I involved myself with whatever was relevant in the body of knowledge called literary criticism. I did so in order to be able to look through as many perspectives as possible at the works I was teaching, so I would be better able to point to aspects of those works, to enable my students to attend to dimensions they might otherwise not have seen. My end in view, of course, was to do what I could to make those works accessible to my students in such a fashion that they could bring them variously alive in their experience. It would never have occurred to me to assign them all the critical studies I had read, although it *did* occur to me to try to make clear to them that criticisms provide a kind of grid, a set of perspectives through which to see. I had to choose from the "stock of knowledge at hand" studies of reading response, criticisms, literary history that which might feed into the kind of teaching that would stimulate my students to interpret for themselves. And so it was with history. I had to look at the modes of explanation, the records, the original sources, the secondary accounts in a certain kind of way. Yes, I had to learn for myself . . . .But then I had to reshape what I thought of as my learning, my research; I had to find an appropriate articulation for it, a way of sequencing and pacing what I had to present. I had to identify what I thought to be the leading questions in the texts I had used, so as to move my

students into their own investigations, their own making sense . . .to move them into
the activity of coming to know, of finding support for their own knowledge claims,
of using evidence and giving good reasons and making connections and seeking out
the meaning, the significance of it all.

Whatever roles computers ultimately play in the classroom, they cannot
fail but contribute honorably by emulating or even approximating this vision of education.

REFERENCES

Amarel, M., & Swinton, S. *Influences of teachers' conceptions on curriculum implementation in a CAI project.* Paper presented at the meeting of the American Educational Research Association, San Francisco, April, 1976.

Anderson, R. The notion of schemata and the educational enterprise: General discussion of the conference. In R. Anderson, R. Spiro, & W. Montague (Eds.), *Schooling and the acquisition of knowledge.* Hillsdale, New Jersey: Lawrence Erlbaum Associates, 1977.

Apple, M. W., Reproduction and contradiction in education. In M. W. Apple, (Ed.) *Cultural and economic reproduction in education:essays on class.* London and Boston: Rutledge & Kegan Paul, 1982.

Barr, R., & Dreeben, R. Instruction in classrooms. In L. Shulman (Ed.), *Review of research in education* (Vol. 5). Itasca, Illinois: F. E. Peacock, 1978.

Brown, J. S. & Burton, R. R., Diagnostic models for procedural bugs in basic mathematical skills. *Cognitive Science,* 1978, *2,* 155-62.

Calfee, R. Cognitive psychology and educational practice. In D. C. Berliner (Ed.), *Review of research in education* (Vol. 9). Washington, D.C.: American Educational Research Association, 1981.

CERL *Demonstration of the Plato IV computer-based education system, final report* (NSF Contract C-723). Urbana, Illinois: University of Urbana, 1977.

Dahllöf, U. S. *Ability grouping, content validity, and curriculum process.* New York: Teachers College Press, 1971.

Doyle, W. Paradigms for research on teacher effectiveness. In L. Shulman (Ed.), *Review of research in education* (Vol. 5). Itasca, Illinois: F. E. Peacock, 1978.

Evertson, E., Anderson, C., Anderson, L., & Brophy, J. Relationships between classroom behaviors and student outcomes in junior high mathematics and English classes. *American Educational Research Journal,* 1980, *17,* 43-60.

Good, T. Classroom research: past and future. In L. Shulman and G. Sykes (Eds.), *Handbook of Teaching Policy* (in press)

Good, T. L., Biddle, B. J., & Brophy, J. E. *Teachers make a difference.* New York: Holt, Rinehart & Winston, 1975.

Goor, J., Melmed, A., & Farris, E. Student use of computers in schools. *Fast response survey system,* U.S. Department of Education, No. 12, March, 1981.

Greene, M. *Teaching teachers.* Unpublished manuscript, 1981.

Hawkins, D. *The informed vision: Essays on learning and human nature.* New York: Agathon Press, 1974.

Kounin, J. S. *Discipline and group management in classrooms.* New York: Holt, Rinehart & Winston, 1970.

Rohwer, W. D., Jr. Decisive research: A means for answering fundamental questions about instruction. *Educational Researcher,* 1972, *1,* 5–11.

Rothkopf, E. Z. Writing to teach and reading to learn: A perspective on the psychology of written instruction. In N. L. Gage (Ed.), *The psychology of teaching methods,* 75th Yearbook of the National Society for the Study of Education, Pt. 1. Chicago: University of Chicago Press, 1976.

Rumelhart, D., & Ortony, A. The representation of knowledge in memory. In R. Anderson, R. Spiro, & W. Montague (Eds.), *Schooling and the acquisition of knowledge.* Hillsdale, New Jersey: Lawrence Erlbaum Associates, 1977.

Sheingold, K. *Issues related to the implementation of computer technology in schools: A cross-sectional study.* Report presented to the National Institute of Education Conference on issues related to the implementation of computer technology in schools, Washington, D.C., February, 1981.

Shulman, L. S. Disciplines of inquiry in education: An overview. *Educational Researcher,* 1981, *10*(6), 5–12.

Sleeman, D. H. Assessing competence in basic algebra. In D. H. Sleeman and J. S. Brown (Eds.), *Intelligent tutoring systems.* New York: Academic Press, 1982.

Swinton, S., Amarel, M., & Morgan, J. *The PLATO elementary demonstration: Educational outcome evaluation.* Final Report (ESS PR 78-11). Princeton, New Jersey: Educational Testing Service, 1978.

3

Evaluating Computer-Assisted Instruction on Its Own Terms*

Richard L. Venezky

INTRODUCTION

Evaluation begins, perhaps, in China in 2200 B.C. with proficiency testing (Dubois, 1965), or perhaps in 1864 with Reverend George Fisher's Scale-Book (Ayres, 1918), or perhaps in the 1890s with J. M. Rice's studies of spelling and math (Rice, 1897). Twentieth-century educational evaluation might be dated from the publication of Thorndike's handwriting scale (Thorndike, 1910), or the Cleveland School Survey of 1915–1916 (Moley, 1923), or Tyler's work on educational objectives in the 1930s (see Merwin, 1969, for a review). Whatever its true origins, educational evaluation is now a major industry, complete with its own terminology, training programs, and publications. Since 1967 or thereabouts, this industry has divided its wares, as suggested by Scriven (1967), into formative and summative tracks, the former applying to evaluation of instructional programs that are, like

---

* Send requests for reprints to Dr. Richard L. Venezky, School of Education, University of Delaware, Newark, DE 19711.

molten iron, still malleable, the latter applying exclusively to solidified products.

When this dichotomy was suggested 14 years ago, educational evaluation was still in the classification stage of scientific development. At that time, the terms provided a convenient organizing algorithm for a seemingly chaotic situation. Instruction, although often organized around behavioral objectives, was still viewed more as art than as science, and instructional programs were generally intended for use without modification. Today, however, the world of instruction (and of the psychology of instruction) has taken on a different hue. Instruction is viewed more and more in terms of specific skills, strategies, and memory structures. And educators, whether by their own choice, or by force of court and legislative action, are becoming more attentive to the structure and consequences of instruction. Instructional programs are no longer seen exclusively as faits accomplis, which one accepts or rejects in toto. Instead, schools and school districts are more and more specifying their own criteria for effective instruction, and requesting that programs be adapted accordingly.

Computer-assisted instruction (CAI), because of its generally high degree of specificity and its potential for saving student responses, offers possibilities for adaptation of instruction and, therefore, for evaluation that are not practical with noncomputer approaches. What these possibilities are, to what degree they are already being realized, and how they can be fully implemented, are the concerns of this chapter. In the next section, a context for discussing evaluation is developed. Then, four levels of CAI evaluation are presented and reviewed in relation to current practice. In this discussion CAI is not restricted to any particular instructional design or hardware configuration. Generative or intelligent CAI is included, along with more traditional modes, whether implemented on large machines (e.g., PLATO), minicomputers (e.g., TICCIT), or microcomputers.

CONTEXT

In this chapter, *evaluation* will be limited to formal or systematic evaluation of curricula, primarily for the benefit of potential users of the curricula. Evaluation of learners, teachers, or schools will not be considered, nor will evaluation of curricula other than for potential users. This orientation parallels that of Popham (1975, p. 8), who defines *systematic educational evaluation* as "a formal assessment of the worth of educational phenomena."

Evaluation in the sense meant here is an adjunct to decision making. It supplies information that supplements what has been learned from other sources, and presumably does so with a high degree of confidence in the validity and reliability of its results. Where sufficient information for a decision exists from informal observation and other nonrigorous procedures, formal evaluation is unnecessary. And where no decision is to be made, evaluation is unwarranted. Thus, the starting point for the design of an evaluation is a clarification of the decisions that the evaluation is to facilitate. From this standpoint, the logic of evaluation parallels the logic of testing as advocated by Cronbach (1966).

Evaluation of CAI generally is done as an aid to institutions and individuals who would use such materials. We might consider, for example, the concerns of a state department of education that plans to implement special instruction for secondary-level students who fail minimum competency examinations in math and reading. Among the options available might be a homemade summer tutorial program using math and reading specialists, an after-school or summer program on a performance contract with an outside agency, and several CAI systems. In reviewing each of these options, information would be gathered on such issues as:

1. Objectives (what each program attempts to achieve)
2. Content covered (the specific materials and skills taught)
3. Instructional design (the approach to instruction, including teaching methods, assessment procedures, and reinforcement techniques)
4. Feedback (the types of information that will be supplied to teachers and others on individual students)
5. Adaptability (how easily each program can be modified to include new skills and materials), and
6. Resources required (initial costs, sustaining costs, personnel, space, and equipment)

Different organizations might assign different weights to these factors. Those, like Florida, that are under court order to demonstrate a relationship between test items and instructional content (*Debra P. v. Turlington*) probably assign the highest priorities to items 2 and 3. States like Wisconsin, which are still considering minimum competency testing, might be more concerned with adaptability and resource requirements. Evaluation studies could provide some of the data required for these considerations, but other sources of information would also be needed. By whatever set of deliberations, the State of Florida decided recently to utilize a CAI system for remediating minimum competency failures for math, whereas New York City selected the summer tutorial route for reading.

Similar decisions are being made throughout the United States on every level of schooling. For example, many elementary schools, in reviewing supplementary materials for reading instruction, are now considering CAI along with kits, minilibraries, film strips, textbooks, and all the other offerings of the publishing trade. Similarly, community colleges are beginning to consider CAI programs for English grammar, and industry and the military are actively comparing CAI to other delivery schemes for instruction in technical areas. These are some of the consumers for CAI evaluation studies. Their needs, although diverse, share a concern for the six factors described previously. How evaluations have been and could be designed to attend to the instructional focus of these concerns is the topic of the remainder of this chapter. The evaluation of costs and other resources required for implementing CAI is left for another time.

FOUR LEVELS OF EVALUATION

Level 1: Pondering the Achievement Gain

The simplest evaluation that can be done looks only at student outcomes. This is, in the terms of Scriven (1967), truly summative evaluation. Fletcher and Atkinson (1971), for example, describe a matched-pairs design used to evaluate the Stanford CAI Initial Reading Curriculum. Twenty-five pairs of first-grade boys and 25 pairs of first-grade girls were matched on Metropolitan Readiness Test scores. The experimental group then received 8–10 minutes per day of CAI instruction for about 5½ months. Various achievement measures taken near the end of the instructional period showed that the experimental group was generally 0.4–0.7 school years ahead of the control group.

This variation on the Pretest–Posttest Control Group Design has been widely used in curriculum evaluation. Less commonly used, but equally valuable, is the Time–Series Design, in which the student outcomes after introduction of a new curriculum (i.e., treatment) are compared not to control group outcomes, but to outcomes in the same context prior to the introduction of the new curriculum (Campbell & Stanley, 1963). Osin (1980) employed this design, among other evaluative techniques, in assessing the outcomes of a middle-grade CAI math program. At each grade level, average yearly gain scores were obtained for several years prior to the introduction of the CAI curriculum. Then, for each of the 3 years following the use of the CAI lessons, yearly gain scores were obtained. Larger increases in yearly gains were recorded in each of the post-CAI assessments than in the pre-CAI assessments; in addition, by the end of the third year, the rate of increase over the pre-CAI outcomes was decreasing, indicating that an achievement asymptote was being reached.

The time series design, although lacking the experimental rigor of the control group design, has higher ecological validity. It approaches more closely than does the control group design the natural conditions under which a curriculum will operate. The time series design also gives some insight into novelty and halo effects by observing outcomes for several years after a change is introduced. Control group curriculum studies require a degree of sanitization that rarely can be obtained in a school setting. Students, teachers, and parents know they are part of a study. Where obviously innovative approaches are used, and particularly where computer terminals are part of the instruction, an aura of privilege is created. Furthermore, schools and students are rarely chosen randomly for such studies. Principals, teachers, and parents must all agree that their children can participate, and the ones most willing to do so are often the ones who also reach out for other approaches to improve student achievement.

Regardless of experimental design, significant differences between a CAI group and a control or base group might not always result directly from the CAI instruction itself. The CAI curriculum, for example, might make the teachers more aware of the specific skills that need to be taught so that they do a better job of teaching these skills in their classroom instruction. This might have happened in the Stanford study cited previously, especially because the CAI students also gained significantly more than the control students in skills not taught by the CAI lessons. Without observing how the human component of the curriculum changes with the introduction of CAI lessons, causal chains are difficult to establish. This is one drawback to the exclusive use of student outcome measures in an evaluation study, but a drawback that is relatively simple to remedy.

Level 2: The Field-Work Additive

Several CAI evaluations have probed beyond outcome differences, generally through the use of teacher questionnaires and classroom observation. A highly readable example of this is a study designed and implemented by CEMREL for a CAI project in the rural highlands (Smith & Pohland, 1974). Three phases of evaluation were carried out during a school year:

1. A standard pre- and posttest achievement-gains comparison, using standard instruments and control groups
2. An affective–attitudinal survey of pupils, teachers, and parents, using questionnaires and interviews
3. A participant–observer anthropological study, using *in situ* observers.

The participant–observer component focused on teachers and students, examining the effects of system changes and system failures, teacher utilization (and frustration), and pupil attitudes and work habits. Of particular interest to the evaluators were the effects of the local culture—its concepts of time, its poverty, and its politics—on the attitudes and activities of the staff and students in the experiment. A similar design was utilized by the Educational Testing Service (ETS) in its evaluation of the PLATO and TICCIT systems (Alderman, 1978; Murphy & Appel, 1977; Swinton, Amarel, & Morgan, 1978).

Observation of classroom behavior and assessment of attitudes add significantly to the interpretation of achievement measures; however, such designs still provide no information on the nature of the instruction itself. First, it is important to know how much instruction was actually received by the students. Although time-on-task by itself is an unreliable predictor of achievement, when it is coupled with instructional content it provides a robust gauge of instructional quality (Harris & Serwer, 1966; Stallings & Kaskowitz, 1974). Gross measures of on-line time have been included in many evaluations of CAI lessons (e.g., Fletcher & Atkinson, 1971; Gentile, 1967; Hansen, 1966); however, few studies have distinguished *on-line time* from *lesson time*. Generally, on-line time is compiled by software functions that record log-on and log-off time. During this time the student may be attending to the CAI lesson; but he or she might also be in the bathroom, tying a shoe, reading a comic book, or even playing on-line games. Poore, Qualls, and Brown (1979), in an evaluation of PLATO Basic Math Skills lessons, found that approximately 2 hours of terminal time were required to register 1 hour of lesson time.

Accurate measurements of lesson time can, for the most part, be obtained on-line. Algorithms could be developed for detecting unusually long response times, and techniques such as occasional "Press RETURN if you are still there" probes could be incorporated in lessons. Furthermore, by carefully designing the frequency of requests for student responses, the probability of detecting nonattending times could be made quite high. (On systems like PLATO, and Apple II with PILOT, students can be routed automatically to a particular lesson, and game-playing and use of alternative lessons can be eliminated. However, where automatic routing is not used, time spent in each lesson must be recorded within the lesson itself.)

With the measurement of lesson time, part of the treatment can be assessed. What remains is specification of the treatment itself. The total potential objectives for a large, adaptive CAI lesson are not necessarily what any particular student will receive. First, the interactive properties of a CAI lesson might lead to a significant portion of the time in each session being taken up with sign-on and sign-off protocols and routing information. These problems, coupled with system failures and overload response delays, may result in some students not completing the CAI course objectives.

Second, where there is complex branching in the CAI program, criterion levels for mastery may be set too high, thus forcing overlearning, or they may be set too low, thus allowing students to progress to objectives they are not prepared for. Osin (1980) describes such a problem with a math test and drill program.

Most, but not all, CAI lessons are designed for specific objectives that can be identified with specific segments of lesson code (units, blocks, algorithms, segments, etc.). In these cases, information on mastery attainment and time can be recorded for each student. Schools that are considering use of such lessons could then determine from the results of an evaluation study not only the relative amounts of time spent on each objective, but also the relationship between time and mastery level on particular objectives and on overall achievement in the course. With the widespread use of behavioral objectives and minimum competency testing, schools today need to know, for any instructional program under consideration, what objectives (i.e., skills) are actually taught in the program and how effective the instruction for each objective is.

As a result of the *Debra P. v. Turlington* decision in Florida, that state must now demonstrate that it in fact teaches the skills that it tests on its minimum competency examinations. The judge in this case has indicated, furthermore, that this requirement cannot be met satisfactorily simply by reference to the objectives ostensibly taught in particular courses (Haney, 1981). CAI evaluations (if they are to assist instructional decision-making in Florida and in other states using minimum competency exams as diploma requirements) must provide performance data on specific objectives within courses, not just on the course as a whole. To declare that such matters are a concern of formative rather than summative evaluation is as naive as declaring a rock to be a tree and expecting it to bear fruit.

The distinction between formative and summative evaluation is not useful in an instructional world that plans its activities around specific objectives. An evaluation that simply tells how well students scored on an overall achievement test at the end of the year is not sufficient for such school systems. Schools are beginning to understand that instruction is their responsibility, and not that of the programs they purchase. More and more, schools are defining the skills they want to teach, and then searching for programs that assist in achieving these ends. Fortunately, some CAI evaluations have already attended to these needs, as is described in the next section.

Level 3: A Glimpse into the Black Box

The third level of CAI evaluation incorporates the measures required for Levels 1 and 2, but adds analyses of performance on specific skills. One model for doing this can be found in an evaluation study of PLATO Basic Math Skills lessons used for Florida high school students (Poore et al., 1979). Three high schools used the math lessons during the 1978–1979 school year, primarily with students who had failed the statewide math assessment on their first try. Nine skill areas were covered by the lessons, ranging from basic number ideas to geometry and area measurement. Each school analyzed the contents of the lessons, and decided on its own how to incorporate them into regular classes.

In one school, for example, 236 students spent 20–30 minutes per day on the terminals, and the remaining remedial instruction time using various types of workbooks. Among the data collected in the evaluation, which was carried out by the Computing Center at Florida State University, were times spent in each lesson objective. These data were reported separately for students who finished the entire curriculum, for students who completed at least the whole number operations (but not the whole curriculum), and for students who did not complete the whole number operations (see Table 1).Pretest and posttest scores were also reported for each of these groups for the entire curriculum. As one would expect if instruction were meaningful, gain scores increased with increasing coverage of the curriculum.

There are obvious faults to this study, particularly in its failing to report on the non-CAI instruction. However, its attention to performance on specific objectives, and to lesson time as opposed to terminal time, are contributions to CAI evaluation. Similar reports on time spent on specific objectives can be found in two evaluation reports from a University of Alberta CAI project; one on COMPS, an introductory, college-level computer sciences course (Romaniuk, 1978), and one on STAT 1, a college-level statistics course (Hunka, Romaniuk, & Maguire, 1976). Evaluation data from these studies are shown in Tables 2 and 3. What none of these studies does that is needed, however, is to relate performance on lesson objectives to performance on external measures of each objective. The question that schools want answered for each CAI course (or any other type of course) is how well the course teaches specific skills. Time measures could provide confirmation of instructional effectiveness if, for example, within a specified range, increased time spent on an objective led to higher achievement on an external assessment of that objective. The shape of the time-achievement curve would also be informative. An early asymptote, for example, would indicate extensive overteaching, whereas a near-zero initial slope (x

TABLE 1

Average Number of Hours (and Number of Students) Spent in Nine Areas of Math for Each Student Group

Area	All students	Students completing entire curriculum	Students completing whole number operations	Students not completing whole number operations
All schools				
Basic number ideas	1.88 (230)	1.55 (58)	1.93 (163)	3.12 (9)
Addition	0.98 (235)	0.86 (58)	1.00 (166)	1.32 (11)
Subtraction	1.21 (235)	0.92 (58)	1.22 (166)	2.73 (11)
Multiplication	1.21 (234)	0.67 (58)	1.29 (166)	2.95 (10)
Division	2.87 (232)	2.03 (58)	3.14 (166)	3.45 (8)
Fractions	7.18 (229)	7.06 (58)	7.40 (165)	2.34 (6)
Decimals	2.65 (209)	3.62 (58)	2.32 (148)	0.20 (3)
Ratio/prop/percent	1.59 (195)	2.50 (58)	1.21 (137)	—
Geometry/measurement	1.37 (193)	2.91 (58)	0.65 (129)	—
Total time	19.74 (236)	22.01 (58)	19.39 (167)	13.12 (11)
At Paxon				
Basic number ideas	2.00 (112)	1.39 (39)	2.12 (69)	5.82 (4)
Addition	0.78 (112)	0.71 (39)	0.74 (69)	2.35 (4)
Subtraction	1.04 (112)	0.75 (39)	0.99 (69)	4.74 (4)
Multiplication	1.16 (112)	0.58 (39)	1.19 (69)	6.41 (4)
Division	2.32 (112)	1.32 (39)	2.72 (69)	5.27 (4)
Fractions	6.13 (111)	4.83 (39)	7.08 (69)	1.09 (3)
Decimals	2.80 (101)	2.62 (39)	2.92 (62)	—
Ratio/prop/percent	1.89 (94)	1.69 (39)	2.04 (55)	—
Geometry/measurement	2.04 (89)	2.70 (39)	1.53 (50)	—
Total time	19.08 (112)	16.49 (39)	20.18 (69)	25.40 (4)

Note. From J. H. Poore, Jr., J. E. Qualls, & B. L. Brown. *Basic skills in math for Florida High Schools.* Final Report. FSU PLATO Project. Computing Center, Florida State University, Tallahassee, Florida, 1979. Reprinted with permission.

= time, y = achievement) would probably indicate inadequate prerequis-
ities (or a poor introduction) for the skill involved.

We could not expect such information from an evaluation of a noncomputer course, due to the heavy cost in hand compilation of the data required. But CAI systems that are intelligently designed should provide such
data as a standard part of their operation. The advantages of CAI will
probably not be realized as long as CAI lessons are seen as black boxes for
which only inputs and outputs are important. The folly of the teacher-proof
curriculum no longer menaces most CAI design, as it did in the 1960s. Lower
(1976), among others, has made convincing arguments for the necessity of
designing CAI lessons to work within a teacher-controlled environment,
rather than apart from it. With powerful computers and intelligently designed courseware, an even higher level of evaluation feedback can be provided than is represented by Level 3.

Level 4: A Paradigmatic Shift

Let us for a moment imagine what the world of CAI might be in 5 to 10
years, as if we believed the most optimistic projections now emanating from
the cognitive-science–intelligent-CAI workshops and the Delphian centers
of the microcomputer industry. Classrooms will abound in networks of
powerful, inexpensive, desktop machines with nearly limitless memories,
print-quality graphics, and voice input and output. Courseware will be
cognitively based, capable of diagnosing student strategies, and will be able
to gain access to enormous information banks and to interpret natural language responses. Consider now what role evaluation could serve in such a
reverie and what information such a role would require.

Undoubtedly we would still want to assess general outcomes and to observe the culture of the classroom or whatever setting would evolve for
learning. We might not divide the instructional world into subject-depend-
ent skills as we do now, but we would probably have learning units smaller
than the total course (or whatever larger unit might replace courses). Performance on these smaller units would need to be monitored just as we
need to monitor subject-related skill performance today, but such monitoring would need to be adapted to the mode of operation of the CAI lessons.

Intelligent CAI

To understand what would be required to do this, consider the state-of-
the-art in intelligent CAI (ICAI). Programs such as ADS (Marshall, 1980),

TABLE 2

Mean Time to Complete COMPS Segments

Segment	Mean	Low	High
10	1:32	0:28	2:19
15	2:21	0:54	3:25
20	2:01	1:02	2:54
25	1:38	0:22	2:11
99	0:17	0:01	0:31

Note. From E. W. Romaniuk, *A summative evaluation of the CAI course "COMPS".* Report DERS-06-049, Division of Educational Research Services, University of Alberta, Edmonton, Alberta, 1978. Reprinted with permission.

and BUGGY (Brown & Burton, 1978) have in common the capability to build a model of the students' abilities, a representation of expert behavior in relation to the skills to be taught, and a representation of the subject matter itself. Through diagnosis of the students' strategies and their relationship to expert strategies, instruction is generated (cf. Case, 1978). There are no predetermined, frame-by-frame sequences, nor are there fixed responses to be given to particular student answers.

Figure 1 shows an information flow diagram for the modeler and tutor developed by Burton and Brown (1979) for the PLATO math game "How the West was Won." For this board game, the modeler generates all possible moves at each choice point and then selects the best possible moves according to a particular play strategy. If the student fails to select one of the optimal moves, the features that were present in the optimal moves but not in the student move (e.g., use of parentheses or negative numbers) are recorded, along with the actual move (and a variety of other information). Through this process, a model of the student is constructed, based upon features (called issues) that the student fails to use. The tutor program decides when a student should receive advice on a particular feature and then generates the advice using frame sentences.

A second characteristic of ICAI is represented by Figure 2, which shows a procedural network for the addition of two fractions, adopted from Marshall (1980; see also Larkin, this volume). Although subskill hierarchies have been used for many years for guiding instruction, the use of procedural networks, directed graphs, and semantic networks to direct both diagnosis of student abilities and generation of instruction is unique to ICAI.

A generalization of ICAI presented by Osin (1980) is shown in Figure 3. Within the ICAI system, a teacher model accesses the student model to

TABLE 3

Time to Complete Various Sections of STAT1 by Students in 1975 and 1976[a]

	Average hours		Minimum hours		Maximum hours	
Topic	1975	1976	1975	1976	1975	1976
Lessons						
Introduction to terminal	—	0.6	—	0.2	—	1.5
Descriptive statistics	6.0	2.1	.27	1.0	12.0	5.9
Prediction & correlation	12.0	9.9	6.5	5.3	19.0	20.8
Multiple & partial correlation	2.9	3.3	0.8	2.1	4.0	5.0
Tests & confidence intervals[b]	2.0	4.8	1.0	2.5	6.0	8.5
Terms of inferential statistics	0.1	0.3	0.1	0.1	0.6	0.7
Random sample of means	1.1	1.1	0.5	0.3	2.4	2.3
Probability of RSD of mean	0.9	1.0	0.2	0.3	2.6	6.1
Hypothesis testing	7.7	6.1	2.3	2.6	15.2	17.5
Anova: purpose	1.1	1.0	0.4	0.3	2.0	1.6
Anova: computation	2.0	1.4	0.7	0.6	4.4	2.8
Anova: intuitive approach	2.5	2.2	1.1	0.7	4.1	4.1
Anova: mathematical	1.2	1.3	0.3	0.7	4.4	2.0
Tukey & Scheffé	6.6	6.3	2.4	3.5	10.2	11.2
Anova: 2-way interaction	3.5	3.6	1.3	1.3	5.7	6.1
Chi-square	1.3	1.6	.5	.8	2.4	2.3
Normal curve and binomial[c]	—	5.7	—	3.0	—	11.6
Data analysis & research design[c]	—	3.1	—	1.0	—	5.8
Examinations						
Descriptive statistics	—	1.1	—	0.4	—	3.2
Prediction	—	1.0	—	0.3	—	2.2
Correlation #1	—	1.1	—	0.4	—	2.8
Correlation #2	—	0.9	—	0.3	—	2.4
Hypothesis testing	—	0.9	—	0.4	—	3.0
	50.9	60.4	20.8	8.1	95.0	129.4

[a]From S. Hunka, E. W. Romaniuk, and T. O. Maguire. *Report on the use of the computer-assisted course Stat 1 as used in Educational Psychology 502, 1975–1976.* Report DERS-06-036, Division of Educational Research Services, University of Alberta, Edmonton, Alberta, 1976. Reprinted with permission.

[b]In 1975 the topic of confidence intervals was not part of this section.

[c]These two sections were added to the 1976 testing and did not appear in the 1975 version of the course.

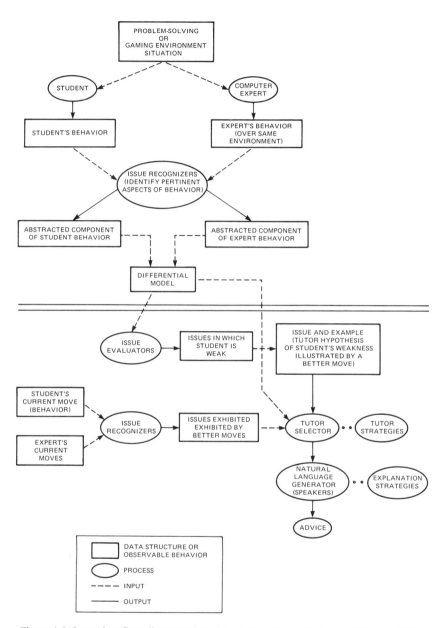

Figure 1 Information flow diagram of modeler/tutor. (From Burton and Brown, 1976; reprinted with permission.)

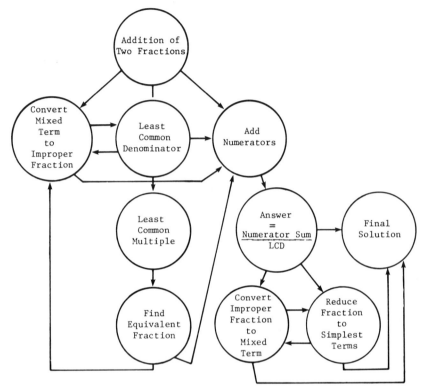

Figure 2 A portion of the procedural network for the addition of two fractions. (From Marshall, 1980; reprinted with permission.)

learn what the student knows and the subject-area (universe) model for what remains to be learned. From these data, the system decides what task to present to the student. Once a task is generated, the student draws upon his or her current knowledge to do the task and presents this decision to the ICAI system. From the student response, the system updates its student model and initiates a new decision cycle.

INTRINSIC EVALUATION

For teachers to decide if such systems meet their instructional needs and are adaptable to the total curriculum, special types of evaluative information will be needed. First, it will be important to know the range of student

ICAI System

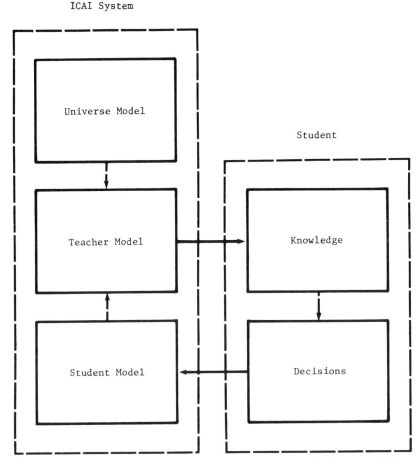

Figure 3 A generalization of intelligent CAI. (From Osin, 1980; reprinted with permission.)

strategies the program is capable of diagnosing and the probability of diagnosing each correctly. Second, it will be important to know for each diagnosis the effectiveness of the instruction that follows, both in terms of achievement outcomes and in terms of time spent learning.

We can characterize ICAI programs as sequences of assertions of the form (S_i, I_{ij}, S_j) where S_i is the learner's current state, S_j is the next desired learner state, and I_{ij} is the instruction generated for moving from state S_i to state S_j. In other words, the program asserts first that, based on its diagnosis, the learner is in state S_i. Furthermore, it asserts that instruction I_{ij} is sufficient to move the learner to state S_j. The role of evaluation in such a model is to assess the validity of both the *state* and *instruction* assertions. To do this effectively, evaluation procedures will need to be designed as an integral part of the lesson itself, that is, be intrinsic to the lesson. In the current ICAI systems, the instructional components are quite weak, generally consisting of simple frame sentences or problems to be worked. For a given skill network and learner state, these systems tend to have an invariant task to present. The next generation of such systems has a wide research literature on instructional approaches to draw upon to begin to produce adaptive, ICAI systems that continually evaluate their own behavior and adjust their instructional paradigms and processes accordingly. To evaluate such systems, it will be necessary to determine how the instructional approach changes with student behavior.

FEASIBLE PROGRAMS

Instructional Tools

It is probable, however, that even with adaptive ICAI, the main use of computers in the classroom over the next decade will not be for delivery of complete curricula. Instead, computers will provide instructional and management tools to support a teacher-directed curriculum. Text editors, spelling checkers, and writing aids (see chapters by Rubin and by Levin, Boruta & Vasconcellos, this volume), along with skill diagnosis systems, learning games, and simulations may become as common supplements to classroom programs as kits, cassette tapes, and board games are today. Such tools may represent the most effective utilization of the current (and coming) generation of microcomputers, given the limited number of machines available to the average classroom and the unproven quality of CAI curricula.

Evaluation of instructional tools can follow the same guidelines as suggested above for courseware, but with an added emphasis on compatibility with the teacher-directed curriculum. A general diagnostic program for elementary reading, for example, would need to provide assessments for all the important skills taught in the major reading programs in use today, and would also need to provide feedback to the teacher in a vocabulary that was compatible with what she or he was accustomed to. Such tools must do their intended tasks well, be friendly to their users, and provide adequate and readable feedback to the instructor.

Hardware Limitations

Both Level 3 and Level 4 evaluation require large-volume, ongoing data collection. They cannot be implemented easily on existing microcomputers, both because of storage and CPU limitations, and because of the impracticability of collecting performance data from stand-alone microcomputers with diskettes. Networked machines, with centralized mass storage are a minimum requirement, but for the present generation of microcomputers (e.g., TRS-80, Apple II), there is probably little possibility of achieving CAI worthy of sophisticated evaluation. With current limitations on graphics resolution, CPU speeds, random-access memory, and disk capacity for low-cost devices, little more than page turning can be implemented for real-time operation. At present, cognitively sophisticated lessons exist only on more powerful machines. The newer generation of microcomputers, with 16-bit word size, and corresponding improvements in other characteristics, may also be inadequate for major implementations. But there are strong indications that sufficient power will be available soon in microcomputers to build and deliver ICAI systems with intrinsic evaluation. What remains is to develop a more adequate cognitive base for both instruction and evaluation.

CONCLUSIONS AND RECOMMENDATIONS

CAI, whether realized as curricular courseware or as instructional tools, should be viewed as a resource within a teacher-directed classroom. The interaction of the computer with the students and teachers, its compatibility with the normal classroom routines and discourse, and its ability to provide timely and interpretable feedback are as important as the intelligence of its programs. Assessment of all of these factors is critical to a complete evaluation. (On the classroom as a social environment, see Amarel, this volume.)

ICAI requires evaluation that assesses beyond the initial and terminal states of the learner. At a minimum, instructional effectiveness and efficiency for identifiable subskills should be determined. A complete evaluation would probe the algorithms and heuristics that drive the program.

Intrinsic rather than extrinsic evaluation should be implemented. That is, evaluation procedures should be designed and coded directly into the lessons themselves, just as debugging and testing circuitry is built into modern integrated circuits. Post hoc, neutral observer evaluation is inefficient for

CAI (intelligent or not). Effective utilization of classroom computers requires a dynamic integration process, whereby programs and users are adapted over time to increase total instructional efficiency. To achieve this, CAI lessons (and tools) must collect and analyze operational information continually.

School districts should include specifications for intrinsic evaluation in their specifications for courseware. By requiring that lessons have built-in collection of performance data, schools can quickly change the current design and evaluation practices of CAI developers.

Research labs and research and development centers, in attending to the problems of integrating computers into classrooms, should provide schools with practical guidelines for evaluating lessons and instructional tools. The recent National Council of Teachers of Mathematics guidelines for courseware evaluation are a major step towards this goal (Heck, Johnson, & Kansky, 1981).

REFERENCES

Adlerman, D. L. *Evaluation of the TICCIT computer-assisted instructional system in the community college,* Vol. 1. Final Report, Educational Testing Service, Princeton, New Jersey, 1978.

Ayres, L. P. History and present status of educational measurements. *The measurement of educational products.* (Seventeenth Yearbook of the National Society for the Study of Education, Part 2). Bloomington, Illinois: Public School Publishing Co., 1918.

Brown, J. S., & Burton, R. R. Diagnostic models for procedural bugs in basic mathematical skills. *Cognitive Science,* 1978, *2,* 155–192.

Bruner, J. S. *Toward a theory of instruction.* New York: Norton, 1966.

Burton, R. R., & Brown, J. S. An investigation of computer coaching for informal learning activities. *International Journal of Man–Machine Studies,* 1979, *11,* 5–24.

Campbell, D. T., & Stanley, J. C. *Experimental and quasi-experimental designs for research.* Chicago: Rand McNally, 1963.

Case, R. A developmentally based theory and technology of instruction. *Review of Educational Research,* 1978, *48,* 439–463.

Cronbach, L. J. New light on test strategy from decision theory. In A. Anastasi (Ed.), *Testing problems in perspective.* Washington, D.C.: American Council on Education, 1966.

DuBois, P. H. A test-dominated society: China, 1115 B.C.–1905 A.D. *Proceedings of the 1964 Invitational Conference on Testing Problems.* Princeton, New Jersey: Educational Testing Service, 1965.

Fletcher, J. D., & Atkinson, R. C. *An evaluation of the Stanford CAI Program in Initial Reading* (grades K through 3). (Tech. Rep. No. 168, Psychology Series). Stanford, California: Stanford University, Institute for Mathematical Studies in the Social Sciences, 1971.

Gentile, J. R. The first generation of computer-assisted instructional systems: An evaluative review. *AV Communication Review,* 1967, *15,*(1), 23–53.

Haney, W. *Validity and competency tests: The Debra P. Case, conceptions of validity and strategies for the future.* Paper presented at The Conference on the Courts and Content Validity in Minimum Competency Testing, Boston College, Boston, October 13–14, 1981.

Hansen, D. N. Computer-assisted instruction. *Review of Educational Research,* 1966, *36,* 588–603.

Harris, A. J., & Serwer, B. L. The CRAFT Project: Instructional time in reading research. *Reading Research Quarterly,* 1966, *2,* 27–56.

Heck, W. P., Johnson, J., & Kansky, R. J. *Guidelines for evaluating computerized instructional materials.* Reston, Virginia: National Council of Teachers of Mathematics, 1981.

Hunka, S., Romaniuk, E. W., & Maguire, T. O. *Report on the use of the computer-assisted course Stat 1 as used in Educational Psychology* 502, 1975–1976. (Report DERS-06-036). Edmonton, Alberta: University of Alberta, Division of Educational Research Services, 1976.

Lower S. K. Making C.A.I. make a difference in college teaching. Paper delivered to the NATO Advanced Study Institute on Computers in Science Education, Louvain-la-neuve, Belgium, July 1976.

Marshall, S. P. Procedural networks and production systems in adaptive diagnosis. *Instructional Science,* 1980, *9,* 129–143.

Merwin, J. C. Historical review of changing concepts of evaluation. In Ralph W. Tyler (Ed.), *Educational evaluation: New role, new means* (Sixty-eighth Yearbook of the National Society for the Study of Education, Part 2). Chicago: University of Chicago Press, 1969.

Moley, R. The Cleveland surveys—net. *The Survey,* 1923, *50,* 229–231.

Murphy, R. T., & Appel, L. R. *Evaluation of the PLATO IV Computer-based education system in the community college.* Final Report, Contract No. NSF–C731. Educational Testing Service, Princeton, New Jersey, 1977.

Osin, L. *Computer-assisted instruction in Israeli disadvantaged elementary schools.* Unpublished manuscript, Centre for Educational Technology, Ramat Aviv, Israel, 1980.

Poore, J. H., Jr., Qualls, J. E., & Brown, B. L. *Basic skills in math for Florida high schools.* Final Report, FSU PLATO Project. Computing Center, Florida State University, Tallahassee, Florida, 1979.

Popham, W. J. *Educational evaluation.* Englewood Cliffs, New Jersey: Prentice–Hall, 1975.

Rice, J. M. The futility of the spelling grind. *The Forum,* 1897, *23,* 163–172; 409–419.

Romaniuk, E. W. *A summative evaluation of the CAI course "COMPS"* (Report DERS–06-049). Edmonton, Alberta: University of Alberta, Division of Educational Research Services, 1978.

Scriven, M. The methodology of evaluation. In R. E. Stake (Ed.), *Curriculum evaluation.* (American Educational Research Association Monograph Series on Evaluation, No. 1.) Chicago: Rand McNally, 1967.

Smith, L. M., & Pohland, P. A. Education, technology, and the rural highlands. In R. H. P. Kraft (Ed.), *Four evaluation examples: Anthropology, economics, narrative, and portrayal.* Chicago: Rand McNally, 1974.

Stallings, J. A., & Kaskowitz, D. *Follow through classroom observation evaluation* 1972–1973. Menlo Park, California: Stanford Research Institute, 1974.

Swinton, S. S., Amarel, M., & Morgan, J. A. *The PLATO elementary demonstration: Educational outcome evaluation.* Final Report submitted to the National Science Foundation. Princeton, New Jersey: Educational Testing Service, 1978.

Thorndike, E. L. Handwriting. *Teachers College Record,* 1910, **11,** 11–21.

PART II

Perspectives from Cognitive Science

The chapters in this section emphasize theory, although some of them also have specific proposals for courseware. In a chapter on students' understanding of physics and chemistry, Jill Larkin begins where the previous section ended. She analyzes the task of learning a science by formulating a cognitive model of two types of knowledge needed by students in science courses: specific knowledge of course content and general knowledge of procedures for solving problems.

Two other chapters continue the theme of formulating a cognitive model, but do so for the domain of learning a language. T. R. G. Green discusses how computer programming languages are learned. He considers what expert programmers know and how the size and structure of a programming language affect its learnability. Robin Chapman, Christine Dollaghan, O. T. Kenworthy, and Jon Miller examine how children learn about verbs of motion in natural language. They also discuss the design of a computer program to be used for teaching and diagnosing knowledge of such verbs with very young children and the handicapped.

Finally, there are two chapters that present cognitive models of students' knowledge of vocabulary. Robert Sternberg, Janet Powell, and Daniel Kaye write about the problem of learning new vocabulary. They discuss alternative methods of improving one's vocabulary, emphasizing psychological processes that underlie effective learning, and they translate their conclusions into an outline of a curriculum. The chapter by Charles Perfetti is also concerned with vocabulary, but more with the benefits of having proficiency in using familiar vocabulary than with techniques for learning new vocabulary. He emphasizes the importance of fluency and rapidity in using one's knowledge of vocabulary, and he applies his analysis to students' reading and writing.

A new theme that emerges from these chapters is the value of understanding what makes an expert proficient. It matters whether the expert is skilled in programming computers, in solving scientific problems, or in using vocabulary. The area of expertise will influence the manner in which a model of the expert's knowledge is formulated. We have no single model that can cover all kinds of expertise. Rather than try to devise a single general model, each chapter in this section presents a model of expertise in a specific domain and uses the model to identify what the novice student needs to learn in that domain.

4

A General Knowledge Structure for Learning or Teaching Science*

Jill H. Larkin

INTRODUCTION

The computer is both a smart beast and a dumb beast. Most applications, especially those in education, view it as a dumb beast: The computer is used to perform, with great reliability and patience, trivial tasks that human beings find tiresome and perform badly. For example, the computer can perform superbly for the writer various trivial tasks, checking spelling and rudimentary grammar or warning the writer about over-long sentences (Frase, Macdonald, Gingrich, Keenan, & Colleymore, 1981). Similarly, the computer can provide continuing, accurate monitoring and pacing of a child's reading practice (Wilkinson, this volume). The computer as dumb

* This work was supported by NSF grant number 1–55035 and by the Defense Advanced Research Projects Agency (DOD), ARPA Order No. 3597, monitored by the Air Force Avionics Laboratory under Contract F33615–78–C–1151. Requests for reprints should be sent to: Jill H. Larkin, Department of Psychology, Carnegie–Mellon University, Pittsburgh, PA 15213.

beast is indeed a wonderful servant, continually taking over one more task that we detest and perform badly.

In addition, however, to being a patient and helpful dumb beast, the computer is also a very smart beast indeed, and that is the aspect of the computer with which I deal in this chapter. Computers operating in their smart mode provide what is called "intelligent" computer-assisted instruction (ICAI). Good examples are the BUGGY and DEBUGGY programs (Brown & Burton, 1978; Brown & VanLehn, 1980), which can look at a child's written work on an arithmetic test, and deduce the erroneous (buggy) algorithms the child used. The intelligent performance of the BUGGY and DEBUGGY programs is at a level far beyond that of even experienced teachers of arithmetic. Another example is the MYCIN program (Davis, Buchanan, & Shortliffe, 1977) and its associated tutoring program (Clancey, 1979) that can, on the basis of explicit rules, diagnose and prescribe treatment for bacterial diseases. In addition, the program can respond intelligently to student questions about how and why the diagnosis was made, or it can intelligently guide students through appropriate steps to make their own diagnoses.

Applications of the computer's intelligence to education need not involve what is ordinarily called computer-assisted instruction. The BUGGY program, for example, provides input to teachers on the nature of the algorithms their students use. How to remedy these deficiencies is up to the teacher.

While programs like these will not be in every pre-college classroom next year, one should not underestimate how quickly the hardware needed to support such intelligent computer applications may become available. Machines able to do important intelligent work should in the next few years be available for a few thousand dollars (Carnegie–Mellon University, 1982). Thus it would be a mistake to believe that all classroom applications of computers will continue to be of the "dumb beast" variety.

The purpose of this chapter is to present one illustrative example of how the computer might function as a smart beast in the classroom. The example is not an implemented program, but a design for a computer-implemented model that could make scientific inferences and guide learners in making such inferences. The design is worked out by considering what general reasoning abilities are necessary to allow a system to use the knowledge presented in textbooks from two different scientific domains (physics and organic chemistry) to solve associated problems.

Such a program could be used as the center of an intelligent CAI program to teach problem solving in science. It would have the virtue that knowledge of a new scientific domain (e.g., astronomy) could be added without writing a whole new program. Furthermore, the instruction itself might stress the general rules of inference, applicable across a variety of scientific disciplines, with the aim that students would learn these important patterns of inference especially well. However, as mentioned in the preceding comments, computer-implemented models (such as BUGGY) may be used in ways that do not involve computer-implemented instruction. The work described here, in fact, has the following major goals that do not involve directly the development of instruction programs.

First, the proposed model explicitly separates knowledge which appears in the textbook from other knowledge that does not appear, but which is necessary to solve problems. There is a lot of this "other" knowledge and it is often not possessed by learners (Larkin, 1982b). Making this other knowledge explicit allows it to be taught directly by teachers, by an expanded textbook, or potentially by computers.

Second, the model includes general knowledge applicable to reasoning in different scientific domains. Explicating this general knowledge allows it to be given special emphasis because of its broad importance. Again, this emphasis can be conveyed by a variety of means.

Finally, the model places knowledge from different scientific domains (here physics and organic chemistry) into a single form (so that the general knowledge in the model can act on both). This common form also allows one to compare and contrast what is required for successful learning and problem solving in each domain. This ability to make systematic comparisons has potential implications for instruction—one might teach very differently depending on the memory and inferencing demands of the domain being taught.

For the purpose of designing the model, I have used scientific material from chapters in two widely-used undergraduate textbooks (Halliday & Resnick, 1970; Solomons, 1978). Science and mathematics at the introductory university (or late high-school) levels provide good domains for research of this kind. The content is well structured, facilitating the difficult task of identifying patterns of general inference. Many students find mastering these domains very difficult, yet society increasingly needs to use scientific knowledge intelligently. Therefore, it is worthwhile to make a substantial research investment to understand these domains well and to design effective instruction for them.

The next section of this chapter gives a general description of the design of the proposed computer-implemented model. The succeeding sections describe the encoding of knowledge from physics and from organic chemistry. The final sections discuss interpretations based on the model of why these two sciences are difficult to learn and teach.

DESCRIPTION OF THE MODEL

The model is designed to be implemented as a *production system,* a type of computer program very different from the familiar structured programs written in FORTRAN-like languages. Production systems have two components: A relatively small *working memory* contains a collection of elements that might be thought of as statements or parts of statements. Each element contains several fields and the contents of one field can be used to point to another working-memory element. Thus, a collection of elements can function together as a composite declarative statement. This working memory is acted on by a usually large collection of condition-action rules called *productions.*

As the production system operates, the contents of working memory are matched against the conditions associated with every production. If the conditions associated with one production are found to match the current contents of working memory, then the associated actions are implemented, actions which ordinarily add, delete, or modify elements in working memory. Because the working-memory contents are now different, ordinarily a different production will have its conditions satisfied, its actions will then be implemented, and the cycles continue. Models written as production systems are thus flexible programs that respond to the current contents of working memory, and are not driven by the rigid hierarchical structure of a FORTRAN-like program. Such programs have repeatedly proved useful for efforts in psychological modeling and in artificial intelligence (Newell, 1977; Newell & Simon, 1972).

For the effort described here, the distinction between working memory and production memory provides a natural distinction between declarative and procedural knowledge. The working memory contains statements describing knowledge about the current problem being solved, both knowledge given in the problem statement, and knowledge developed through the solution process. Working memory also contains declarative statements corresponding to domain-specific knowledge stated in the textbook chapter (physics or organic chemistry). Problems are solved by productions that make comparisons between the current problem situation and statements from the chapter, and use these comparisons to make inferences about the problem situation, thus adding new information to the problem situation. This matching and inferencing is done by general problem-solving knowledge, which is encoded as productions, that is, as procedural knowledge.

Functionally then, the model has three kinds of knowledge: (1) Domain-specific knowledge that parallels statements in the textbook. It is represented as statements in working memory. (2) Knowledge of the problem currently being solved. Some of this knowledge parallels the original problem statement; the rest reflects inferences that have already been made in efforts to solve the problem. This knowledge too is encoded as statements in working memory. (3) Domain-independent knowledge that can compare the current knowledge of the problem with the textbook knowledge, and decide how to apply a textbook statement to generate new knowledge about the problem. This knowledge is encoded as rules of inference in production memory.

We turn now to describing in more detail the problem representation, the domain-specific knowledge statements, and the general problem-solving knowledge. However, this discussion seems easier in the context of specific examples. Therefore, the following sections discuss these issues in turn for sample problems from physics and from organic chemistry.

PHYSICS

Representation of Problems

Consider the following typical physics problem: A bullet of mass 10 *g* strikes a wooden pendulum of mass 2.0 *kg*. The center of mass of the pendulum rises a vertical distance of 12 *cm*. Assuming the bullet remains embedded in the pendulum, calculate its initial speed. The propositions used to represent this problem initially in the working memory of the model compose the following sentences:

Sentence 1: (has mass bullet)

(has-value mass 10 gram)

(has mass pendulum)

(has-value mass 2 kilogram)

(associates bullet pendulum)

(has-time associates time2)

Sentence 2: (has center-of-mass pendulum)

(moves center-of-mass direction)

(moves center-of-mass distance)

(has-value distance 12 cm)

(has-value direction upward)

Sentence 3: (has speed1 bullet)

(has-time speed1 time1)

(has-value speed1 desired)

These propositions are constructed roughly following the system for representing memory structures proposed by Anderson (1980: Chapter 4). For example, the first sentence is reflected by propositions associating the attribute mass with the bullet and pendulum, and the indicated values with each mass. The general relation *associates* replaces the specific word *strikes*. The word *associates* also reflects knowledge actually appearing in Sentence 2 that, after striking the pendulum, the bullet remains associated with it (i.e., does not pass on through it). The initial representation given to the model is thus quite close to the original verbal problem statement. However, I do not address seriously the challenging issues of how to translate natural language statements into initial problem representation, an issue considered in some detail by Novak (1977).

Representation of Textbook Knowledge

As background for the discussion of the knowledge required to solve this problem, the reader may want to study briefly the complete solution given in Table 1, together with the following statements of physics textbook knowledge:[1]

1. We call one-half the product of the mass of a body and the square of its speed the kinetic energy of the body. If we represent kinetic energy by the symbol K, then
$$K = (1/2)mv^2 \qquad (7-12)$$
2. $U(y) = mgy.$ (8-10)
   The gravitational potential energy is then mgy.
3. Total energy—kinetic plus potential plus internal plus all other forms—does not change.   (p. 151)
   a. $E = K + \Sigma U + \Sigma U_{int} + \Sigma U_{other}$
   b. $E = $ constant
4. The *momentum* of a single particle is a vector p defined as the product of its mass m and its velocity v. That is,
$$\mathbf{p} = m\mathbf{v}. \qquad (9-11)$$
5. The system as a whole will have a *total momentum* P in a particular reference frame, which is defined to be simply the vector sum of the momenta of the individual particles in that same frame, or
$$\mathbf{P} = \mathbf{p}_1 + \mathbf{p}_2 + ... + \mathbf{p}_n \qquad (9-14)$$
6. For a system of particles,
$$\mathbf{p}_1 + \mathbf{p}_2 + ... + \mathbf{p}_n = \mathbf{P}_o \qquad (9-18)$$

[1]Notations at the right indicate the equation or page number from Halliday and Resnick (1970).

TABLE 1
Solution to Ballistic Pendulum Problem

Solution step	Textbook statement of physics knowledge	General knowledge
Momentum during collision[a]		
$\mathbf{p}_{bullet} = m\mathbf{v}_O$	4	Rule-application
$\mathbf{p}_{block} = O$	4	Rule-application
$\mathbf{P} = m\mathbf{v}_O$	5	Summation
Total mass $= M + m$	—	Association
$\mathbf{P} = (M + m)\mathbf{V}$	5	Summation
$m\mathbf{v}_O = (M + m)\mathbf{V}$	6	Conservation
Energy after collision[b]		
$K = (\frac{1}{2})(M + m)v^2$	1	Rule-Application
$E = (\frac{1}{2})(M + m)V^2$	3a	Summation
$U = (M + m)gy$	2	Rule-Application
$E = (M + m)gy$	3a	Summation
$(M + m)gy = (\frac{1}{2})(M + m)V^2$		
Initial speed of bullet[c]		
$v_O = [(M + m)V]/m;\ V = 2gy$	—	—
$v_O = (M + m)2gy/m = 308m/s$	—	—

[a]Momentum of the bullet-block system is conserved during the collision. $\mathbf{v}_O$ is the initial velocity of the bullet; $\mathbf{V}$ is the velocity of the bullet-block system immediately after impact; m and M are the masses of the bullet and block. Lower case $\mathbf{p}$ with a subscript denotes the momentum of an individual object; $\mathbf{P}$ is the momentum of the bullet-block system.
[b]Energy of the bullet–block system is conserved after the collision.
[c]Combining results of preceding steps.

The momenta of the individual particles may change, but their sum remains constant if there is no external force.

The textbook does not contain clear separate statements that total energy is a sum of individual kinetic, potential and other energies; and that total energy is conserved. The individual Statements 3a and 3b are not in the text, but are added here for clarity.

Textbook knowledge is encoded in working memory as propositions analogous to those used for representing the problem. Possible propositional representations for textbook Statements 4 and 5 are shown in Table 2. Each of these representations has a *result* that corresponds closely to the main equation of the corresponding statement in the list following Table 1. The rest of the propositions describe a *setting* in which the result is true. For example, the first result $\mathbf{p} = m\mathbf{v}$ is true when $\mathbf{p}$ is the momentum, m the mass and $\mathbf{v}$ the velocity of one particle. Simple statements and settings anal-

TABLE 2

Propositional Representations of Two Pieces of Textbook Physics Knowledge

Statement of physics knowledge	Result	Setting
4	(equals **p** m**v**)	(has particle mass m) (has particle velocity **v**) (has particle momentum **p**)
5	(equals total-momentum sum 1) (summation sum 1 type 1) (is-a type 1 momentum) (has type 1 particle) (in particle system)	(has total-momentum system)

ogous to this one can be formed for all of the textbook Statements 1, 2, and 4.

The second of the textbook statements encoded in Table 2 (statement 5) is considerably more complex. The result is not a simple equality between two algebraic expressions. The equality is between a quantity, total momentum, and an indefinite sum, labeled *sum 1*. This sum includes all items of a particular type (*type 1*) that satisfy three additional propositions: the type is a momentum, it is the momentum of a particle, and the particle is in the system. (This system is the same system that appears in a later proposition in the setting.) Thus, operationally, this bit of textbook knowledge must be interpreted to mean that there is a quantity called *total momentum* that is an attribute of a system and that it is to be found by finding all the particles in the system, associating with each a momentum (using Statement 4), and then adding all these momenta (in fact, adding them as vectors). Illustrations of the application of these two textbook statements to the pendulum problem are shown in the top part of Table 1.

Representation of General Knowledge

We now turn to the general procedural knowledge, encoded as production rules, that acts to match entities in the problem against the statements of the text, and to use these matches to make appropriate inferences about the problem situation.

To see how these rules work, consider the solution to the pendulum problem (Table 1). Each step shows the associated textbook statement on which it was based. We now consider the additional knowledge, summarized in the third column of Table 1, that is required to relate the textbook statements to the problem statement.

The first step in the solution in Table 1 is based on Statement 4 and is merely an expression for the momentum $\mathbf{P}_{bullet}$ of the bullet. This step illustrates two of the five most primitive kinds of general knowledge, described below:

IS-A RELATIONSHIPS

In order to apply the physics Statement 4 to the bullet, one must have some extra general knowledge of the following kind: If a textbook principle concerns some entity (e.g., a particle), and if an entity in the problem statement (here a bullet) can be considered as the entity mentioned in the principle (i.e., a bullet is a particle), then the principle can be applied to the entity in the problem. This general *is-a* inference pattern is separate from the specific knowledge that a bullet is a particle. The former is applied, for example, both in the current situation, and subsequently in this problem to conclude that because the bullet–block composite is a body, textbook Statement 1 is applicable. Later in this chapter, we will also see it applied in organic chemistry to conclude that because propene is a double-bonded hydrocarbon, a textbook rule describing such compounds can be applied. The *is-a* inference pattern allows a problem solver to connect specific entities in a problem to general entities in a textbook statement.

RULE APPLICATION

This category of general knowledge includes knowledge of how to match and apply standardized types of rules (e.g., theorems and postulates, mathematical and reaction equations). The general knowledge involves matching entities in the rule (e.g., the symbols $\mathbf{p}$ m $\mathbf{v}$ in textbook Statement 4) to entities in the problem statement (the mass and speed of the bullet), and then writing an associated inference (here $\mathbf{p}_{bullet} = m\mathbf{v}$). The same general knowledge is applied four times in the problem solution in Table 1, for example, to use the general textbook Statement 1 ($K = \frac{1}{2}mv^2$) to write the specific relation $K = (\frac{1}{2})(M + m)v^2$ relating the kinetic energy, mass, and speed of the bullet–block composite.

ASSOCIATION

If two objects combine, and thereafter are viewed as one object, our natural tendency is to assume that a quantity (i.e., mass associated with the composite object) is equal to the sum of the corresponding quantities associated with each of the substitution objects. Although far from universally true, this general pattern of inference is ordinarily true for a variety of quantities, including mass, charge, and volume (for incompressible substances). The conservation of these quantities really reflects principles of physics, and is occasionally stated in textbooks (cf., Reif, Larkin, & Brackett, 1975). But the more common situation is reflected in the textbook considered here; such assumptions are not always stated, but are left to the solver to make on the basis of general knowledge. In the pendulum problem, this general knowledge is required to conclude that the mass of the bullet-block composite is $M + m$, the sum of the masses of the two substituents.

SUMMATION

In the problem solution in Table 1, application of textbook Statements 3a and 5 requires a special pattern of general inference of the following form: If a textbook statement involves an indefinite sum (or product) over a collection of quantities satisfying certain criteria, then set a subgoal to find all the quantities satisfying the criteria, and then add (or multiply) them. Such general knowledge is required to interpret a wide variety of principles of physics, including Statements 3a and 5. Other work indicates that students often lack this particular piece of general knowledge, and cannot apply such principles correctly (Larkin, 1982b). The applications of this inference pattern to the pendulum problem are, in fact, quite simple. First, the total momentum $\mathbf{P}$ of the bullet–block system before the collision is the sum of the individual momenta $m\mathbf{v}$ and O, or just $m\mathbf{v}$. Second, the total momentum $\mathbf{P}$ of the bullet–block composite after the collision is just the momentum $(M + m)\mathbf{V}$ of this composite considered as a single particle. Similar reasoning produces the results based on Statement 3a later in the problem solution.

CONSERVATION

Many scientific principles, including Statements 3b and 6, are stated by saying that a certain quantity is "conserved," or "doesn't change." General knowledge is needed to apply such statements usefully to a problem situation. This knowledge is of the form: If there is a statement of conservation applicable to the current situation, then set a subgoal to compute expressions for the conserved quantity at two different times (or states), and then equate these expressions. This general knowledge guides the application of textbook Statements 3b and 6 to produce the final relations in each of the two main parts of the problem solution in Table 1. The final section of the solution merely involves algebraic combination of the results of the two preceding parts, and we will not consider it further.

The five kinds of general knowledge listed above are certainly not specific to physics. Three of them will be seen again in the discussion of organic chemistry. One can also easily generate other examples of their use. For example, *association* underlies the postulate that the length of the line is equal to the sum of the lengths of its segments. *Is-a relations* let us rename ideas of a triangle as line segments. *Rule-application* allows one to match the conditions of a geometric theorem or postulate and to conclude the consequent, an application that has been worked out in detail by Anderson (1980b).

Clearly, these five examples do not exhaust the possibility for general patterns of inference used in a variety of sciences. They merely serve to illustrate the kind of inferences that a model that could work in a variety of scientific domains would have to have. To see how these general patterns of inference apply broadly, we now turn to considering a very different scientific domain.

ORGANIC CHEMISTRY

Representation of Problems

As an example, consider the following typical problem in organic chemistry:

$$\text{Propene} + H_2O \quad \xrightarrow{\;\;H^+\;\;} ?$$

The task is to find the products that result when propene and water react in the presence of H^+ ions. The following propositional representation of this problem is analogous to the representation of the pendulum problem in the previous section:

(Reactant Propene)
(Reactant H_2O)
(Reactant H^+)
(Product desired)

Rather than being encoded as a reactant, the H^+ ion, written over the reaction arrow, might have been encoded as a catalyst (something that participates in the reactions, but emerges unchanged). In the interests of simplicity, it is included with reactants.

Summary Representation of Textbook Knowledge

In general, textbook knowledge in organic chemistry is presented at two quite different levels of detail. First, there is what I shall call the summary level of description. For example, the textbook chapter relevant to the propene problem (Solomons, 1978, Ch. 6), lists a summary of 11 major reactions, including:

Addition of water
$$R—CH = CH_2 + H_2O \xrightarrow{\text{H}^+} R—CH—CH_3$$
$$|$$
$$OH$$

In addition, there are statements that relate names, like *propene,* to the associated structural formula:

$$CH_3—CH = CH_2,$$

three carbon atoms, the first two joined by a single bond, and the second by a double bond. Hydrogen atoms are attached to each carbon atom in such a way that each carbon has a total of four bonds. Using the textbook statement, the following solution to the propene problem can be constructed:

1. The general *is-a* pattern of inference lets one conclude that propene ($CH_3—CH = CH_2$) is an example of the general structural formula ($R—CH = CH_2$) because R stands for any collection of carbons and hydrogens.
2. Rule-application applies to match the $CH_3—CH = C_2$, H_2O, and H^+ in the problem to the corresponding symbols in the textbook statement about addition of water, and to conclude that the corresponding matching product is

$$CH_3—CH—CH_3,$$
$$|$$
$$OH$$

thus solving the problem.

Solutions like this one, based on the summary rules in the textbook, are, however, unsatisfactory for several reasons. First, the solution is unmotivated and difficult to understand. Second, there are about 10 summary rules, each with several variants for each of 25 chapters in the 1-year textbook. Thus, a student is potentially faced with the learning and remembering reliably some 500–750 rules, each as complex and unmotivated as the preceding rule for addition of water. Fortunately, there is another way.

Mechanism Representation of Textbook Knowledge

The following are statements corresponding to the textbook statements (Solomons, 1978 p. 197) in the discussion of addition of water to carbon-carbon double bonds:

1. When a nucleus and electron have come together, a bond is formed between the new nucleus and the nucleus with which the electron is associated
2. Double bonds are sites of negative charge
3. Carbon-carbon bonds are smaller (allow less space for charge separation) than do bonds between carbon and other species
4. A water molecule (H_2O) has a negative site at the oxygen atom, and positive sites at the hydrogen atoms
5. Oxygen can sustain just two bonds

These statements differ from those in the textbook in two ways: they are written in sentences rather than as symbols, and they are slightly generalized; for example, carbon-carbon double bonds are *generally* sites of negative charge (not just those bonds in one particular kind of compound). These textbook statements, together with some general knowledge, are used to produce for the propene problem the solution shown in Table 3.

These statements of textbook knowledge are very different in level of detail from the single summary rule listed earlier. The solution, based on the summary rule, depended totally on remembering that rule completely and precisely, and using general rule-application knowledge to apply it exactly. The current solution (shown in Table 3) uses instead several pieces of chemistry knowledge together with the following general knowledge.

General *is-a* and *rule-application* knowledge is used to recognize in the propene problem examples of double bonds, nuclei, etc. Also, the general knowledge of *conservation* discussed in connection with physics is applied to conclude that when a negative charge is removed from a site, the site becomes positively charged. There are two other forms of general inference used in this problem. Neither was seen in the physics problem, although both are used in physics.

Attraction-repulsion knowledge describes the interaction of entities that tend to attract or repel each other. It includes knowledge that entities that attract each other will tend to come together, and entities that repel will move as far apart as possible (e.g., take up as much space as possible). Although this inference pattern applies directly to charged particles, one can more generally apply it to groups of hostile or amorous animals, or to movable boundaries moving so as to enclose as much space as possible. *Attraction-repulsion* knowledge is used three times in Table 3, twice to infer

TABLE 3
Solution to the Propene Problem ˙

Solution step	Textbook statement of organic chemistry knowledge	General knowledge (see text)
$CH_3—CH = CH_2$ H^+		

The H^+ ion moves to the double bond (negative site) and forms a bond involving one of the electrons.

| $\begin{array}{c} H^+ \\ |\ \ | \\ C—C—C \end{array}$ | 1,2 | is-a, Attraction |

The new H, with its bonded electron, moves to the left carbon, where the larger number of carbon-noncarbon bonds provide more room for the electron.

| $CH_3—C^+$ $H—CH_3$ | 3 | Repulsion |

Because the H^+ moved with an electron, a positive site remains at the central carbon.

| $CH_3—C^+$ $H—CH_3$ | — | Conservation |

The negative site at the oxygen of H_2O moves to the positive site at the C, and an O–C bond forms.

| $\begin{array}{c} CH_3—CH—CH_3 \\ | \\ OH^+_2 \end{array}$ | 4 | Attraction |

Oxygen, which can sustain just two bonds, releases an H^+.

| $\begin{array}{c} CH_3—CH_1—CH_3 \\ | \\ OH \end{array}$ | 5 | Maximum |

the coming together of oppositely charged sites, and once to infer the placement of the positive charge.

The general inference pattern labeled *maximum* contains knowledge that if a quantity can be no larger than a certain value, and a component of that quantity changes so as to make the quantity larger, then some other component must change so that the maximum is not violated. In Table 3 *maximum* knowledge is used to infer that because the oxygen atom (maximum number of bonds = 2) bonds with the carbon, it must release one of the hydrogens. This pattern of inference is similar to the *part–whole* knowledge used in solving arithmetic word problems (Briars & Larkin, 1982).

The solution summarized in Table 3 has several advantages over the original rule-application solution. First, the textbook principles apply to many different reactions. Thus, unlike the original summary rule, if these rules are learned they can be used over and over again. Thus a general policy of learning these "mechanism" rules may allow a substantial saving in the amount of memorization required. Second, many of these rules are interpreted by means of general scientific patterns of inference. Thus, less new knowledge must be learned for organic chemistry, and more knowledge is carried by general patterns that might have been learned and used elsewhere.

WHY IT IS HARD TO LEARN SCIENCE

What does our analysis of the underlying inference rules required to apply textbook knowledge in physics and organic chemistry tell us about why these two subject matters are so very difficult to learn?

Both research studies (Clement, Lochhead, & Soloway, 1979; Larkin, 1982a; Larkin, McDermott, Simon, & Simon, 1980) and the experience of most instructors support the idea that science students begin by trying to apply rules. Thus, the basic general inference structure they use is rule-application. This pattern causes difficulties in both physics and organic chemistry for different reasons.

In physics, the first difficulty is that a large number of the most important principles in the discipline (e.g., conservation of energy, Newton's laws) cannot be applied through rule-application alone. Conservation of energy, for example, requires application of the general reasoning patterns of conservation, and of summation. Newton's laws require summation (of forces, torques, etc.). These important principles will cause difficulty to students operating with rule-application knowledge. Indeed, in one study with 12 beginning physics students working 5 simple mechanics problems, of 9 errors made, 7 involved the application of summation (Larkin, 1982a).

In organic chemistry, the extensive use of rule-application causes difficulties for a different reason. Compared with the simple equation rules in physics, each rule in organic chemistry is very complex, and there are many, many rules. I estimate about 500 rules for a 1-year course in organic chemistry, compared to 70 for a one-year course in physics. This amount of knowledge probably simply can not be memorized reliably in rote form (although students certainly try—organic chemistry students are noted for large packages of flash cards with which they attempt to memorize reaction equations). Accomplishing this feat of memory is made more feasible if the arbitrary summary-level reaction rules are decomposed into mechanism rules of the kind in the textbook statements. Because the mechanism rules appear repeatedly in many different reactions, and some are even general beyond chemistry, total memory load is smaller.

There is some evidence that the problem of reliable memory for rules arises also in physics, even though the rules are simpler and the number smaller. For example, there are two principles relating various descriptions of motion, both of which are readily interpretable using the general pattern of inference that a quantity associated with a whole is equal to the sum of quantities associated with its parts; $v = v_o + at$ can be interpreted as "the final speed equals the initial speed plus the amount speeded up"; $x = v_o t + \frac{1}{2}at^2$ can be interpreted as "the distance traveled equals the amount that would have been traveled at the initial speed plus an extra amount traveled because the object was accelerating with acceleration a." There is a third equation, obtained by eliminating t from the preceding two: $v^2 - v^2_o = 2ax$. This rule, which has no ready interpretation, is almost never used by expert solvers, but is commonly used by novices (Larkin *et al.,* 1980; Simon & Simon, 1978). Thus novices seem to make no distinction between interpretable and less interpretable formulas—all are simply rules to be applied with rule-application knowledge. In contrast, experts have recoded even these simple rules so that they have an interpretable form, and can use broadly applicable (and therefore easily remembered) general pattterns of inference.

CONCLUSION

This chapter has described the kind of general scientific knowledge that would be required to enable a computer to make inferences based on sub-ject-matter knowledge from several scientific domains. Physics and organic chemistry, two very different sciences, were considered here.

The purpose of this analysis is to offer an example of how a computer might be sufficiently intelligent to support good instruction in a complex and difficult subject matter. If an intelligent computer-assisted-instruction system produced the kind of general scientific knowledge outlined here, then it could guide learners not in rote rule application, or in following a collection of lessons formulated by a human instructor, but in applying general scientific patterns of inference to new subject matter.

However, the computer is an aid to instruction beyond its role as a class-room tutor. The computer provides a medium in which one can specify explicitly the nature of the knowledge being taught. Even the simple anal-ysis presented here offers several suggestions that could be used by any science instructor or curriculum designer: Instruction in physics must in-clude careful attention to the general patterns of inference that are required in order to apply the most important principles; instruction in organic chemistry must include efforts to replace ad hoc summary-level reaction rules, unconnected to other knowledge, with rules that both have a wider applicability within chemistry and are based on general scientific knowledge that may already be available.

The computer program envisioned here is currently state-of-the-art work in artificial intelligence, not something to be imagined in the school systems next year. However, recent history should convince us that it is almost impossible to overestimate the sophistication of the computation that will become rapidly available at affordable prices.

Thus, the appropriate focus of this volume on currently available applications of computers to instruction should be tempered with attention to the rapidly approaching possibilities for applications of a very different kind. However much we value the role of the computer as a faithful dumb beast, we need also to explore the possibilities for even more exciting roles for the intelligent beast it is so rapidly becoming.

REFERENCES

Anderson, J. R. *Cognitive Psychology and its Implications.* San Francisco: W. H. Freeman, 1980. (a)

Anderson, J. R. *A general learning theory and its application to the acquisition of proof skills in geometry.* (Tech. Rep. 80-81). Pittsburgh: Carnegie–Mellon University, Department of Psychology, 1980. (b)

Briars, D., & Larkin, J. H. *An integrated model of skill in solving elementary word problems* (A.C.P. 1). Department of Psychology, Carnegie–Mellon University, 1982.

Brown, J. S., & Burton, R. R. Diagnostic models for procedural bugs in basic mathematical skills. *Cognitive Science,* 1978, *2,* 71–109.

Brown, J. S., & VanLehn, K. Repair theory: A generative theory of 'Bugs'. *Cognitive Science,* 1980, *4,* 379–426.

Clancey, W. J. *Transfer of rule-based expertise through a tutorial dialogue.* Unpublished PhD dissertation, Department of Computer Science, Stanford University, 1979.

Clement, J., Lochhead, J., & Soloway, E. *Translating between symbol systems: Isolating a common difficulty in solving algebra word problems* (Tech. Rep.). Amherst: University of Massachusetts, Cognitive Development Project, Department of Physics and Astronomy, 1979.

Davis, R., Buchanan, B., & Shortliffe, E. Production rules as a representation for a knowledge-based consultation program. *Artificial Intelligence,* 1977, *8,* 15–45.

Frase, L. T., Macdonald, N. H., Gingrich, P. S., Keenan, S. A., and Colleymore, J. L. Computer aid for text assessment and writing instruction. *The NSPI* [National Society for Performance of Instruction] *Journal,* 1981, *20,* 21–24.

Halliday, D., & Resnick, R. *Fundamentals of physics.* New York: John Wiley & Sons, 1970.

Larkin, J. H. The cognition of learning physics. *American Journal of Physics,* 1982, *49,* 534–541. (a)

Larkin, J. H. *Spatial knowledge in solving physics problems* (C.I.P. 434). Department of Psychology, Carnegie–Mellon University, 1982. (b)

Larkin, J. H., McDermott, J., Simon, D. P., & Simon, H. A. Models of competence in solving physics problems. *Cognitive Science,* 1980, *4,* 317–345.

Newell, A. Knowledge representation aspects of production systems. *International joint conference on artificial intelligence,* 1977, *7,* 987–988.

Newell, A., & Simon, H. A. *Human problem solving.* Englewood Cliffs, New Jersey: Prentice-Hall, 1972.

Novak, G. S. Representations of knowledge in a program for solving physics problems. *International Joint Conference On Artificial Intelligence,* 1977, *5,* 286–291.

Preliminary report of the task force for the future of computing. Carnegie–Mellon University, 1982.

Reif, F., Larkin, J. H., & Brackett, G. *Principles of Physics for the Physical and Biological Sciences.* Preliminary edition. New York: Wiley, 1975.

Simon, D. P., & Simon, H. A. Individual differences in solving physics problems. In R. Siegler (Ed.), *Children's thinking: What develops?* Hillsdale, New Jersey: Erlbaum, 1978.

Solomons, T. W. G. *Organic Chemistry.* New York: Wiley, 1978.

5

Learning Big and Little Programming Languages

*T. R. G. Green**

INTRODUCTION

Which language should beginners learn? BASIC, LOGO, Pascal? A lesser-known beginner's language like SOLO, especially developed for teaching at a distance in the Open University (Eisenstadt, 1978), or COMAL (Atherton, 1982)? Or what? Perhaps the question will be less acute in 10 years' time, or 20, or 30. Perhaps computer toys, computer games, computer aids to information handling, and computer-driven devices will bring their own logic and their own answers. And perhaps not; perhaps it will merely get harder and harder for the young to absorb all that the world has to offer before they have to give up learning. At any rate the question is certainly acute now.

The available hardware and software change very fast. It would almost certainly be pointless to offer conclusions based on today's technology, or even on a guess at tomorrow's. Instead, we shall approach the problem of

*Requests for reprints should be sent to: Dr. T. R. G. Green, MRC/SSRC Social and Applied Psychology Unit, University of Sheffield, Sheffield S10 2TN, United Kingdom.

criteria to guide choices. (For an entirely different approach, with summaries of research on BASIC, Pascal, LOGO, and other languages in the
hands of novices, see du Boulay, O'Shea, and Monk [1981].)

It is not merely a language that is required, in practice, but an environment for programming. There has been considerable progress in redistri-
buting the balance of work between the computer and the novice user, so
that the computer relieves the user of some of the routine work. BASIC
was an early success: where FORTRAN at that time insisted on an explicit
distinction between integer numbers and reals, with special routines to be
used if an integer value had to be passed over to a real variable or vice
versa, BASIC allowed the programmer to ignore the difference, and automatically converted if the context demanded it. Thus, the computer did
more work, the programmer less. The LOGO language (Papert, 1980) offers some features from LISP in an easy-to-use form, making the routine
use of simple list structures much less trouble because the computer looks
after the "housekeeping" automatically. Teitelbaum (1981) has developed
the Cornell Program Synthesizer to allow novices to create syntactically
correct PL/I programs with very little effort. Eisenstadt (1978) is working
towards an automatic debugging assistant for novices' programs, which automatically attempts to guess why a subroutine fails to meet its specifications. And in the commercial world, program generator packages, such as
the famous "The Last One," claim to absolve their users from needing to
know anything at all about programming!

These highly impressive developments in programming aids are not matched
by corresponding advances in the design of languages themselves. There are
many disagreements over many issues, and we cannot possibly deal with all
of them here. Nor can we hope to touch on other important matters, such
as the teaching of programming, the choice of programming techniques, or
the like. Instead, we concentrate on the size and structure of the language
to be learned.

SIZE OF THE LANGUAGE

"Many novices are frightened away right at the start by the amount of
arbitrary and detailed information that they have to remember, as well as
by the problems of typing accurately and quickly" (du Boulay *et al.,* 1981).
There is no question about that; contemporary languages are certainly
frightening. For this reason many teachers like to start with the teaching
of flowcharts, which have a tiny vocabulary: start/stop boxes, action boxes,
and decision boxes are the only possibilities. Unfortunately, the effect is

diffuse and obscure because the programmer has to construct loops and conditionals as they come. For example, in Figure 1, it is by no means clear whether Test 2 is contained within Loop 2; here is a simple illustration of the difficulty of extracting perfectly reasonable information from a very simple language. In Figure 2 the answer is obvious—Test 2 is *not* contained in Loop 2.

Similar comparisons can be made between languages. BASIC is a small language; LOGO and Pascal, though not exactly big, are considerably larger than BASIC. The difference is like that between Figures 1 and 2.

Thus, the simple BASIC program of Figure 3a could be rewritten in the shape of Figure 3b, using Pascal. The segments of program are then much more easily perceived. Observe that the use of identation in Figure 3b closely resembles the "meaningful indentation" system evaluated by Frase and Schwartz (1979). Opinion is mixed as to the importance of supplying indentation schemes in programs—some writers recommend it as a mark of good style, even in BASIC (Nevison, 1978), but empirical tests have not shown any very strong effects. What *has* been shown repeatedly, however, is that it pays to replace the diffuse BASIC style by the Pascal style with its bigger chunks. The Pascal style is more readable. This has been reported in a variety of contexts for very simple languages based on conditionals, for experts (Green, 1979), for novices (Mayer, 1976) and for non-programming tasks (van der Veer & van de Wolde, in press). It is hardly surprising, of course, that a clearly perceived structure is easier to use, and parallel findings have been reported in many other areas, for example, the design of instructional text (Hartley, 1978).

We have a trade-off. Flowcharts have very few different symbols to learn, and the few they have are conceptually very easy to grasp. But flowcharts are diffuse and cluttered. If the clutter is to be reduced and some degree of spatial organization imposed, the vocabulary has to be enlarged and the concepts have to become harder. We have condensed the language into larger chunks, but the chunks are now more numerous in kind and less digestible. Moreover, the ways they can fit together may be less easy to understand. In flowcharts there is no restriction on which arrow goes where; in BASIC there is very little restriction; but in Pascal the organization of chunks is quite severely constrained by factors which are completely invisible to the beginner. Take declarations in Pascal, for instance: constants must obviously precede types, types precede variables, variables precede procedures. Obvious, that is, *if* you happen to see why! Languages with richer ontologies are correspondingly harder still. To the expert, or even to the moderately experienced user, the problems may seem trivial, but at the other end of the scale the problems of understanding a few "trivial" concepts may be sufficient to frighten learners away for good.

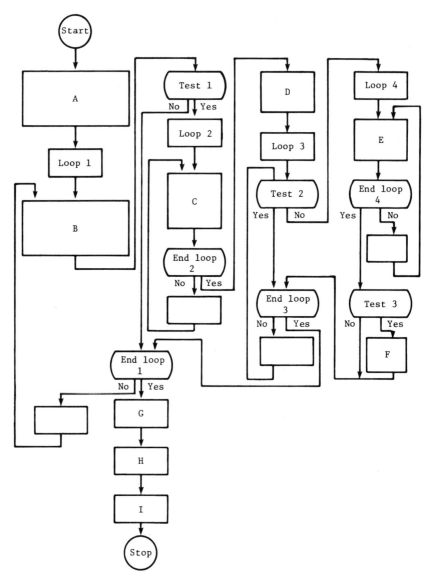

Figure 1. A flowchart in skeletal form. Reproduced from a published flowchart; the actions have been reduced to single letters. Boxes marked Loop 1, etc., contained instructions for initializing counters; empty boxes contained instructions for incrementing counters. In a more powerful notation only one box would be required for each loop, instead of three. (From Green, 1982; Reprinted with permission.)

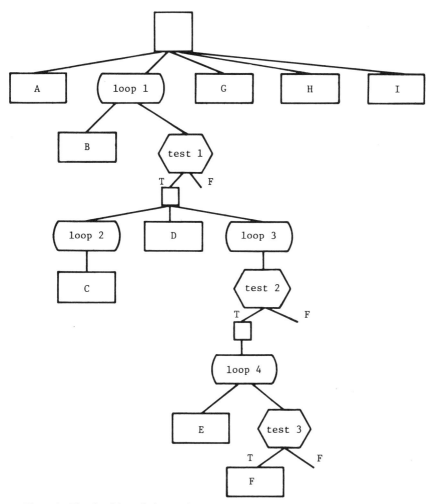

Figure 2. The algorithm of Figure 1 is here redrawn in the notation used by Bowles (1977). Execution proceeds from left to right and downwards; do A, then do Loop 1 (which contains B, and then Test 1 (which, if true, starts Loop 2 .....)), then do G, H, and I. (From Green, 1982; Reprinted with permission.)

Small languages make for long, diffuse programs. Big languages can shorten the programs by chunking up the language, but the result is a larger vocabulary to be learned, harder concepts, difficult interrelationships between the items in the language, negative facts, and kludges. Moreover, the actual size of the language is not at all easy to discern; what counts is the

```
10 REM Determines whether a supplied positive integer is prime or composite
20 INPUT N : PRINT N ; "  " ;
30 IF N <> FIX (N) THEN PRINT "is not an integer" : STOP
40 IF N < 1 THEN PRINT "should not be less than 1" : STOP
50 IF N < = 3 THEN GOTO 140
60 IF N MOD 2 = 0 THEN GOTO 130
70 SQROOTOFN = FIX ( SQR ( N ) )
80 POTFACTOR = 3
90 IF N MOD POTFACTOR = 0 OR POTFACTOR > = SQROOTOFN THEN GOTO 120
100 POTFACTOR = POTFACTOR + 2
110 GOTO 90
120 IF N MOD POTFACTOR <> 0 THEN GOTO 140
130 PRINT "is composite" : STOP
140 PRINT "is prime" : STOP
```

Figure 3. (a) A program in BASIC to determine whether a number is prime. The structure is unclear, although the program is quite short.

effective size, the mental lexicon, not the vocabulary as defined in the reference manual. Some attempts to discover the mental lexicon are described in the following section.

WHAT PROGRAMMERS KNOW

Nonprogrammers are perfectly able to describe algorithms, but not in the usual programming terms. One possibility for evading some of the difficulties described in the previous section might be to examine how nonprogrammers describe algorithms, and then to base a programming language on the outcome. Such a language would presumably be very natural. Alternatively, if that fails, another possibility might be to discover more exactly what expert programmers know, and make that knowledge explicit in the design of a new language. These two possibilities are united by their presuppositions that one can discover the knowledge base, either of novices or of experts, and that a language designed around that knowledge base would be natural and thus easy to use. All the studies in this section fit into this framework.

Miller (1981) reports experiments on natural-language programming, where participants were invited to devise and describe procedures for well-specified operations. These participants were nonprogrammers, and their efforts were very unlike programs.

> One has only to glance over a few well-written programs to see the dominant textual style of programs: great massive control structures of DOs and IFs, with the primary data-manipulation activities embedded deep within these. For this reason, we characterize this style as 'conditionalized action.' However, natural language provides

```
program Prime (input, output);
    {Determines whether a supplied positive integer
     is prime or composite.}

  var
    n, potfactor, sqrootofn : integer;
begin
  read (n); write (n, '  ');

  if n<1 then
    writeln ('should not be less than 1')

  else
    if n<=3 then
      writeln ('is prime')

    else
      if odd (n) then
      begin
        sqrootofn := trunc (sqrt (n));

        potfactor := 3;
        while (n mod potfactor<>0) and (potfactor<sqrootofn)do
          potfactor := potfactor+2;

        if n mod potfactor=0 then
          writeln ('is composite')
        else
          writeln ('is prime')
      end else
        writeln ('is composite')
end.
```

Figure 3. (b) The same program in Pascal. Here the structure is displayed much more clearly at the cost of making the program longer. The two programs do in fact have the *same* structure, but it is hard to tell. (From Atkinson, 1980; Reprinted with permission.)

almost a reverse emphasis: they almost always begin with those primary actions that are so deeply embedded within programs; special conditions or circumstances that control if and how the action is to be applied are expressed rather as 'qualifications,' usually following the action words. We therefore characterize natural 'programming' style as 'act on qualification' [p. 210].

Figure 4 illustrates the differences. Later, Miller reports that he and his co-workers were not prepared for the magnitude of the differences: "Programming language style is simply alien to natural specification," and he reports other differences as well.

But is that the case? Has Miller not shown, perhaps, that a procedural information structure is ill-suited to novice programmers? Maybe they would have performed in a style less alien to programming had they been

```
DO END UNTIL TIME = 5:00 PM
  I = 0
  DO END.OUT WHILE I<200
    I = I + 1
    OPEN BOX(I)
    J = 0
    DO END.IN WHILE J<12
      GET NEXT BALL
      IF RED THEN
        IF LARGE THEN
          IF UNBROKEN THEN
            J = J + 1
————————————————————————▶ PACK BALL IN BOX(I)CELL(J)
            RETURN(END.IN)
          ELSE RETURN(END.IN)
        ELSE RETURN(END.IN)
      ELSE RETURN(END.IN)
    END.IN
    CLOSE BOX(I)
  END.OUT
END
```

(A) *Program Normal Form*

————————▶ PACK LARGE RED DECORATIONS TWELVE TO A BOX.
MAKE UP A TOTAL OF 200 BOXES.
STOP AT 5:00 PM IF NOT FINISHED.
BE SURE TO PACK ONLY THE UNBROKEN ONES.

(B) *Natural Normal Form*

Figure 4. Comparison of "normal forms" for programs versus natural language specifications. The task is to pack Christmas decorations into boxes. (A) illustrates typical *conditioned action* style of programming; (B) illustrates natural *action qualification* style. The arrow points to the primary action to be accomplished by the program. (From Miller, 1981; reprinted with permission.)

using a declarative structure instead.[1] This idea is appealing but at present cannot be supported. Figure 4 shows that such heavy use was made of the context and the environment that the problems lie deeper than any question of procedural or declarative structure. It is taken for granted in Figure 4 that the computing system knows how to pack things twelve to a box without being told which cell to use. Miller lays some considerable stress on the

---

[1]Procedural information concerns the sequence of steps taken to achieve a purpose or perform an action. Declarative information concerns the propositions of fact and statements of relatedness that give cohesion to a set of ideas.

degree to which natural-language style assumes semantic knowledge of the world.

There are also two studies that cast doubt on the idea that the declarative paradigm is naturally predominant. Gould, Lewis, and Becker (1976) showed that patterns of typing and arrangements of children's blocks were described about as quickly and accurately with declaratives as with procedures. More important, they found that their subjects were ready to switch styles with very little prompting.

> Mild variations in task environment and expressional constraints lead to large variations in the way subjects express themselves. In designing a hypothetical computer system dealing with block figures, for example, one could not just find the 'natural' way of referring to them and implement it, since there is not a single natural way. Human linguistic and cognitive systems are better characterized as adaptive than as having strong 'natural tendencies.' Discovering 'natural ways' people think has ethological value and sometimes psychological value, but may have little value for systems design [p. 21].

Finally, Hoc (1979) investigated the performance of novices in designing the rules for an algorithm to give change for metro tickets. In one condition, where no strategies were imposed, he found "le débutant exprime spontanement les règles du processus en suivant *l'order d'une exécution*" (the learner spontaneously expresses the rules of the process following *the order in which they are executed*) (p. 256).

It would be reasonable to conjecture that in natural-language programming, there is no fundamental difference between procedural and declarative structures, but that either can be deployed at will. Where a sequence of events happens to the same physical object, say, the procedural method would be used; where many exceptional cases must be considered, the declarative method would be used as well. There is no great difficulty here because the reliance on semantics and on what is actually possible or reasonable makes it unnecessary to use the same degree of precision in specifying a procedure as a computer requires, and the human reader can integrate declaratives and procedures in appropriate ways.

There is no prospect of introducing such powerful semantic mechanisms into everyday programming in the immediate future, and we must therefore continue to concentrate on the problems of ordinary programming, rather than magicking up a quick exit from them. Mayer (1979) has attempted to analyze the knowledge that must be acquired by the beginner at BASIC. Noticeable in his description is the importance of making operations concrete. For instance, among the important locations of a computer is the "ticket window" where numbers can be handed in, one at a time (i.e., the input operation). Mayer's analysis includes "transactions," in which objects are moved to locations, etc.; "prestatements," such as setting counters

(LET X = 1); mandatory chunks, such as FOR. .NEXT; and nonmandatory chunks, or techniques, such as forming the total of a set of numbers.

Mayer's work is well done and is backed up with experimental evidence showing the importance of concrete metaphors. But it gets more vague as soon as we get away from the notation and into the higher-order objects, the nonmandatory chunks. Yet it is just these that are the interesting end of the lexicon.

One may make the same objection to recent attempts to discover the mental lexicon empirically. McKeithen, Reitman, Reuter, and Hirtle (1981) used cluster analysis techniques operating on free recall of program material. In their abstract they write:

> We infer the details of individual programmers' chunks of key programming concepts . . . . Beginner programmers' organizations show a rich variety of common-language associations to these programming concepts; intermediate programmers show mixtures of programming and common-language associations; and experts show remarkably similar, but not identical, organizations based clearly on programming knowledge [p. 307].

Without wishing to belittle their research, it cannot be said to go as far as we would like in identifying the terms of mental lexicon. Their experts certainly show Algol-based chunking, as they claim, grouping together if-then-else, case-of, for-step, and while-do, and so on; but that can hardly be said to display key programming concepts. They have shown us what the beginner does not know, rather than what the expert does know. Adelson (1981) also used sophisticated techniques of cluster analysis with free recall, and found slightly higher levels of organization amongst experts than did McKeithen *et al.* The material to be recalled could be perceived as being organized in three distinct programs, and the recall strategies of experts, but not of beginners, reflected that organization; but that tells us what could be done with the material, not what experts know.

In short, there is no reservoir of natural computing concepts identified so far, and empirical techniques have displayed the problems of beginners but not the solutions of experts. Thus, it seems difficult, at present anyway, to propose realistically that the mental lexicon can be used as a basis for design.

STRUCTURE OF THE LANGUAGE

In the previous two sections we have seen that to make programs less diffuse we have to make them more complex internally, and have examined the possibility of developing natural (and therefore noncomplex) types of chunking. A very different approach is to develop types of chunking which are mathematically simple, even if not in any way natural. The well-known developments of structured programming started in just this way. The usual argument is that the nested loops and conditionals found in Pascal are structurally simpler than the tangles of overlapping jumps and loops found in many beginners' BASIC programs. We need to avoid programs like Figure 5.

This proposal should be compared carefully with the previous argument for nesting. Earlier, we considered the argument that among programs of *identical structure,* the easiest ones to comprehend were those which used Pascal-like systems, because the segments of program were then more easily perceived. The present argument is that among programs using *identical languages,* the easiest ones to comprehend will be those where the structure is hierarchically nested, because the strategy of divide-and-rule can be followed: understand the outermost levels, then the inner ones at leisure. The present argument maintains that the program in Figure 5 would be easier to understand if it were restructured, even if the language were still BASIC. The virtues of Pascal and COMAL are that they impose a nested structure. The fact that the structure is also more visible than the same structure in BASIC is given less weight, or even in some cases no weight at all. Kernighan and Plauger (1974) dismiss the choice of language as "parochial," and concentrate solely on structure.

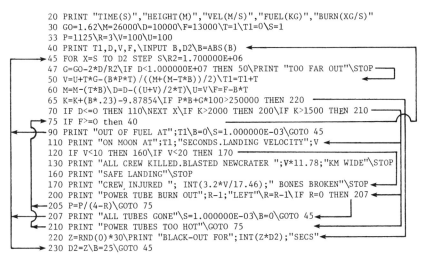

```
20  PRINT "TIME(S)","HEIGHT(M)","VEL(M/S)","FUEL(KG)","BURN(XG/S)"
30  GO=1.62\M=26000\D=10000\F=13000\T=1\T1=0\S=1
33  P=1125\R=3\V=100\U=100
40  PRINT T1,D,V,F,\INPUT B,D2\B=ABS(B)
45  FOR X=S TO D2 STEP S\R2=1.700000E+06
47  G=GO-2*D/R2\IF D<1.000000E+07 THEN 50\PRINT "TOO FAR OUT"\STOP
50  V=U+T*G-(B*P*T)/((M+(M-T*B))/2)\T1=T1+T
60  M=M-(T*B)\D=D-((U+V)/2*T)\U=V\F=F-B*T
65  K=K+(B*.23)-9.87854\IF P*B+G*100>250000 THEN 220
70  IF D<=0 THEN 110\NEXT X\IF K>2000 THEN 200\IF K>1500 THEN 210
75  IF F>=0 then 40
90  PRINT "OUT OF FUEL AT";T1\B=0\S=1.000000E-03\GOTO 45
110 PRINT "ON MOON AT";T1;"SECONDS.LANDING VELOCITY";V
120 IF V<10 THEN 160\IF V<20 THEN 170
130 PRINT "ALL CREW KILLED.BLASTED NEWCRATER ";V*11.78;"KM WIDE"\STOP
160 PRINT "SAFE LANDING"\STOP
170 PRINT "CREW INJURED "; INT(3.2*V/17.46);" BONES BROKEN"\STOP
200 PRINT "POWER TUBE BURN OUT";R-1;"LEFT"\R=R-1\IF R=0 THEN 207
205 P=P/(4-R)\GOTO 75
207 PRINT "ALL TUBES GONE"\S=1.000000E-03\B=0\GOTO 45
210 PRINT "POWER TUBES TOO HOT"\GOTO 75
220 Z=RND(0)*30\PRINT "BLACK-OUT FOR";INT(Z*D2);"SECS"
230 D2=Z\B=25\GOTO 45
```

Figure 5. A program with severely tangled control paths. Modifying this program would be extremely difficult. Recent developments in structured programming are aimed at avoiding programs like this. (From Atherton, 1982; reprinted with permission.)

There has been considerable resistance to this argument. Amongst computer scientists the position is widely accepted, so much so that it is difficult at times to discuss contrary possibilities; but among the readers of popular computing magazines, who are considering the merits of BASIC versus The Rest Of The World (COMAL, LOGO, and Pascal), it is frequently maintained that nesting is conceptually harder to learn and that there is no evidence of benefit. The former point is obviously correct, and is exactly the theme of an earlier section. Evidence of benefit, however, is another story.

Sime, Green, and Guest (1977) showed that novices made fewer logical errors writing conditional-structure programs in a hierarchical language than in an unstructured language which, like BASIC, allowed free jumps to labels. One reason was that in the jump-happy language the programs got tangled, like Figure 5 above. This problem can, in theory, be attacked by imposing rules of style, as espoused by Kernighan and Plauger (1974), Nevison (1978), and others, using jumps to labels *only* to mimic nested structures and *never* in any other way.

Do rules of style work? Yes and no. Yes, in that when novices were either constrained or advised to use hierarchic structure in a jump-happy language, their logical errors were reduced (Arblaster, Sime, & Green, 1979). No, in that the debugging effort of those same novices was not reduced. In contrast, Sime *et al.* (1977) had found that the debugging effort could be reduced by a factor of ten: not, indeed, solely by using the hierarchic language, but by adding to it the mystery ingredient X which I shall reveal shortly. Without X, the debugging effort was very similar for hierarchic and for jump-happy languages. Again, Green (1977) found that the answer times of professional programmers are greatly influenced by ingredient X. Even nonhierarchic structures can be used, such as decision-table structures, and will prove better than total lack of structure (Arblaster *et al.*, 1979), clearly showing that hierarchy alone is not the solution to comprehensibility.

The answer to all this lies in the procedural–declarative distinction, or sequential–circumstantial distinction, as it is also called. Conventional programming languages reveal the sequential information: what order the statements are performed in. Circumstantial information, telling us the conditions which must be met for a certain action to be performed, is obscured in conventional programming languages. Ingredient X is nothing more than a syntactic device that reveals a certain amount more circumstantial information. (Figure 6). Thus, what Green (1977) found was that circumstantial questions need a good structure and also ingredient X, while sequential questions need only a hierarchical structure. Supporting evidence has now been found by other groups, modifying details of the story in ways that

```
CHOP AND GRILL:   All things which are green and juicy.
CHOP AND ROAST:   All things which are green and not juicy.
PEEL AND BOIL :   All things which are not green and hard.
FRY :             All things which are not green and not hard.
```

Solutions

Nest-BE	Nest-INE	Jump

```
If green THEN            IF green: chop           If green GOTO L1
  BEGIN chop               IF juicy: grill        If hard GOTO L2
  IF juicy THEN            NOT juicy: roast        fry stop
    BEGIN grill END       END juicy            L2 Peel boil stop
  ELSE                   NOT green:             L1 chop
    BEGIN roast END        IF hard: peel boil      IF juicy GOTO L3
  END                      NOT hard: fry          roast stop
ELSE                      END hard             L3 grill stop
  BEGIN                  END green
  IF hard THEN
    BEGIN peel boil END
  ELSE
    BEGIN fry END
  END
END
```

Figure 6. In these three notations, the *sequential* information is about equally visible; but the *circumstantial* information ("what things get fried") is far more visible in Nest-INE. (From Arblaster, Sime, & Green, 1979; reprinted with permission.)

need not be discussed here (e.g., Sheppard, Kruesi, & Curtis, 1980; van der Veer & van de Wolde, 1983).

If, therefore, we hope to make a good language, it is not enough to recommend rules of style. They must be built into the language. More: The circumstantial information needed for debugging must also be built in.

From a lexical point of view, we have just made an important decision. It is more important to make structure visible than to keep the language small. The emphasis on the visibility of information ties in closely with recent explorations of program comprehension as a problem in psychological theory; for instance, Brooks (1980) has attempted to formalize the process of comprehending a program, and makes great play with the process of searching through a program seeking clues to its behavior. The programmer needs both to anticipate what sort of clue might be found and to recognize it when it is encountered, as well as interpreting it accurately enough to take the next step. Conversely, the programmer as viewed by Brooks also needs to be able to avoid areas of the program that are unpromising, in relation to the information being sought. Processes such as these will patently be eased if the information is made more visible.

The problems of understanding the flow of data within a program cannot be discussed here at any length, important though they clearly are. (It has even been claimed that perceived data flow is *more* important than perceived control flow, although this is a rather facile statement and certainly demands more than one simple experiment to support it.) It would seem remarkable if the same principles of visibility did not apply, rather than any appeal to mathematical elegance.

Earlier we saw a trade-off between diffuse languages with a small vocabulary, and compact languages with a larger and difficult vocabulary. This trade-off becomes more complex when the need to create visible structure is considered, because when a program is altered, the structure must be maintained. Simple experience tells us that it is easy enough to slip a quick jump into a BASIC program to modify a slight bug or to meet a new requirement, when the same change in LOGO or Pascal would need much more extensive reworking.

Once again, to an experienced hand this may seem piffling. But to the beginner, the difficulty of changing the program is extremely important. Struggling to make a simple change, and introducing a few new mistakes in the process, drains the motivation and kills the interest. BASIC may have no structure, but at least that means one cannot create mistakes which are solely due to slips in the structuring.

Fortunately, recent developments can relieve users of much of the tedious part of program editing and maintenance. Some of the impressive developments in programming aids were noted in the Introduction, such as Teitelbaum's Cornell Program Synthesizer, which gives users very powerful tools for writing and editing programs. Templates are used extensively for writing. During editing, substructure can be "clipped out," stored, and reinserted elsewhere with a minimum of difficulty, and the system automatically takes care of indenting and syntax checking. To make programs readable on a 24-line screen, there is an ellipsis command to suppress the inner loops and replace them by a row of dots. Mikelsons (1981) takes ellipsis a stage further with a "multiple focus mode," which displays the program structure that connects phrases selected by the programmer, thus revealing how $x : = x + y$ is related to $x : = 1$, etc. Morris and Schwartz (1981) and Waters (1982) describe yet other approaches to language-directed editing. Work of this sort (no longer, thank goodness, confined to mainframes running LISP) is clearly going to soothe many of the beginner's headaches.

The position we arrive at, therefore, is that highly structured languages should be assessed by whether the structure reveals anything helpful to the programmer, not by whether they meet certain arbitrary mathematical standards; and that they will be acceptable to novices if, and only if, sufficiently powerful tools are provided to manipulate the programs. The indications are that adequate tools are possible on classroom computers, but only recently has there been enough interest in their development outside mainframes.

REGENERABILITY: COPING WITH SIZE

In the previous section we saw that the performance of programmers was improved by imposing structure on the language. Contrary to the arguments of many computer scientists, the effects depended less on the particular type of structure than on its visibility, at least in small-scale experiments. We also saw that developments in programmers' aids may take care of much of the clerical labor in debugging and modifying highly structured languages, by means of "knowledge-based editing." Novices will therefore be able to take advantage of the benefits of large languages—less diffuse programs and visible structures—without experiencing so much of the costs.

The problem remains of *learning* a large language. There has been fragmentary research on the problem, but no unified view has emerged: instead, it has been suggested in one place that concrete metaphors are needed, in another place that English-likeness is needed, etc. In this section I shall propose that the existing research can be unified by one very simple proposition. Languages are easy to learn when those bits that are forgotten or not yet learned can readily be regenerated from the other bits. Forgotten how feature A works in some particular context? Well, feature A seems to work like feature B most of the time, so let us assume it does so here as well.

In a well-known type of intelligence test, a grid is presented with one square blank, as in the fictional example of Figure 7. The task is to discover the missing component from the others, by finding the rules of composition and using them to regenerate it. By the regenerability of a system, I mean the extent to which it is systematic rather than arbitrary; the saliency of the rules; and the difficulty of deriving missing elements, given the rules.

One extremely effective way to increase the regenerability of a system is to base it on a familiar prototype. The work of Mayer (1979) includes numerous demonstrations of the effectiveness of giving novice programmers help in the form of concrete images. Du Boulay *et al.* (1981) also develop this theme, but they also warn us against trusting our own intuitions rather than our observations of the real difficulties of novices: "We have found that some highly experienced programmers find special languages for novices quite distasteful, and regard pedagogically simple explanations as not

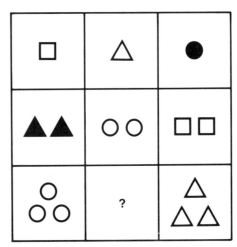

Figure 7. In a well-designed ensemble, a missing member can be generated from the remaining members.

telling the 'truth.' We believe that this arises from their attempts to use such languages in ways that they were not designed for, and from their concern for elegance and generality rather than human factors" (p. 240). Because a novice language makes it hard to attack problems that appeal to experienced programmers, experienced programmers condemn it—a sad but familiar tale.

Naturally, if an explicit concrete prototype is used to help novices, it must match the programming domain very well. A prototype that invites incorrect analogies will be a hindrance rather than a help. At an anecdotal level, the power of ill-matched prototypes to *inhibit* performance has been frequently brought home to me when trying to explain a text-editing system to secretaries with no computing background. Being used to the properties of paper, they found it impossible to insert a new line into a text, even though the editor possessed a clearly labeled "insert" command. Why? Because on *paper* one cannot type a new line over an old one; one needs to create a blank line first, and the editor had no way they could discover, try as they might, to create a blank line on which to type their insertion. Rumelhart and Norman (1981) report exactly similar problems in teaching the use of an editor, and describe how different concrete prototypes create different problems. Similar problems in a rather difficult domain are reported by Plum (1977), who shows how an interactive system using mathematical notation can fool the user into thinking that it is far more powerful than it really is.

The well-learned patterns of English can also provide a usable prototype:

Ledgard, Whiteside, Singer, and Seymour (1980) report that modifications to a text editor, making its commands interpretable as short English sentences, greatly improved performance. Instead of RS:/TOOTH,/TRUTH/ the subjects would write R "TOOTH"W "TRUTH," interpreted as Replace . . . With . . . , and although the precise interpretation of the results has aroused some discussion, it is surely clear that English-likeness of this sort will help learners to generate the argument order.

Regenerability need not rest solely on prototypes. Figure 7 works because simple rules can be inferred from the eight patterns present, which ought to predict the missing one, but none of these rules rely on previously familiar ones. The same effect has been observed with lexicon design. Barnard, Hammond, Morton, and Long (1981) have shown that novices learning a command system remember the order of arguments best if there is a consistent pattern across all command words. Failing that, their subjects presumably cast around for some other rule, and where order was inconsistent, the most successful cases relied on the usual pattern of English, in which the direct object precedes the indirect. Another type of within-lexicon structure has been demonstrated by Carroll (1980), who pointed out the problem of congruence: ADVANCE/RETREAT is a congruent pair, whereas GO/BACK, and MOVE ROBOT FORWARD/CHANGE ROBOT BACKWARD, are both noncongruent. Congruent sets are easier to learn because missing elements can readily be regenerated.

All these studies combine to demonstrate that if there is a simple and effective rule, learners will find it and use it. The set of names, the set of operations named, and the mapping between them can all be made more regenerable and hence more learnable.

Grammar, however, is a different story. Whereas there have been several studies on command terms, there have been few indeed on grammar. Our ignorance of regenerability in grammar is indeed regrettable, since it is the mental grammer—the building up of larger assemblies from smaller—which defines the skilled programmer.

Green (1979) compared dialects of a nonsense language, Jabberish, in which the proportion of marker elements was varied. All dialects had the same fundamental structure, with a simple phrase structure, but in some dialects each word class was preceded by a marker word unique to that class, as though in English all animate nouns were signalled by a preceding word "animal." (Compare these markers to a gender system, where masculine nouns are frequently given a different ending from the feminine.) In other dialects of Jabberish, *phrases* were given their own unique markers, as though in English all noun phrases were signaled by the word *the*. (It is known that much of the structure of English sentences can in fact be derived solely from such function words.) Finally, there were conditions with no markers and with all possible markers. Figure 8 illustrates some of these dialects. By varying which words and which phrases were marked, a number of delicate predictions could be derived and tested, given the basic assumption that subjects could and would use the markers. The experiment was highly successful in showing that the dialects were in general learned better when markers were present, and more particularly, that those aspects of the grammar signaled by markers were learned better. We conclude that when a grammar is hard to learn, it might often be improved by inserting markers to signal the phrase structure.

The intuitive expectations would be that a more complex grammar should make learning harder. Reisner (1981) certainly believes this, and has produced some degree of supporting evidence. She used an interactive graphics system as a testbed, putting a plausible case for regarding actions at a terminal as subject to rules of grammar in the same sense as programming

Learning phase

Condition 1: indicative markers

| ERD | LOTHOG | ALT | STINY | ETH | DOOB. |
| ALT | FENGLE | IRP | GORT | ERD | FLEAM. |

Condition 2: no markers

| LOTHOG | STINY | DOOB. |
| FENGLE | GORT | FLEAM. |

Test Phase

Condition 1:

ERD _____ ALT STINY ETH DOOB.

Condition 2:

_____ STINY DOOB.

Figure 8. When a nonsense language was learned, test scores were much higher when markers (ERD, ALT, IRP, ETH) occurred as "signals" of the grammatical class of each word, than when no markers were used (Condition 2) or when markers were randomized (Condition 3). In a subsequent study, the results were extended to markers signaling the class of particular phrases, and similar results were found. Grammars appear to be easier to learn when it is easy to perceive the syntax. (From Green, 1979; reprinted with permission.)

languages. One system, called ROBART 1, required fewer control actions of the user at the price of a more complex grammar than in the competing system ROBART 2. In several places Reisner identified "structural inconsistency" in ROBART 1, places where different sequences of steps are required depending on what is being drawn, so that at least two rules have to be learned, whereas in ROBART 2 a single general rule sufficed. In ROBART 1, users tended to apply the wrong rule, and Reisner compared the problem with the child who has learned that "verb + -ed makes past tense" and then insists on saying "yesterday I goed." In general, users made more mistakes with ROBART 1 at the points identified by Reisner. She concludes that whereas common practice is to minimize the number of terminal symbols (the lexicon size), one should instead minimize the number of grammatical rules.

More exactly, Reisner recommends minimizing the number of *forms* of rules. It is not the absolute number of rules that causes problems, but the number of unrelated rules. This view ties in very well with the way computer people talk about languages, using terms like *harmonious, consistent,* and *orthogonal.* Inconsistent features cause problems; harmonious features are easy to learn.

Some rules share a family resemblance at a fairly abstract level. For instance, the notion of "a *sequence* of As separated by Bs" is a notion that turns up time and again. A program is a sequence of statements separated by semicolons, a declaration is a sequence of identifiers separated by commas, and an expression is a sequence of operands separated by operators. So here we have only one *form* of rule, but we have three rules sharing a family resemblance.

A convenient formalism has been invented to describe these family resemblances, the van Wijngaarden two-level grammar (van Wijngaarden, 1966; for an introductory account see Pagan, 1981). The language is rather horrifying, as we have to distinguish between protonotions and metanotions, production rules, hyperrules, and metarules, but the idea is simple enough: one level of rules, the hyperrules, generates the other level, the ordinary rules. So if we forget the ordinary rules of a language we can regenerate them from the hyperrules—always assuming that we understood them.

No direct research has been reported on the regeneration of grammatical rules, but it seems very promising. Reisner's recommendation (to minimize the number of forms) suffered from supplying no definition of the number of forms; it could now be rephrased as advice to minimize the number of hyperrules. My hypothesis, or rather my restatement of Reisner's hypothesis, is that people observe family resemblances between rules and capitalize on them in learning, exactly as they capitalize on external concrete prototypes or on English-likeness. The two-level grammar provides the most nearly equivalent formal machinery to learning by family resemblance. The intuitions of computer people about harmony and consistency can be seen in the same light—in a harmonious language, a few hyperrules are sufficient; but in an unharmonious one the ordinary rules will not be amenable to generalizations, and there will be as many hyperrules as ordinary rules. The notion of a hyperrule is consistent with the idea of a higher-order rule in problem solving (Scandura, 1977).

It is the lot of psychologists to be told that their thoughts are unsurprising. To forestall such a comment as "everybody knew that," let me ask why, if everybody knew about harmony in syntax, Pascal has the design it does. The semicolon in Pascal is intended as a statement separator, but it can equally well be viewed as a statement terminator in most contexts. The difference is evident in the *if-then-else* construction, where the statement before the *else* must not be terminated with a semicolon. But in the context of *begin-end*, the statement before the end can be terminated with a semicolon if desired, and the compiler views that as a separator for a nonexistent statement. Now, grammars allowing nonexistent elements are difficult (Green, 1980, p. 289), and so it is not surprising that students come to regard the semicolon as a terminator in such a context. They have thus created a higher-level rule which is incorrect. As a result, many of their syntax errors have to do with semicolons (Pugh & Simpson, 1979; Ripley & Druseikis, 1978).

To summarize, we can apply the criterion of regenerability both to the vocabulary of programming and to the grammar. The regenerability of vocabularies may depend on prototypes, such as concrete metaphors or well-learned patterns in English, or may depend on interrelations between components, such as Carroll's congruence. In grammars, regenerable systems require highly visible and distinct cues to the grammatical rules, as in the good dialects of my Jabberish studies, and they require a set of hyperrules as simplifications and abstractions of the ordinary rules.

CONCLUSIONS

Those programming languages that use a few simple constructions make for diffuse and difficult programs. If the programs are shortened by chunking the languages, the language gets harder to learn. One way to escape from the trade-off, some writers have suggested, is to investigate natural programs, either as performed by novices or as performed by experts; this chapter argues that the knowledge possessed by programmers is not yet accessible, and that the development of natural systems is not yet practicable.

However, the psychological rather than formal bent of the naturalness school is well justified. In the realms of program structure, it is argued that the structure must be psychologically helpful as a first priority, rather than formally elegant. The problems of modifying highly structured programs, which are considerably greater than the slip-a-quick-jump-in style of beginners' BASIC, may be alleviated by programmers' aids that are now becoming available.

The last section of the chapter attempts to unify research on language learnability and on the rubric of regenerability, a notion that ties in well with the psychology of recall and memory in other fields. Regenerability can successfully be based on explicit concrete prototypes or on interrelations between elements. A novel proposal is that the regenerability of grammatical rules should be assessed by writing a two-level grammar; if the original grammar can be learned by learning just a few hyperrules, which apply consistently, then even a larger grammar should be easy to learn. This view has clearly not been adhered to strictly in existing languages.

REFERENCES

Adelson, B. Problem solving and the development of abstract categories in programming languages. *Memory and Cognition, 1981, 9,* 422–433.

Arblaster, A. T., Sime, M. E., & Green, T. R. G. Jumping to some purpose. *Computer Journal, 1979, 22,* 105–109.

Atherton, R. *Structured programming with COMAL.* London: Ellis Horwood, 1982.

Atkinson, L. V. *Pascal programming.* New York: Wiley, 1980.

Barnard, P. J., Hammond, N. V., Morton, J., & Long, J. P. Consistency and compatibility in human-computer dialogue. *International Journal of Man-Machine Studies, 1981, 15,* 87–134.

Bowles, K. L. *Microcomputer problem solving using Pascal.* New York: Springer–Verlag, 1977.

Brooks, R. A. *A behavioral theory of program comprehension.* Unpublished paper, Department of Psychiatry, University of Texas, Galveston, Texas, 1980.

Carroll, J. M. *Learning, using, and designing command paradigms.* Report No. RC 8141, IBM Watson Research Center, New York, 1980.

du Boulay, B., O'Shea, T., & Monk, J. The black box inside the glass box: Presenting computing concepts to novices. *International Journal of Man-Machine Studies, 1981, 14,* 237–250.

Eisenstadt, M. *Cognitive psychology: Artificial intelligence project.* Milton Keynes: Open University Press, 1978.

Frase, L. T., & Schwartz, B. J. Typographical cues that facilitate comprehension. *Journal of Educational Psychology, 1979, 71,* 197–206.

Gould, J. D., Lewis, C., & Becker, C. A. *Writing and following procedural, descriptive, and restricted syntax language instructions.* Report No. RC 5943, IBM Watson Research Center, New York, 1976.

Green, T. R. G. Conditional program statements and their comprehensibility to professional programmers. *Journal of Occupational Psychology,* 1977, *50,* 93–109.

Green, T. R. G. The necessity of syntax markers: Two experiments with artificial languages. *Journal of Verbal Learning and Verbal Behavior,* 1979, *18,* 481–496.

Green, T. R. G. Programming as a cognitive activity. In H. T. Smith & T. R. G. Green (Eds.), *Human-computer interaction.* London: Academic Press, 1980.

Green, T. R. G. Pictures of programs and other processes, or how to do things with lines. *Behavior and Information Technology,* 1982, *1,* 3–37.

Hartley, J. *Designing instructional text.* New York: Nichols, 1978.

Hoc, J-M. Le probleme de la planification dans la construction d'un programme informatique. *Le Travail Humain,* 1979, *42,* 245–260.

Kernighan, B. W., & Plauger, P. J. *The elements of programming style.* New York: McGraw-Hill, 1974.

Ledgard, H., Whiteside, J. A., Singer, A., & Seymour, W. The natural language of interactive systems. *Communications of the ACM,* 1980, *23,* 556–563.

McKeithen, K. B., Reitman, J. S., Reuter, H. H., & Hirtle, S. C. Knowledge organization and skill differences in computer programmers. *Cognitive Psychology,* 1981, *13,* 307–325.

Mayer, R. E. A psychology of learning Basic. *Communication of the ACM,* 1979, *22,* 589–593.

Mayer, R. E. Comprehension as affected by structure of problem representation. *Memory and Cognition,* 1976, *4,* 249–255.

Mikelsons, M. *Pretty printing in an interactive programming environment.* Research report RC 8750, IBM Watson Research Center, New York, 1981. *ACM SIGPLAN Notices,* 1981, *16*(6), 108–116.

Miller, L. A. Natural language programming: Styles, strategies, and contrasts. *IBM Systems Journal,* 1981, *20,* 184–215.

Morris, J. M., & Schwartz, M. D. The design of a language-directed editor for block-structured languages. *ACM SIGPLAN Notices,* 1981, *16*(6), 28–33.

Nevison, J. M. *The little book of BASIC style.* Reading, Massachusetts: Addison–Wesley, 1978.

Pagan, F. G. *Formal specification of programming languages: A panoramic primer.* Englewood Cliffs, New Jersey: Prentice–Hall, 1981.

Papert, S. *Mindstorms: Children, computers, and powerful ideas.* Brighton, Massachusetts: Harvester Press, 1980.

Plum, T. Fooling the user of a programming language. *Software-Practice and Experience,* 1977, *7,* 215–221.

Pugh, J., & Simpson, D. Pascal errors - empirical evidence. *Computer Bulletin,* 1979, *19,* 26–28.

Reisner, P. Formal grammar and human factors design of an interactive graphics system. *IEEE Trans. Software Engineering,* 1981, *7,* 229–240.

Ripley, G. D., & Druseikis, F. C. A statistical analysis of syntax errors. *Computer Languages,* 1978, *3,* 227–240.

Rumelhart, D. E., & Norman, D. A. Analogical processes in learning. In J. R. Anderson (Ed.), *Cognitive skills and their acquisition.* Hillsdale, New Jersey: Erlbaum, 1981.

Scandura, J. M. *Problem solving.* New York: Academic Press, 1977.

Sheppard, S. B., Kruesi, E., & Curtis, B. *The effects of symbology and spatial arrangement on the comprehension of software specifications.* Report No. TR-80-388200-2, Information Systems Programs, General Electric, Arlington, Virginia 1980.

Sime, M. E., Green, T. R. G., & Guest, D. J. Scope marking in computer conditionals - a psychological evaluation. *International Journal of Man-Machine Studies,* 1977, *9,* 107–118.

Teitelbaum, T., & Reps, T. The Cornell program synthesizer: A syntax-directed programming environment. *Communications of the ACM,* 1981, *24,* 563–573.

van der Veer, G. C., & van de Wolde, J. Individual differences and aspects of control flow notation. In T. R. G. Green, S. J. Payne, & G. C. van der Veer (Eds.), *The Psychology of Computer Use.* London: Academic Press, 1983.

van Wijngaarden, A. Recursive definition of syntax and semantics. In T. B. Steel (Ed.), *Formal description languages for computer programming.* Amsterdam: North-Holland, 1966.

Waters, R. C. The programmer's apprentice: Knowledge based program editing. *IEEE Transactions on Software Engineering SE,* 1982, *8,* 1–12.

6

Microcomputer Testing and Teaching of Verb Meaning: What's Easy and What's Hard?*

Robin S. Chapman,
Christine Dollaghan,
O. T. Kenworthy,
Jon F. Miller

We are developing microcomputer programs to test and teach motion-verb meaning in developmentally disabled, physically handicapped, and language-disordered children. In this chapter we explore what is easy and what is hard in this application of microcomputers to education. Three different perspectives are considered in turn: (1) the programmer's view; (2) the child's view; and (3) the adult's view. Each of these perspectives creates its own constraints on the materials to be developed. Our task is to account for each in program design.

*Preparation of this chapter was supported in part by funding from the Wisconsin Center for Education Research, which is supported in part by a grant from the National Institute of Education (Grant No. NIE G-81-0009); and by the facilities of the Waisman Center on Mental Retardation and Human Development. The opinions expressed in this chapter do not necessarily reflect the position, policy, or endorsement of the National Institute of Education. T. M. Klee carried out the analyses of mothers' requests; A. Heintzelman assisted in diary data analyses; and C. Bilow provided programming advice.

OVERVIEW

We selected motion verbs for study because they are an important and infrequently assessed aspect of semantic development in preschool children. They are important because they constitute a vocabulary central to early syntactic development that differs in organization and development from object language. Specific verbs or restricted semantic classes become foci for early sentence construction (Bloom, Miller, & Hood, 1975; Braine, 1976). Thus, the teaching of verb meaning should have consequences for syntactic growth in young language-delayed children.

Despite the centrality of motion verbs to language acquisition, they are infrequently assessed because action is difficult to depict in static pictures. An efficient and flexible means for evaluating and teaching comprehension and use of motion verbs by developmentally disabled children is needed to differentiate patterns of language delay and to augment programming of early sentence development.

Interactive microcomputers programmed to test and exemplify spoken sentences offer such a means. With them, the researcher can provide action; use the same contexts for testing understanding and getting the child to talk; create action alternatives that the child can choose among (a recognition test paradigm); allow the child to carry out the action by moving objects on the screen (a recall test paradigm); construct yes–no switches or joy sticks that can be activated by orthopedically handicapped individuals; and use the same action stimuli in exemplifying sentences in testing and teaching modes.

Here we take up the problems of developing such programs from three perspectives in turn:

1. The programmer's problem of achieving rapid and believable animation and a program that the child can interact with
2. The child's problem of relating what it sees and hears to prior knowledge (and hence our problem of finding out what form that prior knowledge takes)
3. The adult's problem of ensuring that all the nuances of motion-verb meaning available to him are adequately sampled by the materials

THE PROGRAMMER'S PERSPECTIVE

Animation

The microcomputer is well suited to the task of random or contingent selection of the events to be shown. It is also an ideal tool with which to ring consistent minimal changes in the motion events displayed. Creating the illusion of movement and synchronizing movement with spoken stimuli, however, tax the limits of current microcomputers.

Both the limited speed of programming languages and the inability of many microcomputers to perform simultaneous tasks limit the application we have in mind. Approximately 2 seconds are required, for example, to complete a new drawing on the screen. Thus, the use of the multiple frame technique of cartoon animation, which requires rates of approximately 40 frames a second to achieve smooth motion, is not presently possible on microcomputers; what can be achieved introduces flicker and jerky movement.

Some of the problem can be overcome by creating either shape tables or character fonts. Shape tables involve storing shapes to be flashed successively on small parts of the screen; character fonts call for altering the form associated with each keyboard letter and using these new characters to "write" the animated figure on the screen. When the latter technique is employed using Pascal on an Apple II, for example, images are created on the screen sufficiently quickly to convey the illusion of smooth movement with little flicker. The creation of each brief event, however, requires the collaboration of a skilled programmer and artist and may take up to a week.

Machine language, which would allow even faster presentation rates, has the practical disadvantage that few skilled programmers are available. Nor would use of machine language shorten the time-consuming collaboration between programmer and artist that is required. One still faces the artist's problem of what the successive shapes should be to achieve convincing impressions of moving figures—people walking, birds flying, horses galloping.

One method developed as a cartooning aid for convincing animation is to take movies or videos of the motion to be represented. Successive frames can then be traced for transformation to character-font elements. The resulting motion is convincing because it is based on actual models. Books of still frames representing common methods of locomotion also exist and can be used as a basis for many animated events.

A second alternative emerges from motion perception studies. Johansson (1973) showed that adults, at least, can easily interpret moving patterns of light as different human gaits when the lights correspond to 10 to 12 joints (shoulder, elbow, wrist, hip, knee, ankle). A compelling illusion of human locomotion could then be created simply through programming the motion of dots.

A third alternative to achieving the impression of motion is suggested by the pioneering work of Michotte (1963) on the perception of causality, and by the recent work of Levelt, Schreuder, and Hoenkamp (1978). Michotte demonstrated that adults will attribute agency to moving geometric forms under specific conditions of speed, path, and contact. That is, they will see one shape as the cause of the second shape's motion: for example, pusher and thing pushed. Adults use the vocabulary of change-of-location verbs *(push, carry, follow)* to describe the simplified interactions that they see.

A fourth alternative would be to abandon animation attempts and to use the microcomputer to control selection of videotaped events. Random-access videodisks that plug into current microcomputers are available at relatively little ($700) expense. The master disks, holding over 100,000 frames, could be made from videotape at a current cost of approximately $5000. Programs have been developed, for example, to explore a town: north, south, east, and west views are available on the master disk for every intersection. Similarly, one could create a set of fixed alternatives for moving an object through space.

The second and third alternatives to representing motion on the microcomputer have the advantage of shorter implementation time but the possible disadvantage, for young children, of being unusually abstract. If children's verb meanings are learned with respect to specific contexts, only the creation of recognizable figures in realistic motion (the first and fourth alternatives) may be a fair test of comprehension. One of the questions we will be exploring is the extent to which children's performance is affected by the prototypicality of the scenes shown.

If the simplified, abstract solutions to the presentation of motion verbs do not work initially for children, it may still be possible to teach the meaning of verbs within simplified and restricted motion universes, by providing the child with experience. Children's use of the LOGO program, (Papert, Watt, diSessa, & Weir, 1979), for example, allows arbitrary movement patterns on the screen to be created and given a name which evokes them. By providing the necessary immediate experience, the computer creates its own contexts for word meaning. The need for programming, however, introduces unnecessary task complexity for preschoolers. Control of a joystick to move objects on the screen would provide an easier task with some of the virtues of user control, initiative, and creativity that LOGO offers the older child.

Sound

To test and teach the meaning of motion verbs, the program must provide rapid random access to high fidelity speech. Of the possibilities we have examined, synthetic speech devices seem too low in fidelity for naive listeners. The Super-Talker, which creates a digitized representation of speech, seems to provide good quality, but it requires too much memory (4K per second of speech) in conjunction with the graphics memory requirements. Further, graphics and speech can not be provided simultaneously. A good alternative is the Instavox, a rapid random-access device with high fidelity, 27 minutes of recording time per disk, and variable-length records. It requires no storage space within the microcomputer, permits messages of variable length, and allows simultaneous presentation of picture and sound.

Response System

The application of microcomputers to assessment and teaching of language in preschoolers represents a novel endeavor. Most computer applications have focused upon adults and school-aged children (e.g., the LOGO project; Osberger, Moeller, Kroese, & Lippman, 1981). In working with preschoolers, we must resolve uncertainty about their interactions with the computer.

For example, our pilot work has indicated that children below the age of 3 need direct selection systems to indicate their choices. Two-year-olds can easily name or point to two different objects on the screen but do not learn to press the correct button to indicate their choice even with demonstration and 70 training trials. This is true even when button position (top, bottom) corresponds to picture position and button color to the framing color, and even when the buttons are mounted alongside the picture choices.

Touch screens that permit the children to make direct selections of the answer offer a solution for normal children (light pens appear to require too much fine motor control). Severely physically handicapped children, however, may not be able to use touch screens. Evaluation then becomes a problem for children functioning intellectually at 2- to 3-year-old levels. Direct selection devices (e.g., through looking, head pointers) are preferable to indirect switch selections for assessing children of this developmental level.

Motivation

If the child is allowed to interact with computer representations of motion and to learn the alternatives the computer offers through direct experience, one may be able to reap the additional and powerful benefits of motivation that computer games offer. Malone (1981) describes the properties of computer games—and other intrinsically motivating learning environments—that make them preferred to others by school-aged children. These properties include freedom to choose the activity, challenge of an appropriate level, fantasy elements in the game, and outcomes that can pique curiosity.

The implications of Malone's theory for the design of intrinsically motivating computer games from which children might learn include the following:

1. The learning activity should be embedded in an overall fantasy goal arising out of the material and appealing to children of the target age. Visual and auditory feedback of overall goal progress should be provided. Visual and auditory feedback about individual trials should also be provided.
2. The materials should be scaled in difficulty level. The level presented to the learner should be adjusted to one at or just above his current skill level, depending on whether he is consolidating or extending skills.
3. Novelty and surprise should be built into the game relative to the cognitive structures (e.g., event representations) one wishes the child to acquire.

For children in the preschool age range, typical themes of spontaneous fantasy play include telephoning, playing house, playing doctor, and monster's coming (Garvey & Berndt, 1975). The last theme includes a group of games in which threat arises at every turn, to be averted by running away or, among older children, finding a safe place to hide. The game suggests an overall fantasy goal appropriate for motion verbs. Looking for hidden treasure or rescuing people in distress are other fantasy goals typical of early elementary school play in which motion verb elements could be embedded.

The child's task, to pilot a figure through scenes on the screen, can be cued by instruction. Variations in the number of trials and length of time allowed, and the movement alternatives permitted by the computer, can be introduced as ways of building in variable skill levels. Difficulty can also be altered by varying the words themselves, and the ways in which instructions must be applied to contexts. For example, does the context permit an easy inference about the proper location of an object? Do the contexts contrast in observable properties such as rate, path, and end result of motion? Or do they contrast in inferred properties of intent and belief?

How to create cognitive curiosity in a game of motion-verb instruction is less obvious. For example, one way would be to vary the probability of the instructed moves—the difference between going out the door or up the door. A second way, for a "Monster's Coming!" version, would be to make the monster's movements unpredictable at a surface level but predictable at a deeper one. The child could discover, for example, that certain places or distances were always safe. A third way, used in games like "Adventure,'' but possibly too complicated for preschoolers, would be to provide clues to a consistent spatial configuration of an area that could be used to select a path on trials that did not show what would come next—what area, for example, would be found beyond a door, or outside the window, or up the stairs? A fourth method to introduce elements evoking curiosity would be to determine some event sequences randomly.

It is a hypothesis to be tested that learning words within the same script—or, in this case, interactive computer game—will provide for acquisition of contrastive compotential meaning in ways that learning words in different contexts may not.

THE CHILD'S PERSPECTIVE

To create motion events that are recognized as instances of motion verbs by children, we need to be able to guess the meanings of these words for children and to learn how meanings might change with experience. What makes motion verbs, and motion events, easy or hard to understand and describe from the child's point of view? Several bases for prediction are suggested by existing literature (e.g. Bowerman, 1978; Gallivan, 1981; Gentner, 1978; Huttenlocher & Charney, 1982).

1. Salient and frequent events that children observe will determine which motion-verb meanings they learn first.
2. Those actions which children themselves carry out frequently will be meanings that they learn first.
3. Those motion events that are consistently commented on by caretakers will be first learned.
4. The more semantic components required to describe a motion verb's meaning, the harder it will be to learn the full meaning of the verb.
5. Some semantic components may be harder than others (for example, those requiring inference about the other person's beliefs or intents, rather than observation).
6. Those motion events that have more obligatory situational elements than others may be later talked about or understood.
7. Verbs emerging later in children's talk may also have entered their comprehension vocabularies later, in comparison to early acquired verbs.

These differing approaches to predicting verb difficulty are not mutually exclusive; all may be right to some extent. Further, there is some evidence for developmental change in the way the child's representation of events, and hence representation, of motion-verb meanings is organized. Schank and Abelson (1977) suggest that early event representations are of action, shifting to scripts (summaries of what usually happens) at age 2 and to plans by age 4. Bowerman points to syntactic over-generalizations of word use (e.g., *You sad me)* as evidence of lexical reorganization around semantic components occurring toward the end of the 2–4-year period.

The theoretical issues would be unnecessary to resolve if all we wanted were an assessment instrument with a range of difficulty, but we also want to use the microcomputer displays as a basis for teaching verb meaning; and here the theoretical issues are important. Exemplars conforming to the child's current mode of event representation, sequenced to allow easy integration into the current organization of its lexicon, should prove the best teaching materials.

In this section, therefore, we examine three bodies of evidence that may help us to make predictions about which motion verbs will be easy and hard to understand, and which verbs children might want to learn: (1) the action words that very young children use during bathtime, and the contexts in which they use them; (2) the action comments and requests that young children hear from their mothers during free play; and (3) the three most common responses that school-age children give to verbs in word association tests. We ask what aspects of events young children talk about and mothers encode; and what contexts verbs bring to mind in the association data.

Evidence from Bathtime: What Children Talk About

What aspects of an everyday activity do young children come to talk about? We can raise this question in the specific context of bathtime for 31 children between 10 and 21 months whose mothers kept a diary of their utterances during the event. We can correlate what children say during bathtime with the usual sequence of bathtime events to learn what events children have chosen to communicate about: actions, scripts, plans, or all three? We can ask whether these are events of some novelty in the ordinary course of bathtime, or the usual events themselves. Early speech has been characterized as informative (Greenfield, 1978) in the sense that it ordinarily marks what the child has noticed; but events can be perceptually salient in their own right or novel relative to one's expectations. To the extent that novelty plays a role in determining what the child chooses to talk about, we will learn only of departures from the usual script. To the extent that children mark usual but salient aspects of the routine verbally, we will learn about its content.

All children's utterances related to action during bathtime, and the associated contexts, are listed for 31 children in the Appendix. The following summary is constructed for these entries.

Up through 19 months, the total number of words per child paired with different contexts during bathing is small, ranging from 2 to 12. The usual event can begin with a request for it: BATH. After that, few of the routine aspects receive comment. No children talked about the necessary preparatory activities of running the water or undressing, except to protest the latter (NO). Getting into the water received comment only if it was unexpectedly hot (HOT; OWIE). Once in, vocalization or talk accompanied splashing (WHEE) and play with toys, usually as a request for or comment on the object (BOAT; DUCK). Other language accompanying toy play marked attainment of the toy, or unexpected failure to attain it (OH); its transfer to another person (HERE), or the water (BOOM); a completed construction (I-DID-IT); the unexpected disaster when water spilled on the floor, boats sank, or toys came apart (UH-OH); and the unexpectedly bad taste of soap or wash cloth (ICKY).

Standing up in the tub was frequently accompanied by talk, either to repeat the mother's injunction (DOWN), to recognize the prohibited nature of the activity spontaneously (NO-NO), or label it (UP). People and animals entering the room were greeted (HI) and, after they left, inquired about (BYE-BYE?). Washing and shampooing, in contrast, were noted only by occasional protest. Readiness to get out was frequently signaled (MAMA; PLEASE; UP; OUT); and the end of bathtime marked by watching the water drain out of the tub (ALL DONE).

SCRIPTS, PLANS, AND TALKING.

From the foregoing summary we can draw three conclusions. First, children do not routinely talk about the usual temporal sequence of events accompanying bathtime, except to protest them: getting undressed, getting in, getting washed or shampooed. Only the initiation and the end of the activity are marked.

Second, the children do comment on novel events for which they are only observers: entrances and exits of others; the unexpected behaviors of toys and water. These events are coded differently as a function of appearance–disappearance (HI–BYE) and types of undesirable outcome (UH-OH; HOT; ICKY); but not as a function of the specific action that led to the resulting state. It is the unexpected end result that occasions comment rather than the method of achievement.

Third, children also, and most frequently, talk about their plans: objects that they want or do not want; events that they want to bring about or prevent; reaching or failing to reach their desired goals; and the conflicts between their plans and the activities permitted by their mothers. Farwell (1977) and Gopnik (1981) drew similar conclusions from data collected during free play. Gopnik (1981) concludes that children talk about disappearance (GONE) or changes in location (UP, DOWN, IN, OUT, ON, OFF) that they are attempting to bring about; success or failure of a plan (THERE, OH DEAR); rejection of a plan (NO); and repetition of a plan (MORE). Uses related to the child's own plans precede comments on similar outcomes in other people's activities in Gopnik's longitudinal data. Perhaps children learn to extend language for their own plans to the actions of others through observing similar outcomes in their own and others' actions.

By these analyses, plans or goal structures are characteristic of children's representation of words associated with action even before the first transitive verbs are observed, and well before the age of 4 years, at which Schank and Abelson (1977) place the emergence of plan-based memory structures. Toddlers talk about ends and outcomes relative to expectations, rather than means and actions, in event-related language.

These conclusions do not necessarily mean that children approaching 2 years of age lack conceptual representation of actions or routine events. Children may know the bathtime script well (might be surprised, for example, to be put in the water with clothes on), but we cannot demonstrate it from what they say. Nor can we be certain, lacking records of mothers' input during these episodes, whether the mothers have commented to their children on the routine aspects of the event; although this, too, is probable. Thus, we see that what young children choose to talk about may systematically exclude that portion of the language that they hear in reference to usual events: The very aspects of input that are likely to be most easily understood are not sufficiently unusual to talk about. By this argument, free-speech samples can give a biased view of the child's linguistic mapping of the world.

Alternatively, mothers may not encode the usual aspects of their actions either, limiting the child's opportunity to learn the relevant language; or children in the sensorimotor period may have no scripts for extended event sequences, as Schank and Abelson suggested (1977). To decide among these alternatives we need studies in which the child's talk, the child's comprehension, and the mother's talk are all elicited for the same event sequence; and we need event sequences that introduce unexpected variations. These could easily be carried out for computerized event sequences.

Evidence from Play: What Mothers Say

The verbs that children come to understand will be a subset of the verbs that they hear. The fact that they talk about their own plans, unexpected events, and event outcomes raises the question whether mothers similarly limit their own input. Mothers' vocabulary addressed to language-learning children is reported to be less diverse (Phillips, 1973; Snow, 1972) and more concrete than speech to older children and adults; but specific characteristics of verb use have not been described.

Is There a "Basic Event" Language?

Brown (1977, pp. 1–30) proposes that the labels used by mothers are more likely to designate basic object categories (Rosch, Mervis, Gray, Johnson, & Boyes-Brahem, 1976) than superordinate or subordinate terms. A similar argument could be made that *natural categories* of events exist for children and that mothers also restrict their verbs to basic event labels in talking to children. Our review of young children's event-related language suggests at least three bases of natural-event categorization: (1) by goals or the intended outcome; (2) by success or failure of outcome relative to expectation; and (3) by the desirability of the outcome. One could then argue that the coincidence between natural event category and basic event language would increase the probability of comprehension.

Children between the ages of 1 and 2 command a small but growing repertoire of actions that they carry out on objects. Although they do not comment on them, the mother may; alternatively, she may comment extensively on her own actions, which may not correspond with the child's developmental level. Huttenlocher and Charney (1982) have argued that children have no particular reason to equate their own goal-directed actions with observed, perceptually based ones; if so, one needs to consider separately the input associated with child and other action.

Chapman (1981) has proposed that later comprehension (Miller, Chapman, Branston, & Reichle, 1980) and production (Goldin-Meadow, Seligman, & Gelman, 1976) of action verbs by English-speaking children may stem in part from the difficulty of segmenting them from the speech stream. In this hypothesis, action words modeled in single words at the ends of utterances would have an increased probability of being learned.

To predict a motion verb's acquisition, then, one may need to consider not only its frequency of use by the mother, but the pragmatic contexts in which it occurs (e.g., comment or request for action), its linguistic context (utterance medial or final), and who is carrying out the action (child or mother).

MOTHERS' INPUT: ACTION AND OUTCOME

These questions can be better appraised if we have a description of the verbs that language-learning children hear. We can provide such a summary for 12 mothers' comments on action during free play to 10- to 21-month olds (see Table 1); and for 48 mothers' requests for action to 10- to 21-month olds (see Table 2). Inspection of Table 1 shows that mothers not only comment frequently on the same outcome-oriented aspects of events that children do; they also explicitly encode the child's action on objects. They almost never comment on their own actions exclusively with a word.

In the requests for action that mothers address to children (Table 2), actions as well as goals are made explicit. The actions requested correspond closely to the repertoire to be expected from children in the late sensorimotor stages; they include most of the following from the Uzgiris-Hunt scales of developmentally sequenced schemes in relation to objects: hold, mouth, look, hit, bang, hit together, shake, wave, push, pat, throw, look at (examine), spin, crumple, squeeze, drop, put on, take off, show, stack, knock down, put in, take out (dump), put together, take apart, conventional actions on objects (eat with spoon, drink from cup, hug doll, brush with brush, etc.), point, give.

It is clear, then, that the absence of verbs focusing on means, rather than

TABLE 1

Verbs in Mothers' Comments on Children's Actions to 10- to 21-Month-Olds ($n = 12$)

Total Frequency	Action verbs
10	go (34), put (25), got (17), fell/fall (16), *get* (14), look (10)
9	have/has
8	fit
7	come, see
6	find, make, want
5	do, oink-oink, take
4	all gone, boom, gallop, move
3	*knock,* lost, *open,* stand
2	*beep,* blow, bring, *dance,* drop, jump, nibble, *peek,* roll, say, *sit,* try, work
1	*bang, break, climb,* crash, *crush,* deliver, fly, *hammer,* keep, like, *pile, play, pull, rattle, reach,* show, spin, *squish,* stick

Note. From 10-minute free play sessions. Catenatives gonna (8) and wanna (6) omitted, verb particles omitted; italicized words occur exclusively with children's actions, not adults'. Only *show* occurred exclusively with adult action.

TABLE 2

Action Verbs in Mothers' Requests for Action to 10- to 21-Month-Olds ($n = 48$)

Number of mothers using verbs	Action verbs
20	put on (23), put in (22)
11–19	come (18), get (16), give (16), do (15), come on (14), no (14), put together (13), have (11), try (11)
10	go get
9	make go, put
8	push
7	bring, give kiss, stand up
6	find, get out, go, let's see, put back, turn around
5	hold, leave alone, make, pound, show, sit, squeeze, take, take off, turn
4	get in, pick up, put back together, put inside, roll, see, shake, take out, throw
3	catch, don't bite, don't put in, dump out, go on, kiss, patticake play, put away, turn over
2	blow, bring back, bring over, brush, build, can't have, come here, come on over, dance, don't fit, give hug, give ride, goes, help, hit, hold on, hug, leave, line up, make fly, make noise, make run, make talk, not to play with, open, open up, over here, pull, pull over, put down, rock, set up, sit down, spit, stay, tip up, use
1	balance, bang, bang on, beat, be careful, bring here, can't go, climb, climb up, comb, come get, come off, come out, come over, crawl, do you have to, doesn't want to have, don't chew, don't eat, don't do, don't hit, don't hurt, don't open up, don't play, don't put in, don't pound, draw, feel, flip, fix, gallop, get apart, get back, get down, get 'em up, get off, give love, give me 5, go ahead, go bzz, go do, go in, go like this, go nite nite, go rock, go up, go when, hang on, here, hold still, hold up, how big are you, how 'bout this one, in here, jump, keep, leave on, let have, look, make gallop, make jump, make spin, make stand, move, move away, not gonna go, pull apart, pull out, push around, push in, push together, put down on, put on top, put over, reach, rockabye, roll around, send, shake up, sing, sit in, spin, spread, spread out, stack, stack up, stick, stick in, talk, the other end, the other way, this one, tickle, tip out, tip over, tip upside down, toss, turn on, twirl, wave, wait, wanna do.

Note. From Chapman, Klee, and Miller (Ms.); 10-minute free play samples. Requests for action coded from videotapes; specific verb and particles (or other) used noted for each mother.

ends, in children's second year cannot be attributed to their exclusion from their mothers' talk to them. This observation makes it more probable that omission of action encoding words in children's talk stems from the reasons for which children choose to communicate, rather than lack of comprehension. Only direct assessment of action word comprehension, however, can confirm or disconfirm this speculation.

Evidence from Word Games: Children's Word Associations

A child's comprehension of a given verb's meaning develops over time. For example, *come* and *go* are understood to refer to movement long before the directionality of movement can be correctly inferred on the basis of relative spatial location of speaker and listener (Clark & Garnica, 1974). Indeed, one influential theory of semantic development (Clark, 1973, pp. 65–110; 1975) has held that the meanings of the first words to be acquired in a semantic domain will consist of one or a few of the most general features of the domain. Other investigators studying children's comprehension of relational terms such as *younger* or *older* (Kuczaj & Lederberg, 1977), or *more* and *less,* have shown that the child's understanding of the word may not be just incomplete, but different from the adult's, as the child incorrectly focuses on a more salient aspect of the referential situation. For example, height or gray hair may become the child's meaning for *older*.

That the meaning of a word is often only partially—or even incorrectly—acquired has been illustrated through limitations and errors in word use (e.g., *yesterday* for any time not the present). Bowerman (1978) has proposed, on the basis of extensive data on her two children's use of words in specific contexts over the 2–4-year range, that early word meaning is holistic and limited in situations of use. Word use, when it occurs, is usually appropriate. Errors arising toward the end of the fourth year suggest that the child has belatedly come to analyze the components of word meaning in a domain, and to reorganize its lexicon along these componential dimensions.

The errors that Bowerman cites support the inference that the child has incorrectly added a component of meaning by analogy to other constructions; for example, a causative component, as in *You sad me* or *Who deaded my kitty?* Alternatively, of course, the child may be making the best use of limited lexical means, an explanation that seems reasonable for 2-year-olds' errors in labeling objects. Comprehension testing is needed to decide the issue.

ORGANIZATIONAL SHIFTS IN CHILDREN'S VOCABULARIES

There are other paradigms that can yield information on shifts in the child's lexical organization. Children's word associations have been reinterpreted as evidence for a shift from episodic to semantic organization in memory (Petrey, 1977). We examined Entwisle's (1966) word-association data for the three most common responses of each sex to 24 high-, middle-, and low-frequency verbs to see what evidence of changes in semantic organization they yielded.

Among kindergartners, 47% of the common responses named elements playing combinational semantic roles in that verb's meaning: *mix-a cake; obey-your mother; join-club; give-present; sit-chair; move-car; gallop-horse.* Objects of action, locative, actor, and recipient roles all occurred; the first was most frequent. We call these responses *episodic* because they provide other elements of the event in which the action is embedded. They could be viewed as scripts themselves or fragments of larger scripts. These episodic responses suggest that kindergartners still frequently call to mind particular event contexts when they hear verbs that lack a context.

Semantic responses that revealed a focus on componential meaning, including synonyms, antonyms, and manner components, were far less frequent (13%) among the 200 kindergartners and were given more often to the high-frequency verbs. They included, for example: *move-walk, begin-start, listen-be quiet, obey-be good.* Only one antonym was actually offered: *begin-end.* These findings suggest that the lexicon's reorganization is a slower process than we originally believed.

Five other categories among the kindergartners' three most common responses were identified: (1) rhyming associates (14%), for example, *give-live;* (2) responses indicating that the child had interpreted the verb differently, for example, *restore-food* and *inquire-church;* (3) verb particles that made the action more specific (6%), for example, *move-away, sit-down;* (4) associated events (3%), for example, *tell-show 'n tell;* and (5) uncategorized responses (8%), for example, *allow-paper.*

Similar categorizations were carried out for first-, third-, and fifth-grade data. The results are in Table 3 for three of the six categories: episodic responses, semantic responses, and responses indicating that the stimulus word had been misunderstood. One can see that episodic responses become infrequent at 3rd and 5th grade, depending on verb frequency. Among semantically related responses, antonyms constitute about 30% of the responses with little change with grade.

These results suggest that episodic representation of verb meaning will continue to be the dominant pattern of lexical organization for verbs until

TABLE 3

Percentage of Three Most Common Responses Episodically or Semantically Related to Verbs of High-, Middle-, or Low-Frequency

Verb frequency	Response	Grade			
		K	1	3	5
High	Episodic	52%	46%	12%	10%
	Semantic	21%	38%	62%	73%
	Diff. word	4%	0	0	0
Middle	Episodic	42%	52%	10%	10%
	Semantic	17%	15%	69%	69%
	Diff. word	6%	15%	0	0
Low	Episodic	46%	38%	19%	10%
	Semantic	2%	10%	40%	52%
	Diff. word	17%	21%	27%	21%
All words	Episodic	47%	45%	14%	10%
	Semantic	13%	21%	57%	65%
	Diff. word	10%	12%	9%	7%

Note. Responses analyzes are from Entwisle (1966); responses of both sexes.

mid-elementary school, despite the beginning of the transition in preschool years. The implication, for comprehension testing, is that verbs should be blocked into sets that correspond to episodic structure and outcome. Such an organization is developed for motion verbs from the adult's perspective in the following section. To learn which scripts children think of in connection with motion verbs, we will need to ask them.

THE ADULT'S PERSPECTIVE

To learn how children understand and use verbs in a recognition–elicitation paradigm requires more than the development of an event sequence depicting each motion verb. It requires the systematic construction of alternative events contrasting with the "correct" one in components of the verb's meaning and the situation to which it is applied. Only in this way can one discover whether a verb is understood and used across activities or episodes, which components of the adult's meaning are present in the child's representation, and whether components not present in the adult meaning have been added by the child. In this section, we define motion verbs from the adult point of view, divide them into groups corresponding to the basic motion situations that they represent, and discuss the range of variations within situations that correspond to componential contrasts in meaning.

Defining Motion Verbs

The definition of *motion verb* depends on the theorist, but most agree that motion verbs comprise a subcategory of action verbs, and that motion verbs have reference to changes in location or spatial orientation. Miller and Johnson-Laird (1976) and Talmy (1975; in press) have devoted some of the most concentrated attention to the specific question of motion verbs, and their emphases are helpfully complementary.

Talmy is concerned with three components of a motion event, in addition to the component of "motion" (i.e., the presence per se of motion or location). These three he terms the *Figure* (the object moving or conceptually moveable or located), the *Ground* (the object with respect to which the Figure is moving or located), and the *Path* (the course followed or site occupied by the Figure). According to Talmy, a motion event can also have a *Manner* or a *Cause*—both of which he views as distinct events. Finally, Talmy sees two deep verbs which underlie motion events: MOVE and BE.

Miller and Johnson-Laird (1976), on the other hand, are particularly interested in the notion of change of location, which is codified in the core concept of TRAVEL: something has traveled if it appears where it was not before or if it is no longer where it was before. Miller symbolizes the concept of travel using the notation of logical calculus; his choice of symbols reveals that his view of the general motion situation contains one entity and one location which the entity either arrives at or leaves.

Variation between Situations: Combinatorial Aspects of Motion Verb Meaning

The situations in which absolute change of location occur can be divided according to the number of elements present (one, two, or three) and whether each element moves or stays still. Some elements can be further distinguished as having their own motive power (people, cars, animated figures); these are designated as SELF. Five important motion situations are then defined: (1) situations in which one element is present and moves (MOVE SELF); (2) situations in which two elements are present and one moves (MOVE SELF IN RELATION TO ENTITY1); (3) situations in which two elements are present and one moves both itself and the other (MOVE SELF AND ENTITY 1); (4) situations in which two elements are present and one moves the other (MOVE ENTITY 1); and (5) situations in which three elements are present and one moves the second in relation to the third (MOVE ENTITY 1 IN RELATION TO ENTITY 2).

These situations group motion verbs according to their combinatorial properties—the relations among elements that figure in their meanings. They also define animation problems of differing degree—the number of simultaneously moving elements that would have to be displayed in depicting any two motion events.

In Table 4, motion verbs are grouped by situation for the words appearing in 5- and 6-year-old children's stories (Wepman & Hass, 1969) and Wells's (1975) coding manual for child language. Stimuli for our own studies of motion verbs will be drawn from verbs belonging to these five sets. Selection will include both those motion verbs likely to be acquired early because mothers use them to very young children (see Tables 1 and 2) and those verbs not present in samples of mother's early input that children are using by school age, according to Wepman and Hass (1969) norms.

TABLE 4

Motion Verbs for the 5 Motions Situations

Situation	Motion verbs
Move self	crawl, dash, disappear, explore, fall, fly_1, go, hop, jump, move, $roll_1$, run, $sink_1$, skate, ski, skip, $slide_1$, slip, sneak, step, swim, swing, travel, walk
Move self in relation to entity 1	approach, arrive, bump, chase, climb, come, escape, follow, $get back_1$, $hide_1$, hunt, knock, into, $leave_1$, pass, $return_1$, visit
Move self and entity 1	bring, carry, drive, fly_2, paddle, ride, sail, take
Move entity 1	bounce, drop, fly_2, get, get rid of, grab, knock, lay, lift, $move_2$, pick up, pour, pull, push, $return_2$, $roll_2$, ship, shove, $sink_2$, $slide_2$, spill, $swing_2$, take, throw
Move entity 1 in relation to entity 2	attach, cover, crash, dump out, empty, fill, fit, give, hand over, hang, hide, put, rob, screw on, send, set, steal, stick in, take apart, take off

$Verb_1$ = intransitive form.
$Verb_2$ = transitive form.
Note. Compiled from Wells's (1975) Coding Manual and Wepman and Hass (1969) 5- and 6-year-olds' verb lists.

Variation within Situation: Componential Aspects of Motion Verb Meaning

In addition to combinatorial aspects of motion-verb meaning, there are also various component meanings which further specify the nature of the motion labeled. These component meanings, which are differentially important for various verbs, include Talmy's (1975; in press) MANNER (*walk* vs. *run),* PATH *(enter* vs. *exit)* and FIGURE *(rain).* Additional component meanings that may distinguish among motion verbs include the following:

1. Variations in the number of entities in motion: (*go* vs. *swarm*)
2. Variations in whether the entire entity or part of it is in motion: (*go* vs. *wave*)
3. Variations in intentionality of motion: (*lie down* vs. *fall down*)
4. Variations in directionality of motion: (*ascend* vs. *descend*)
5. Variations in the medium involved in motion: (*crawl* vs. *swim*)
6. Variations in the instrument involved in motion: (*walk* vs. *ride*)
7. Variations in starting and ending location: (*throw* vs. *bounce*)
8. Variations in goals of motion (*run* vs. *chase*)

Given the situational blocking, one can ask whether children comprehend contrasts within the situations in a predictable order. For example, contrasts in locative outcomes (e.g., *put in, put on, put under* for verb + locative particle) should show a predictable sequence of acquisition. From cross-cultural research on comprehension and use of locative prepositions (Conner, 1981; Johnston & Slobin, 1979), we know that words for topological relations (those preserved in the absence of measured distance and angle), for example *in, on, under,* are understood before projective and Euclidean-based relationships (e.g., *in front of* for nonfronted objects). We can predict that verbs within a motion-event grouping that differ in locational outcome should show a similar sequence in acquisition.

As a second example, contrasts in observable components of meaning *(walk* vs. *run)* are likely to be understood before componential contrasts in the mental state of the actor (e.g., *walk around* vs. *explore; follow* vs. *chase).* The latter requires more inferential work. We will not know until such studies are completed whether that which children understand in the preschool period differs systematically from the plans and outcomes that they talk about.

CONCLUSION

Three sets of constraints on microcomputer programs designed to test and teach motion verb meaning have been reviewed:

1. The problems faced by the programmer in creating believable animation and sound in a program that children can and will interact with
2. The ways in which children's understanding and use of motion verbs are likely to change with experience and
3. The full range of adult knowledge of motion verb meaning that must eventually be explored in testing or teaching of comprehension and use.

These three perspectives converge in placing constraints on the representation of motion events. For the programmer, animation is hard—time-consuming to create and memory-consuming to use. For the child, animation is necessary if comprehension is to be tested, rather than complex inferences about the events leading up to a static scene. Further, animation may need to be of those specific events that young children think of in association with a motion verb, if early comprehension is to be tested adequately. For the adult, animation must create minimally different motion events that capture the differential semantic components of meaning and the combinatorial properties of individual motion verbs.

Our problem, in short, is the same one arising in any laboratory study of lexical development: that of linking the experimenter's task with the child's knowledge of the world, inference strategies, and usual reasons for talking. By providing animation or video action rather than static representation, we can reduce the inferential requirements of the motion verb test. By learning what scripts children think of when they hear motion verbs, and by using these scripts as the context for motion-verb testing, we can tap the young child's knowledge. By creating new contexts for motion-verb meaning through the child's interactive control of events on the screen, we can examine factors affecting the process of motion-verb acquisition and create the expectations that lead to pragmatic reasons for motion-verb use. By using the microcomputer to control videodisks of real people carrying out actions, we could provide realistic sets of the gestural, facial, and situational cues that may be needed to infer intent and belief, features of meaning that are critical to complete understanding of later-acquired motion verbs.

With microcomputer solutions to motion-event animation, we will be able to study systematically, for the first time, the way that preschoolers understand motion verbs and talk about motion events. The role of familiar scripts in facilitating comprehension, the roles of novelty in facilitating talk, the relative difficulty of the different motion situations, and the relative difficulty of different semantic components of meaning can be investigated systematically for both normal and handicapped children. The information obtained should give us insight into how to teach motion-verb meaning.

REFERENCES

Bloom, L., Miller, P. & Hood, L. Variation and reduction as aspects of competence in language development. In A. Pick (Ed.), *Minnesota Symposia on Child Psychology* (Vol. 9). Minneapolis University of Minnesota Press, 1975.

Braine, M. D. S. Children's first word combinations. *Monograph of the Society for Research in Child Development,* 1976, (Serial No. 164).

Bowerman, M. Systematizing semantic knowledge: Changes over time in the child's organization of word meaning. *Child Development, 1978, 49,* 977–987.

Brown, R. Introduction. In C. Snow & C. Ferguson (Eds.), *Talking to children: Language input and acquisition.* New York: Cambridge University Press, 1977.

Chapman, R. S. Mother–child interaction in the second year of life: Its role in language development. In R. Schiefelbusch & D. Bricker (Eds.), *Early language: Acquisition and intervention.* Baltimore, Maryland: University Park Press, 1981.

Chapman, R. S., Klee, T. M., & Miller, J. F. *The development of pragmatic comprehension skills in 10- to 21-month-olds: responses to requests for attention and action.* Unpublished manuscript.

Clark, E. What's in a word? On the child's acquisition of semantics in his first language. In T. E. Moore (Ed.), *Cognitive development and the acquisition of language.* New York: Academic Press, 1973.

Clark, E. Knowledge, context and strategy in the acquisition of meaning. In D. P. Dato (Ed.), *Georgetown University Round Table on languages and linguistics.* Washington, D.C.: Georgetown University Press, 1975.

Clark, E., & Garnica, O. K. Is he coming or going? On the acquisition of deictic verbs. *Journal of Verbal Learning and Verbal Behavior, 1974, 13,* 559–572.

Conner, P. S. The development of locative comprehension in Spanish-speaking children. Unpublished masters thesis, University of Wisconsin, Madison, Wisconsin, 1981.

Entwisle, D. *Word associations of young children.* Baltimore, Maryland: Johns Hopkins Press, 1966.

Farwell, C. B. The primacy of goal in the child's description of motion and location. *Papers and reports on child language development* (Stanford University) 1977, *13,* 126–133.

Gallivan, J. *The acquisition of English motion verbs.* Unpublished doctoral dissertation, Waterloo, Ontario: University of Waterloo, 1981.

Garvey, C., & Berndt, R. *The organization of pretend play.* Unpublished manuscript, 1975.

Gentner, D. On relational meaning: The acquisition of verb meaning. *Child Development,* 1978, 49, 988–998.

Goldin-Meadow, S., Seligman, M., & Gelman, R. Language in the two-year-old. *Cognition,* 1976, *4,* 189–202.

Gopnik, A. Development of non-nominal expressions in 1–2-year-olds: Why the first words aren't about things. In P. Dale & D. Ingram, (Eds.), *Child language: An international perspective.* Baltimore, Maryland: University Park Press, 1981.

Greenfield, P. M. Informativeness, presupposition, and semantic choice in single-word utterances. In N. Waterson & C. Snow (Eds.), *Development of communication: Social and pragmatic factors in language acquisition.* London: Academic Press, 1978.

Huttenlocher, J., & Charney, R. *Children's verb meanings: Evidence about the emergence of action categories.* Unpublished manuscript, 1982.

Johansson, G. Visual perception of biological motion and a model for its analysis. *Perception & Psychophysics,* 1973, *14,* 201–211.

Johnston, J., & Slobin, D. I. The development of locative expressions in English, Italian, Serbo-Croation, and Turkish. *Journal of Child Language,* 1979, *6,* 529–546.

Kuczaj, S., & Lederberg, A. Height, age and function: Differing influences on children's comprehension of 'younger' and 'older.' *Journal of Child Language,* 1977, *4,* 395–416.

Levelt, W. J. M., Schreuder, R., & Hoenkamp, E. Structure and use of verbs of motion. In R. N. Campbell & P. T. Smith (Eds.), *Recent advances in the psychology of language* (Vol. 4b). New York: Plenum Press, 1978.

Malone, T. W. Toward a theory of intrinsically motivating instruction. *Cognitive Science,* 1981, *5,* 333–369.

Michotte, A. *The Perception of Causality.* New York: Basic Books, 1963.

Miller, G. A., & Johnson-Laird, P. N. *Language and perception.* Cambridge, Massachusetts: Belknap Press of Harvard University Press, 1976.

Miller, J. *Assessing children's language production: Experimental procedures.* Baltimore, Maryland: University Park Press, 1981.

Miller, J. F., Chapman, R. S., Branston, M., & Reichle, J. Comprehension development in sensorimotor stages V and VI. *Journal of Speech and Hearing Research,* 1980, *25,* 243–260.

Osberger, M. J., Moeller, M. P., Kroese, J. M., & Lippman, R. P. Computer-assisted speech training for the hearing-impaired. *Journal of the Academy of Rehabilitative Audiology,* 1981, *14,* 145–158.

Papert, S., Watt, D., diSessa, A., & Weir, S. Final Report of the Brookline LOGO Project, Part 2: Project Summary and Data Anslysis. *LOGO MEMO* 53: *AIM* 545. Cambridge, Massachussetts: Artificial Intelligence Laboratory, Massachusetts Institute of Technology, 1979.

Petrey, S. Word associations and the development of lexical memory. *Cognition,* 1977, *5,* 57–71.

Phillips, J. R. Syntax and vocabulary of mother's speech to young children: Age and sex comparisons. *Child Development,* 1973, *44,* 192–195.

Rosch, E., Mervis, C. B., Gray, W., Johnson, D., & Boyes-Braehm, P. Basic objects in natural categories. *Cognitive Psychology,* 1976, *8,* 382–439.

Schank, R., & Abelson, R. *Scripts, plans, goals and understanding: An inquiry into human knowledge structures.* Hillsdale, New Jersey: Lawrence Erlbaum Associates, 1977.

Snow, C. E. Mothers' speech to children learning language. *Child Development,* 1972, *43,* 549–565.

Talmy, L. Semantics and syntax of motion. In J. P. Kimball (Ed.), *Syntax and semantics* (Vol. A). New York: Academic Press, 1975.

Talmy, L. Lexicalization patterns: Semantic structure in lexical forms. In T. Shopen, S. Anderson, T. Givon, E. Keenan & S. Thomson (Eds.), *Language typology and syntactic field work (Vol. 3).* in press.

Wells, G. *Coding manual for the description of child speech.* Bristol, England: University of Bristol, 1975.

Wepman, J., & Hass, W. *A spoken word count.* Chicago: Language Research, 1969.

APPENDIX: CONTEXTS OF CHILDREN'S EARLY ACTION WORDS
DURING BATHING OF 10- TO 21-MONTH-OLDS (*n* = 31)
(FROM PARENTS DIARIES)

Age in months	Utterance recorded	Specific context recorded
Interpreted meaning:		ALL DONE/ALL GONE
11	a da	`C had just finished bath; watching water go out of tub
20	gaw gone	C drank entire glass of bath water
21	aw done	C didn't want to be shampooed
	ba no	C finished bathing
	all done	Repeat of above
Interpreted meaning:		BATH
10	ba (I)	Repeating after F
11	ba	C standing in bathroom
12	ba	M running water for bath
20	bas (I)	C responding to M asking "Are you having a bath?"
	bauts	C watching tub fill with water
	ba	M running water into tub
21	ba	C requesting bath as M prepares bathroom
Interpreted meaning:		BYE-BYE/NIGHT-NIGHT
10	bye-bye	All of family saying goodnight to sibling
		1) C waving to self in mirror
12	ba by (2x)	2) F leaves room
17	bye-bye, wa wuh	C waves to water in bath as it goes down drain
	bye-bye, dada	C Wants to leave bathroom and go see F
Interpreted meaning:		DON'T/NO-NO
15	no	C wanted M to stop undressing him
	no	C didn't want to get out of bathtub
16	oo na na	C standing up in bathtub and knew he shouldn't
17	no-no-no	C admonishing F not to wipe C's nose
20	no!!	C didn't want hair washed
	no!	C didn't want bottom washed
21	no, no	C responding to parents saying "Don't do that" as C stood up in tub
	no _____	C asking Brother for toy
	_____, don't	C didn't want Brother to pour water on C
Interpreted meaning:		DOWN
10	don (I)	M told C to sit down while C standing in tub
15	down (I?)	C responding to M's request for C to sit down in tub
Interpreted meaning:		FALL
20	boom, boom	C throwing toys in bathtub

(*cont.*)

Age in months	Utterance recorded	Specific context recorded
Interpreted meaning:		GO
21	a go?	C looking for toy boat
Interpreted meaning:		HAVE (= WANT)
21	have it	C points to sponge; wants M to retrieve it
Interpreted meaning:		HI
11	hi	C had just climbed in tub
	hi	C addressing dog as it walked into bathroom
	a (as in apple) (I)	In response to M; said while standing up in tub
13	Hello	F entered room
19	Hi	M walks into bathroom while F bathing C
20	Hi ya,	C sees self and M in mirror
Interpreted meaning:		LOOK (+ AT)
21	ahkut, Mom	C shows M an empty cup
Interpreted meaning:		OPEN
18	ie	C standing in bathroom by door; just finished
	pin	bath; wants out of bathroom
Interpreted meaning:		OUT/OUTSIDE
17	out (repeated with different intonation several times)	C standing up in bath; asking to get out C declaring he is out of bath after M removes him
21	out	C sitting in tub; want to leave
	out	Repeats above
	ow	C points to faucet while water running
Interpreted meaning:		SEE
18	sa	C remarks as F knocks over stack of bowls in bath tub
Interpreted meaning:		SIT
21	sit	C responding to M asking C to sit down in tub
Interpreted meaning:		UH-OH/OOPS
14	uh-oh	C spilled water
15	oooh	C splashing around in water
16	oh-oh	Toys on side of bathtub fell into water
17	oh!	Toy boat falls apart
20	oh-oh	C sank toy boat

Age in months	Utterance recorded	Specific context recorded
Interpreted meaning:		UP
15	up	C stands up alone in bathtub
	uh	C wanted to be lifted into bathtub
16	uh	C standing near bathtub; wanted to get in
	ga uh, (get up)	C finished with bath; wanted to get out of tub
19	up	C wants out of tub
Interpreted meaning:		WANT + (Object Action)
11	ahm	C reaching for toothbrush
12	bath	C reaching for brush toothbrush
15	un ah	C holding cup while playing in water
20	eh, eh	C pointed to soap and shampoo

7

Teaching Vocabulary-Building Skills: A Contextual Approach*

Robert J. Sternberg,
Janet S. Powell,
Daniel B. Kaye

Vocabulary-building skills are techniques for increasing one's sight vocabulary. They differ from techniques for teaching specific vocabulary in that they are intended not only for learning specific words (whose definitions are explicitly given), but also for learning words encountered in real-world contexts without explicit definitions. The purpose of our chapter is to consider some alternative methods for vocabulary-building skills, and to discuss in some detail the method we prefer, learning from context.[1]

---

*Preparation of this chapter was supported by Contract N0001478C0025 to Robert J. Sternberg from the Office of Naval Research.
[1]All of the methods discussed in this chapter have relevance to both first- and second-language learning. In order to keep the scope of the chapter within manageable bounds, we shall deal here only with first-language learning.

The theory of learning from context is described in relation to the theory of verbal comprehension in general in Sternberg, Powell, and Kaye (1982). The theory of external decontextualization represents a collaborative effort between Powell and Sternberg; the theory of internal decontextualization represents a collaborative effort between Kaye and Sternberg.

Our chapter is divided into three parts. First, we briefly review three methods for teaching sight vocabulary. Next, we outline a theory of learning from context. Finally, we suggest how our approach could be implemented in a computer-assisted instructional package. Our general claim is that it is possible to learn vocabulary from context by a method that is theoretically based, practically feasible, and of great value to students in improving their skills of verbal comprehension.

ALTERNATIVE METHODS FOR VOCABULARY BUILDING

A number of different methods have been proposed for teaching vocabulary (see Gipe, 1979; Johnson & Pearson, 1978; Levin, 1981; O'Rourke, 1974). A full review of even a subset of these methods deserves a book-length presentation; indeed, the books by Johnson and Pearson and by O'Rourke are devoted almost exclusively to a consideration of methods for teaching vocabulary. We shall review here the three methods that seem to be of greatest interest today: (1) rote learning, which, despite its slightly unsavory connotations, remains by far the most widely-used method for teaching vocabulary; (2) the keyword method, which is a mnemonic method that makes heavy use of interactive imagery; and (3) learning from context, which is an extremely popular method of teaching vocabulary, but which is now being challenged by advocates of the keyword method. Our description of each method will have three parts. First, we shall briefly describe the method. Then we will evaluate it by three "armchair" criteria. Finally, we will review empirical data regarding the efficacy of the method.

Before discussing the methods, it would be worthwhile for us to describe the three armchair criteria we shall use in evaluating the methods. These are internal connectedness, external connectedness, and practical ease of use. The first two criteria, internal and external connectedness, derive from Mayer and Greeno (1972). These criteria are important because internally and externally connected knowledge tends to be durable and generalizable. By *internal connectedness* we refer to the richness and degree of integration attained for the cognitive structure built to define a single new vocabulary word. Rich and well-integrated definitions exhibiting high internal connectedness are found in references such as etymological dictionaries, which contain expansive accounts of the subtleties of word meanings and their derivations. Sparse and poorly integrated definitions exhibiting low internal connectedness are typically found in pocket dictionaries, especially for multiply defined words. By *external connectedness* we refer to the richness and degree of integration attained between the cognitive structure built to define the new vocabulary word and other cognitive structures. Definitions that relate new words to old concepts, and thereby exhibit high external connectedness, are found in specialty dictionaries that list features such as etymologies, rhymes, antonyms, synonyms, and cognates for words. Definitions that only sparsely or ambiguously relate new words to old concepts are found in pocket dictionaries and some "junior" level dictionaries. We use *practical ease of use,* our third criterion, to refer to the extent to which an individual encountering a new word in the course of everyday experience could use a given method to learn and then retain the meaning of a given new word. The less time and effort expended to learn a new word, the more likely the individual is to employ the method and thereby have a chance of learning from the method.

Rote Learning

There are a number of variants of the rote-learning method for acquiring meanings of new words, but the basic idea is simple. The individual is somehow exposed to a word and its definition, and commits the word, the definition, and the association between them to memory. In some cases, the definition is supplied; in other cases, the definition must be sought after, for example, by consulting a dictionary. But in all cases, there is heavy reliance upon associative memory.

This method does not fare particularly well on the three armchair criteria. Definitions provided for words in pocket dictionaries or in test-coaching books are typically short and concise to make it easier to remember them. But these single-word synonyms and unelaborated short phrases, while perhaps memorable, limit the reader's opportunity to build a highly internally connected cognitive representation for the word, reducing the likelihood that subtleties of the word's meaning will be understood and that the word will be used. On the other hand, richer, more elaborative definitions, while meeting the internal connectedness criterion, are difficult to memorize. So regardless of the type of definition provided for rote learning, odds are against the reader's constructing and retaining an elaborate cognitive representation of the word's meaning.

Poor elaboration in many definitions also reduces opportunities to develop an externally connected cognitive structure. The learning of word lists typically leads to the formation of some degree of subjective organization (Tulving, 1962, 1966) between pairs, triples, or higher-order units of new words, such that recall of a new word or a new word and its definition also touches off recall of other words and their definitions (Bower, 1970; Mandler, 1967; Tulving & Pearlstone, 1966). Operationally, the existence of subjective organization is measured by words consistently tending to be recalled together or in close succession. The association between recalled words may be appropriate and even useful within the impoverished semantic context of a word list; but the associated words may have little semantic relation to each other, and the associations formed are not likely to have much long-term benefit when it becomes necessary to understand the new words outside the episodic and largely arbitrary context of the list in which they were learned.

The ease of applying the rote method is variable, depending upon the variant used. A word list with words and their definitions is easy to use; requiring individuals to look up words in a dictionary is cumbersome. But whatever source is used for definitions, a problem arises when one's goal is to train for vocabulary-building skills as well as for specific vocabulary. By far the largest amount of vocabulary one learns is acquired through everyday interactions with words in conversation, newspapers, books, lectures, and the like. There is usually no dictionary readily available, and even if one makes a note to look up a specific word or list of words later, such notes are notoriously easy to misplace. It is extremely rare for a definition to be given directly in our daily interactions with words, other than in vocabulary-instructional programs. Consequently, rote learning by itself is unlikely to be sufficient for acquiring and retaining the meaning of a previously unknown word, or for enabling the reader to apply the word's meaning to its current context.

Some empirical evidence bears upon the usefulness of rote learning. Gipe (1979) compared two rote methods to a category-learning method and a context-learning method. One rote method presented a new word paired with a brief definition; the other rote method required the individual to look up the meaning of the new word in a dictionary. In this latter method, individuals were also required to write down the definitions, and to write sentences containing each word. Gipe found that for both third- and fifth-grade children, the association method was better than the dictionary method, but both methods were inferior to learning from context. Pressley and Levin (1981) and Pressley, Levin, and Miller (1981) compared the keyword method (to be described) to a control condition that encouraged, but did not require, rote recall of new vocabulary words. Subjects in both studies were college students. The investigators found that under specified conditions, the control group (which, presumably, employed primarily rote learning) performed at a lower level than did the keyword group. Thus, the admittedly skimpy evidence comparing rote learning to alternative methods of learning does not show favorable results for the rote method. These results, combined with the armchair analysis, encourage one to investigate alternative methods of teaching vocabulary and vocabulary-building skills. One such alternative method is the method we consider next, the keyword method.

The Keyword Method

The keyword method was originally introduced for the purpose of teaching foreign languages (Atkinson, 1975; Atkinson & Raugh, 1975; Raugh & Atkinson, 1975), but has been adapted to teaching first-language vocabulary by Levin, Pressley, and their colleagues (Levin, 1981; Pressley & Levin, 1981; Pressley, Levin, & Miller, 1981a, 1981b, 1982). The keyword method is a mnemonic technique based upon the finding that interactive imagery can facilitate learning (Bower, 1972; Paivio, 1971). (See Paivio & Desrochers, in press, for a critical review of the literature on mnemonic techniques in *second-language* learning.)

The keyword method consists of two stages, an *acoustic-link stage* and an *imagery-link stage*. We shall illustrate the method for acquiring English vocabulary with the example, *carlin,* which means *old woman* (Pressley & Levin, 1981). In the acoustic-link stage, the individual acquires a "keyword," which is a familiar English word that (1) sounds like a salient part of the unfamiliar word and (2) is visualizable through a mental image. For the word *carlin,* one might use *car* as a keyword, in that *car* is both a salient phonetic part of the word to be learned and a visualizable concept. In the imagery-link stage, one forms a visual image in which the familiar keyword and the unfamiliar word are visualized as interacting in some manner; for example, one might imagine an old woman driving a car.

The keyword method has a solid foundation in learning theory. Psychological principles drawn upon by the keyword method are that (1) meaningful stimuli are more reliably encoded than are nonmeaningful stimuli; (2) interacting items are more reliably associated than noninteracting items; (3) the greater the similarity between two stimuli, the more reliably one will evoke the other; and (4) thematic interactions are reliably retrieved from appropriate cues (Levin, 1981). Given this base of psychological theory, one might expect the keyword method to fare better than the rote method on both our armchair and our empirical criteria, and, in fact, it does.

The definitions provided in the keyword method are no more verbally elaborated than the definitions provided in the rote method, but they are more visually elaborated through the use of imagery. In the *carlin* example, for instance, not only is the definition of a carlin as an old woman learned, but the old woman is visualized, in this case driving a car. If one assumes a dual memory system with both visual and verbal codes (Paivio, 1971), then one would expect the addition of the visual information to provide an additional retrieval cue for recall of a word and its definition. Almost any other multicomponent model of memory traces (e.g., Bower, 1967) will also predict improved memory by the addition of the visual component to the memory trace. The more elaborate and richer memory trace provides an integration between verbal and imagery components of the word's representation, and would thus seem to be more internally connected than the trace typically provided by rote learning.

Formation of an interactive image also provides increased external connectedness via the interaction of the image of the target word with some other well-known word. In the example, an old woman is associated with a car. This external connection offers no meaningful semantic association, but does provide a visual association. Again, the use of visual imagery is responsible for an improvement over the rote method.

The ease of using the keyword method seems to be variable. Generally, subjects are provided with keywords; providing them facilitates use of the method. In normal reading and listening, however, keywords are not automatically supplied, and especially for abstract words, the keywords may be hard for students spontaneously to generate. This is not, however, to say that the keyword method will not work for abstract words (see Delaney, 1978; Pressley, Levin, & Miller, 1981b). The method requires some mental effort to generate and use the keyword for each new word, and also assumes that somehow the individual has a definition of the word to be learned. As noted earlier in our discussion of the rote method, this assumption is rarely true. Thus, the keyword method, like the rote method, is less useful in everyday situations than in academic situations where preformed word lists are explicitly provided for the learner.

The keyword method has been empirically tested by Levin, Pressley, and their colleagues (Levin, McCormick, Miller, Berry, & Pressley, 1982; Levin, Pressley, McCormick, Miller, & Shriberg, 1979; Pressley & Levin, 1981; Pressley, Levin, & Delaney, 1982; Pressley, Levin, Kuiper, Bryant, & Michener, 1982; Pressley, Levin, & Miller, 1981a, 1981b, 1982). The method has been compared both to control conditions in which no explicit instruction is given (and in which subjects presumably employ rote learning) and to several variants of the learning-from-context method to be described. The outcome of these studies is that the keyword method is at least as effective as, and usually more effective than, the alternative methods against which it has been compared. This finding holds up over age levels and across some variation in word types. But Hall, Wilson, and Patterson (1981), using simultaneous rather than the usual successive presentation of (Spanish) vocabulary words, but also group rather than individual presentation of words, found free study to be superior to keyword study. The data thus appear not to be wholly conclusive. Moreover, we shall claim that the extant tests of the learning-from-context method are not wholly adequate.

Learning from Context

The learning-from-context approach to vocabulary teaching has its theoretical origins in research on incidental learning of vocabulary. Werner and Kaplan (1952) proposed that children acquire the meanings of words primarily in two ways: by explicit reference to names of objects and concepts, and by implicit contextual reference. Their now-famous monograph examined how learning in context takes place for children ranging from 8 to 13 years of age. This early work has given rise to many subsequent studies of contextual learning of vocabulary (e.g., Cook, Heim, & Watts, 1963; Daalen-Kapteijns & Elshout-Mohr, 1981; Keil, 1981; Marshalek, 1981).

In typical studies of learning from context, individuals are presented with several sentences that employ the word to be learned in ways that help elucidate the word's meaning. The individual is required to infer the word's meaning, and then often to use the word in a sentence that shows comprehension of the meaning but is different from the given sentences. An example of this approach is given by Gipe (1979) for the word *barbarian:* "The *barbarian* kicked the dog and hit the owner in the nose. Any person who acts mean to anybody or to anything is a *barbarian. Barbarian* means a person who is very mean (p. 630)." After reading these sentences, the individual is asked to write something that a *barbarian* might do at a dinner table. Gipe's example, especially in the last given sentence, is more directive regarding the meaning of *barbarian* than is sometimes the case, which may account for the success of the context method in Gipe's work (to be discussed below).

The learning-from-context method, like the keyword method, fares reasonably well on our armchair criteria. The method can be strong with respect to facilitating the development of an internally connected cognitive structure for the meaning of the word because one is exposed to some of the richness of the word in its various possible uses in real-world contexts. The individual is thus encouraged to learn the shadings of meaning associated with the word, and to interconnect these meanings by relating the various presented sentences. However, the learning-from-context method can also have some problems with respect to internal connectedness, because the degree to which an individual can form an internally connected representation depends on the ability of the individual and the facilitation provided by the context. Because most occurrences of words in context are less directive as to the word's meaning than is the case in the example from Gipe (1979), a student may get only a rough idea of the word's meaning, especially if the student is unskilled in using context. This potential problem could be overcome, however, as we will argue later, by training people in how to use context.

The method is especially strong in its facilitation of the development of an externally connected cognitive representation of word meaning. The given sentences generally relate the new word to a variety of other concepts, so that it is possible to understand how the concept represented by the word interacts with other concepts. Indeed, it is from its emphasis on the inter-relation of the word to the conceptual environment surrounding the word that the method of learning-from-context takes its name. If the given sentences are highly imageable, then the learner is provided with the additional benefit of being able to supplement verbal learning with visual imagery. For example, the sentence, "The barbarian kicked the dog and hit the owner in the nose," potentially provides a rich visual image to associate with the meaning of the word *barbarian.*

The ease of use of the learning-from-context method depends upon the degree of facilitation provided by the context in which the word occurs: Some contexts (such as Gipe's) essentially define the word; others leave its meaning murky. Training contexts will probably tend to be more defining than natural contexts. Thus, vocabulary building programs may not always provide the learner with realistic expectations regarding the ease of learning from context in real-world verbal environments. But the learning-from-context method does have the advantage that it can always be used (with greater or lesser success) in real-world environments that provide words in context but that rarely give explicit definitions.

As noted earlier, Gipe (1979) compared learning from context to two rote methods and a category-learning method. The third- and fifth-graders in the study did better in the learning-from-context condition than in any of the other conditions. This finding must at present be interpreted with some caution because it is based only on a single data set whose replicability is not clear. But Pressley *et al.* (1982) compared several variants of the context method to the keyword method, and found that the keyword method worked better for college students. The conclusion they would have us draw is that the keyword method is superior, at least when explicit definitions can be available. The question therefore arises of whether the very popular learning-from-context method has been oversold. Our own belief is that current versions of the method may well have been oversold, but that better versions can be devised. We are not arguing that *any single* method of teaching vocabulary is best for all purposes. We do think, however, that the learning-from-context method can be an important component in a comprehensive vocabulary teaching program. In the next section, we discuss modifications of the learning-from-context method, and explain our belief in its potential.

A THEORY OF LEARNING FROM CONTEXT

A vocabulary training program that uses learning from context is incomplete if it fails to provide instruction in how to use the context. According to the theory to be proposed here, utilization of context is a distinctly nontrivial feat. The instructional programs tested by Pressley *et al.* (1982) were incomplete, as were many others (but not all others; see e.g., Johnson & Pearson, 1978). In the keyword method, one is specifically taught how to form and use keywords. Fair comparison of this method to the context method requires comparable instruction in the context method regarding how context can be used to infer word meanings. Although individuals can be expected to have some ideas about how to use context, just as they can be expected to have some ideas about how to use images, these ideas will almost certainly be incomplete and, in some cases, may be incorrect. Thus, we propose here the specific cues we believe individuals should be taught to use prior to their actual learning from context, and certainly prior to their being tested in research on the effectiveness of the method. We divide our system of cues into two subsystems: *external cues,* found in the context surrounding the word, and *internal cues* provided by the morphemes within the word (see also O'Rourke, 1974). Some of the cues draw directly upon aspects of the text; others draw upon the usefulness of these in various situations.

Decoding of External Context

By external context, we refer to the verbal context surrounding a given new word. The methods of learning from context that we have discussed all have dealt exclusively with external context.

TEXTUAL CUES

Our model specifies the particular kinds of cues that individuals can use to figure out the meanings of new words from the contexts in which the words are embedded. Not every cue can be applied in every situation, and even when a given cue can be utilized, its usefulness will be moderated by factors to be described shortly.

Context cues are hints contained in a passage that can facilitate, but might also impede, deciphering the meaning of an unknown word. We propose that context cues can be classified into eight categories, depending upon the kind of information they provide (cf. Ames, 1966; McCullough, 1958; Miller & Johnson-Laird, 1976; and Sternberg, 1974). Our eight categories are:

1. Temporal cues. Cues regarding the duration or frequency of X (the unknown word), or regarding when X can occur; alternatively, cues describing X as a temporal property (such as a duration or frequency) of some Y (usually a known word in the passage).

2. Spatial cues. Cues regarding the general or specific location of X, or possible locations in which X can sometimes be found; alternatively, cues describing X as a spatial property (such as general or specific location) of some Y.

3. Value cues. Cues regarding the worth or desirability of X, or regarding the kinds of affects X arouses; alternatively, cues describing X as a value (such as worth or desirability) of some Y.

4. Attribute cues. Cues regarding the properties of X (such as size, shape, color, odor, feel, etc.); alternatively, cues describing X as a descriptive property (such as shape or color) of some Y.

5. Functional cues. Cues regarding possible purposes of X, actions X can perform, or potential uses of X; alternatively, cues describing X as a possible purpose, action, or use of Y.

6. Enablement cues. Cues regarding possible causes of or enabling conditions for X; alternatively, cues describing X as a possible cause or enabling condition for Y.

7. Class cues. Cues regarding one or more classes to which X belongs, or other members of one or more classes of which X is a member; alternatively, cues describing X as a class of which Y is a member.

8. Equivalence cues. Cues regarding the meaning of X, or contrasts (such as antonymy) to the meaning of X; alternatively, cues describing X as the meaning (or a contrast in meaning) of some Y.

An example of the use of some of these cues in textual analysis might help concretize our descriptive framework. Consider the sentence, "At dawn, *sol* arose on the horizon and shone brightly." This sentence contains several external contextual cues that could facilitate one's inferring that *sol* refers to the sun. "At dawn" provides a temporal cue, describing when the arising of *sol* occurred; "arose" provides a functional cue, describing an action that *sol* can perform; "on the horizon" provides a spatial cue, describing where the arising of *sol* took place; "shone" provides another functional cue, describing a second action that *sol* can do; finally, "brightly" provides an attribute cue, describing a property (brightness) of the shining of *sol*. With all these different cues, it is no wonder that most people would find it easy to figure out that *sol* refers to the sun.

We make no claim that the categories we have suggested are mutually exclusive, exhaustive, or independent. Nor do we claim that they in any sense represent a "true" categorization of context cues. We have, however, found this classification scheme useful in understanding people's strategies in deriving meanings of words from context. Collectively, they are some tools that comprise a person's competence in inferring word meanings.

FACTORS MODERATING THE USEFULNESS
OF THE TEXTUAL CUES

Consider some moderating variables that can affect, either positively or negatively, the application of the textual cues in a given situation.

1. Number of occurrences of the unknown word. A given kind of cue may be absent or of little use in a given occurrence of a previously unknown word, but may be present or of considerable use in another occurrence. Multiple occurrences of an unknown word increase the number of available cues and can actually increase the usefulness of individual cues if readers integrate information obtained from cues surrounding the multiple occurrences of the word. For example, the meaning of a given temporal cue may be enhanced by a spatial cue associated with a subsequent appearance of the unknown word, or the temporal cue may gain in usefulness if it appears more than once in conjunction with the unknown word. On the other hand, multiple occurrences of an unfamiliar word can be detrimental if the student has difficulty integrating the information gained from cues surrounding separate appearances of the word, or if the student notices only peripheral features of the unfamiliar word.

2. Variability of contexts in which multiple occurrences of the unknown word appear. Different types of contexts, such as different topics or writing styles, and different contexts of a given type, such as two illustrations within a given text of how a word can be used, are likely to supply a variety of information about the unknown word. Variability of contexts increases the likelihood that a wide range of cues will be supplied about a given word, and thus increases the probability that a reader will get a full picture of the scope of a given word's meaning. In contrast, mere repetition of an unknown word in essentially identical contexts is unlikely to be helpful, because few or no really new cues are provided regarding the word's meaning. Variability can, however, present a problem in some situations and for some

individuals: If the information is presented in a way that makes it difficult to integrate across appearances of the word, or if a given individual has difficulties in making such integrations, then the variable repetitions may actually obfuscate rather than clarify the word's meaning. In some situations and for some individuals, the overload of information may reduce rather than increase understanding.

3. Importance of the unknown word to understanding the context in which it is embedded. If a given unknown word is judged to be necessary for understanding the surrounding material in which it is embedded, the student's incentive for figuring out the word's meaning is increased. If the word is judged to be unimportant to understanding what one is reading or hearing, one is unlikely to invest much effort in figuring out what the word means. Although in explicit vocabulary building situations the individual may always be motivated to infer word meanings, in real-world situations, there may be little such motivation. Thus, a question of interest from the perspective of our model is the extent to which an individual reader can recognize which words are important to a passage, and which are not. In some cases, it may not be worth the individual's time to figure out a word's meaning. It is possible to distinguish between importance at different levels of text organization. We distinguish between the sentence and paragraph levels, that is, the importance of a given word to understanding the meaning of the sentence in which it occurs, and to understanding the meaning of the paragraph in which it occurs. The ability to recognize the importance of a word to understanding context may be seen as a form of comprehension monitoring (Collins & Smith, 1982; Flavell, 1981; Markman, 1977, 1979, 1981).

4. Helpfulness of surrounding context in understanding the meaning of the unknown word. The helpfulness of a cue depends upon the nature of the word whose meaning is to be inferred and upon the location of the cue in the text relative to the word whose meaning is to be inferred. For example, a temporal cue describing when a *diurnal* event occurs would probably be more helpful than a spatial cue describing where the event occurs in aiding an individual to figure out that *diurnal* means *daily*. In contrast, a spatial cue would probably be more helpful than a temporal cue in figuring out that *ing* means *a low-lying pasture*. It is unrealistic to expect a given kind of cue to be equally helpful in figuring out the meanings of all words. Although the nature of the word is important in these examples, the location of the cue can also be important. If a given cue occurs close to the word whose meaning is unknown, then it is probably likely to be recognized as relevant to inferring the unknown word's meaning. If the cue is located far from the unknown word, the relevance of the cue may never be rec-

ognized. The helpfulness of context cues may also be mediated by whether the cue comes before or after the unknown word. Rubin (1976), for example, found that context occurring before a blank was more helpful to figuring out what word should go in the blank than was context occurring after the blank.

5. Density of unknown words. A reader who is confronted with a high density of previously unknown words may be overwhelmed and be unwilling or unable to use available cues to best advantage. When the density of unknown words is high, relatively more text is occupied by unknown and therefore unhelpful words (for figuring out meanings of other words), and it can be difficult to discern which of the available cues apply to which of the unknown words. In such a situation, utilization of a given cue may depend upon figuring out the meaning of some other unknown word, in which case the usefulness of that cue is decreased.

6. Concreteness of the unknown word and the surrounding context. Concrete concepts are generally easier to apprehend, in part because they have a simpler meaning structure. Familiar concrete concepts such as *tree, chair,* and *pencil* are relatively easy to define in ways that would satisfy most people, but familiar abstract concepts such as *truth, love,* and *justice* are extremely difficult to define in ways that would satisfy large numbers of people. Moreover, the ease of inferring the meaning of the word will depend upon the concreteness of the surrounding description. A concrete concept such as *ing* might appear more opaque in a passage about the nature of reality than in a passage about the nature of food sources; similarly, an abstract concept such as *pulchritude* (i.e., *beauty*) might be more easily apprehended in a passage about fashion models than in one about eternal versus ephemeral qualities.

7. Usefulness of previously known information in cue utilization. Inevitably, the usefulness of a cue will depend upon the extent to which past knowledge can be brought to bear upon the cue and its relation to the unknown word. The usefulness of prior information will depend in large part upon a given individual's ability to retrieve the information, to recognize its relevance, and then to apply it appropriately.

Decoding of Internal Context

By internal context, we refer to the morphemes within a word that combine to give the word its meaning.

TEXTUAL CUES

What particular kinds of context cues can individuals use to figure out the meanings of new words? Because internal context is much more impoverished than is external context, the diversity of kinds of cues is much more restricted (see, e.g., Johnson & Pearson, 1978; O'Rourke, 1974). The four kinds of cues constituting our scheme are:

1. Prefix cues. Prefix cues generally facilitate decoding of a word's meaning. Occasionally, the prefix has a special meaning or what appears to be a prefix really is not (e.g., *pre-* in *predator*); in these cases, the perceived cue may be deceptive.
2. Stem cues. Stem cues are present in every word, in the sense that every word has a stem. Again, such cues may be deceptive if a given stem has multiple meanings and the wrong one is assigned.
3. Suffix cues. Suffix cues, too, generally facilitate decoding of a word's meaning; in unusual cases where the suffix takes on an atypical meaning, or in cases where what appears to be a suffix really is not (e.g., *-s* in *dais*), the perceived cue may be deceptive.
4. Interactive cues. Interactive cues are formed when two or even three of the word parts described above convey information in combination that is not conveyed by a given cue considered in isolation from the rest of the word.

The usefulness of internal cues in decoding meaning can be shown by an example. Suppose one's task is to infer the meaning of the word *thermoluminescence* (see Just & Carpenter, 1980). The word is probably unfamiliar to most people. But many people know that the prefix *thermo-* refers to heat, that the root *luminesce* is a verb meaning *to give off light,* and that the suffix *-ence* is often used to form abstract nouns. Moreover, a reasonable interpretation of a possible relation between *thermo-* and *luminesce* would draw on one's knowledge that heat typically results in some degree of light. Note that this cue derives from an interaction between the prefix and stem. Neither element in itself would suggest that the light emitted from heat would be a relevant property for inferring word meaning. These cues might be combined to infer that *thermoluminescence* refers to the property of light emission from heated objects. This inference would be correct.

We make no claim that this simple (and unoriginal) parsing of internal contextual cues represents the only possible classification scheme, although we think it represents one plausible parsing. Collectively, internal cues provide a basis for a person to exercise his or her competence in inferring word meanings.

FACTORS MODERATING THE USE OF THE TEXTUAL CUES

Again, consider some relations between a previously unknown word and the context in which it occurs that moderate the usefulness of cues. Our model includes five variables that affect cue usefulness. These variables are similar but not identical to those considered for external context:

1. Number of occurrences of the unknown word. In the case of internal contextual analysis, the context cues are the same on every presentation of a word. However, one's incentive to try to figure out the word's meaning is likely to be increased for a word that keeps reappearing.

2. Importance of the unknown word to understanding the context in which it is embedded. Again, a word that is important for understanding the context in which it occurs is more likely to be worth the attention it needs for figuring out its meaning. One can easily skip unimportant words, and often does. As before, importance can be subdivided into the importance of the unknown word to the sentence and to the paragraph in which it is embedded.

3. Density of unknown words. If unknown words occur at high density, one may be overwhelmed at the difficulty of having to figure out so many words and give up. Yet, it is possible that the greater the density of unfamiliar words in a passage, the more difficulty the reader will have in applying external context cues, and hence the more important will be internal context cues. A high density of unfamiliar words may encourage word-by-word processing and a greater focus on cues internal to the unfamiliar words. This performance variable interacts with the next one to be considered.

4. Density of decomposable unknown words. Because internal decontextualization may not be a regularly used skill in many individuals' repertoires, individuals may need to be primed for its use. The presence of multiple decomposable unknown words can serve this function, helping the individual become aware that use of internal context cues is possible and feasible. In this case, the strategy is primed by repeated cues regarding its applicability.

5. Usefulness of previously known information in cue utilization. Again, one's knowledge of words, word cognates, and word parts will play an important part in use of internal cues. The sparsity of information provided by such cues almost guarantees an important role for prior information.

To summarize, our theory of learning from context specifies kinds of external and internal cues that individuals can use in inferring meanings of previously unknown words. It also identifies variables that affect how well these cues can be utilized in actual attempted applications. We have outlined a set of variables that (according to our theory) might be present in a given external or internal context. However, these variables are not sufficient for describing *actual* utilization of context. We have therefore specified additional variables that will determine the differential application of the set of textual cues both across texts for a single individual, and within a single text across individuals.

Tests of the Theory

Our theory of learning from context has been tested in its role as a description of what people actually do in inferring meanings of words from context, but not in its role as a prescriptive model for teaching vocabulary and vocabulary-building skills. We plan to conduct research on the prescriptive model among Venezuelan school children. The research on the descriptive model has been conducted among United States students in junior high school (internal context), high school (external context), and college (internal context). These tests are described in detail in Sternberg, Powell, and Kaye (1982), Sternberg and Powell (in press), and Kaye and Sternberg (1981).

The theory of external decontextualization was tested by asking 123 students to read passages of roughly 125 words in length that contained embedded within them from 1 to 4 extremely low-frequency words. A given word could be repeated either within a given passage or between multiple passages, but not both. The students' task was to define as best they could each of the low-frequency words occurring within each passage (except for multiple occurrences of a single word within a given passage, which required only a single definition). Ratings of various competence and performance variables as they applied to the low-frequency words in the set of 32 passages were used to predict ratings of definition goodness via linear multiple regression. Separate regressions were computed for each of four types of passage style, because preliminary analyses showed regression weights to be different in each case. At issue was how much of the variance in the difficulty of the low-frequency words could be accounted for by a model combining the competence and performance variables. The combined model accounted for 84% of the variance in the difficulty of words in literary passages, for 55% of the variance in the difficulty of words in newspaper passages, for 72% of the variance in the difficulty of words in science passages, and for 60% of the variance in the difficulty of words in history passages. All of these values of R^2 differed significantly from zero. The mean rated quality of subjects' written definitions on the learning-from-context task were correlated with scores on standardized tests of intelligence, vocabulary, and reading comprehension. Correlations for the various passage types combined were .62 with IQ, .56 with vocabulary, and .65 with reading comprehension, suggesting that the task provided a good measure of verbal skills. Correlations with standardized tests were quite similar for learning-from-context scores computed for the individual passage types.

The theory of internal cue use was tested by asking 58 secondary-school students and 50 college-level students to figure out meanings of words such as *exsect* and *promove* on the basis of internal context cues. All of the 58 words were real, but of very low frequency. All words were prefixed, but none were suffixed. Subjects were tested on the meanings of the words via a multiple-choice format, where one option was totally correct (e.g., *to cut out* for *exsect*), one option was correct with respect to the prefix but not the stem (e.g., *to throw out* for *exsect*), one option was correct with respect to the stem but not the prefix (e.g., *to cut against* for *exsect*), and one option was totally incorrect (e.g., *to throw against* for *exsect*). A hierarchical multiple regression procedure was used to predict scores both on the learning-from-context cognitive task and on meaningfulness ratings of stems and of prefixes. The results suggested that college students, but not high-school students, were able to use internal context to help infer word meanings. Values of R^2 for the college students were generally lower than in the external context study. Significant R^2 values for the college students ranged from .32 to .61. A few of the analyses failed to yield significant results.

To summarize, the data we have collected so far suggest that our theory has some promise in accounting for how individuals learn from context. Obviously, the tests are incomplete, and are presented only as preliminary indications of theoretical validity. We believe that the results are sufficiently auspicious to encourage further tests of the theory, and to suggest that the theory may indeed have implications for how vocabulary can be taught. These implications are discussed next.

INSTRUCTIONAL PACKAGE FOR TRAINING IN VOCABULARY-BUILDING SKILLS

In this final section, we describe the tentative format of a training program based upon the theory we have proposed. The program seeks to increase both vocabulary and, more importantly, verbal comprehension skills needed for vocabulary building (see Curtis, 1981; Sternberg *et al.,* 1982). This training program has not yet been implemented, and, indeed, is still in its planning stage. However, our present thinking suggests that the final program might look something like the following.

The training program will consist of three parts. The first and second parts of the program teach the use of the competence cues for internal and external contexts, respectively. The third part of the program teaches a general strategy for using context to infer the meanings of unfamiliar words; this part teaches the application of performance cues to the already learned competence cues. Overall, the program relies heavily on the use of examples and guided practice for teaching each type of cue, and for teaching the general strategy for combining internal and external competence and performance cues. The program is intended for secondary-school students.

Internal Context

The internal-context module consists of a four-step sequence for learning each cue in the competence model and how to use it. There is a heavy emphasis upon teaching specific roots and affixes.

1. Introduction to the cue. A given type of cue, for example, prefix, suffix, or root, is named and described.
2. Exemplification of the cue. Examples of the kind of cue and how it can be used are presented.
3. Cue training. A given affix or stem, according to the cue being trained, is presented and defined. Examples of the word part are given embedded in real words, and the meanings of these words plus the relation of the cue to the meanings are given. Students are given practice in recognizing and constructing word meanings on the bases of the cue embedded in real words and of knowledge about the other word parts. Emphasis is placed on logical integration of word parts. Further examples of the word part are given in conjunction with other previously learned word parts. The student must use all of his or her prior knowledge based upon learning of word parts to infer the meaning of the new word. This step is cycled through for as many different word parts as are relevant for teaching of a given cue. For example, it would be cycled through 20 times if one wished to teach 20 different prefixes.
4. Cue review. Each of the specific instantiations (e.g., individual prefixes) of the cue are reviewed via re-presentation of meaning and possible use in decontextualization. This step occurs only after all instantiations of a given cue have been taught.

External Context

The external-context module consists of a five-step sequence for learning each cue in the competence model.

1. Introduction to cue. A given cue is named and described.
2. Exemplification of cue. Examples of the use of the cue are presented.
3. Cue finding. Short passages with single low-frequency words are presented exemplifying the given cue; location of the cue with respect to the low-frequency word is varied. Students must locate the cue in each passage. Practice is provided for both single and multiple appearances of a cue type within a passage.
4. Cue utilization. Students are given practice in recognizing correct inferences drawn from the cue, and in actually finding and utilizing cues to infer features of unfamiliar words.
5. Multiple cue utilization. Students are given practice in locating and using multiple types of external context cues presented for a given unfamiliar word in a single passage. This step progresses from the recognition of defining features inferred from external cues, to construction of definitions using external context cues.

General Strategy for Context Usage

The general strategy for context usage is derived by combining the textual cues and variables affecting use of cues in actual specific contexts. The following presentation follows the format needed for a training module, rather than the format outlined in our presentation of our theory; that is, specific performance components are combined for the student into a suggested optimal strategy for using context, rather than being presented separately. However, the performance components involved in some of the steps are listed parenthetically. In the general strategy training module, the student is guided through the following seven steps for applying internal and external textual cues to infer the meaning of an unfamiliar word.

1. Attempt to infer the meaning of the unknown word from the general context preceding the word. (This step combines the mediating variables of helpfulness of the surrounding context, concreteness of the word and its context, and application of previous knowledge.) The student is guided in identifying and summarizing the main ideas expressed in the passage up to the encounter with the unfamiliar word, and in making hypotheses, based on this general context and on his or her world knowledge, as to the domain to which the word's meaning might apply.

2. Read on: Attempt to infer the meaning of the unfamiliar word from the general context that follows the word. (This step combines the same mediating variables as the preceding one: helpfulness of the surrounding context, concreteness of the word and its context, and application of general world knowledge.) The student is guided in recognizing what additional general ideas have been presented in the part of the passage following the unknown word, and in reassessing the main ideas of the sentence or passage involved.

3. Attempt to infer the meaning of the unknown word by looking at the word parts. The student is reminded of the internal textual cues trained in the first of the context training modules.

4. Judge whether or not it is necessary to understand the word's meaning in order to understand the passage or the sentence in which it is used. If it is necessary, estimate how definite a definition is required; if it is not necessary, further attempts to define the word are optional. (The performance variables, number of occurrences of the unknown word, density of the unfamiliar words, and importance of the word to passage and sentence understanding, come into play in this step of the general strategy.) This step teaches the student to assess his or her comprehension, and if a lack of comprehension is occurring, to locate the source of the trouble. Students are asked to locate and attempt to connect the key concepts in the passage. Practice is given in recognizing inconsistencies and abrupt transitions in the main ideas expressed. Students are taught to backtrack in the case of poor understanding, and to attempt to decide whether the poor understanding was due to careless reading or to inability to understand a central concept expressed by an unfamiliar word.

5. Attempt to infer the meaning of the unknown word by looking for specific cues in the surrounding context. In this step the student is reminded of the external textual cues taught in the preceding module.

6. Attempt to construct a coherent definition, using internal and external cues, as well as the general ideas expressed by the passage and general world knowledge. (A large number of the variables are combined in this step of the general strategy, including the number of occurrences of the unknown word, the variability and helpfulness of the contexts, the concreteness of the unknown word and its surrounding context, the density of the unfamiliar words, and the application of previous world knowledge.) Students are introduced to the concept of internal connectedness of a definition. They are then given practice in recognizing definitions that are not internally consistent, and in attempting to reconcile such definitions by (1) re-checking to see that features were correctly inferred from the internal and external contexts, and (2) marking those features that are unreconcilable as tentative information.

7. Check definition to see if meaning is appropriate for each appearance of the word in the context, and with general knowledge concerning the passage. (Here the performance variables of number of occurrences, variability of contexts, and application of world knowledge, are combined.) Students are introduced to the concept of external connectedness of a definition. They are given practice in applying a definition to multiple contexts, and in recognizing the need for, and implementing, modifications in the definition when appropriate. If modifications are required, the student is instructed to recheck for internal connectedness of the modified definition.

Following the presentation of the general strategy training module, students are given practice in internal and external context cue finding and utilization. Emphasis in this practice is on integrating cues from multiple sources. Students are asked explicitly to describe how they use the cues in different instances, as well as to provide definitions. Along with the computer-assisted practice, students are asked to find examples of unknown words in their everyday reading, and to share with other class members the strategies they used to infer the meanings of the unknown words, and the criteria they used for evaluating the necessity of defining the word and for assessing internal and external connectedness.

To summarize, we have presented an outline of a computer-assisted training program for the development of vocabulary-building skills. We believe that this theoretically based method, used in combination with other vocabulary-building methods (such as rote learning and the keyword method), can provide potentially significant benefits to students learning to learn vocabulary. The thrust of our work has been primarily theoretical and pedagogical rather than technological: We do not present our program as a new innovation in computer-assisted instruction. Yet, we see such instruction as providing a way of presenting the instructional package in an individualized and interesting way.

REFERENCES

Ames, W. S. The development of a classification scheme of contextual aids. *Reading Research Quarterly*, 1966, *2*, 57–82.

Atkinson, R. C. Mnemotechnics in second-language learning. *American Psychologist*, 1975, *30*, 821–828.

Atkinson, R. C., & Raugh, M. R. An application of the mnemonic keyword method to the acquisition of a Russian vocabulary. *Journal of Experimental Psychology: Human Learning and Memory*, 1975, *104*, 126–133.

Bower, G. H. A multi-component theory of the memory trace. In K. W. Spence & J. T. Spence

(Eds.), *The psychology of learning and motivation: Advances in theory and research* (Vol. 1). New York: Academic Press, 1967.

Bower, G. H. Organizational factors in memory. *Cognitive Psychology,* 1970, *1,* 18–46.

Bower, G. H. Mental imagery and associative learning. In L. W. Gregg (Ed.), *Cognition in learning and memory.* New York: Wiley, 1972.

Collins, A., & Smith, E. E. Teaching the process of reading comprehension. In D. K. Detterman & R. J. Sternberg (Eds.), *How and how much can intelligence be increased?* Norwood, New Jersey: Ablex, 1982.

Cook, J. M., Heim, A. W., & Watts, K. P. The word-in-context: A new type of verbal reasoning test. *British Journal of Psychology,* 1963, *54,* 227–237.

Curtis, M. *Word knowledge and verbal aptitude.* Unpublished manuscript, 1981.

Daalen-Kapteijns, M. M. van, & Elshout–Mohr, M. The acquisition of word meanings as a cognitive learning process. *Journal of Verbal Learning and Verbal Behavior,* 1981, *20,* 386–399.

Delaney, H. D. Interaction of individual differences with visual and verbal elaboration instructions. *Journal of Educational Psychology,* 1978, *70,* 306–318.

Flavell, J. H. Cognitive monitoring. In W. P. Dickson (Ed.), *Children's oral communication skills.* New York: Academic Press, 1981.

Gipe, J. Investigating techniques for teaching word meanings. *Reading Research Quarterly,* 1979, *14,* 624–644.

Hall, J. W., Wilson, K. P., & Patterson, R. J. Mnemotechnics: some limitations of the mnemonic keyword method for the study of foreign language vocabulary. *Journal of Educational Psychology,* 1981, *73,* 345–357.

Johnson, D. D., & Pearson, P. D. *Teaching reading vocabulary.* New York: Holt, 1978.

Just, M. A., & Carpenter, P. A. A theory of reading: From eye fixations to comprehension. *Psychological Review,* 1980, *87,* 329–354.

Kaye, D. B., & Sternberg, R. J. *The development of lexical decomposition ability.* Unpublished manuscript, 1981.

Keil, F. C. *Semantic inferences and the acquisition of word meaning.* Manuscript submitted for publication, 1981.

Levin, J. R. The mnemonic '80s: Keywords in the classroom. *Educational Psychologist,* 1981, *16,* 65–82.

Levin, J. R., McCormick, C. B., Miller, G. E., Berry, J. K., & Pressley, M. Mnemonic versus nonmnemonic vocabulary-learning strategies for children. *American Educational Research Journal,* 1982, *19,* 121–136.

Levin, J. R., Pressley, M., McCormick, C. B., Miller, G. E., & Shriberg, L. K. Assessing the classroom potential of the keyword method. *Journal of Educational Psychology,* 1979, *71,* 583–594.

Mandler, G. Organization and memory. In K. W. Spence & J. T. Spence (Eds.), *The psychology of learning and motivation: Advances in theory and research* (Vol. 1). New York: Academic Press, 1967.

Markman, E. M. Realizing that you don't understand: A preliminary investigation. *Child Development,* 1977, *48,* 986–992.

Markman, E. M. Realizing that you don't understand: Elementary school children's awareness of inconsistencies. *Child Development,* 1979, *50,* 643–655.

Markman, E. M. Comprehension monitoring. In W. P. Dickson (Ed.), *Children's oral communication skills.* New York: Academic Press, 1981.

Marshalek, B. *Trait and process aspects of vocabulary knowledge and verbal ability.* (NR 154–376 ONR Technical Report No. 15.) Stanford, California: Stanford University, School of Education, 1981.

Mayer, R., & Greeno, J. G. Structural differences between learning outcomes produced by different instructional methods. *Journal of Educational Psychology,* 1972, *63,* 165–173.

McCullough, C. M. Context aids in reading. *Reading Teacher,* 1958, *11,* 225–229.

Miller, G. A., & Johnson-Laird, P. N. *Language and perception.* Cambridge, Massachusetts: Harvard University Press, 1976.

O'Rourke, J. P. *Toward a science of vocabulary development.* The Hague: Mouton, 1974.

Paivio, A. *Imagery and verbal processes.* New York: Holt, 1971.

Paivio, A., & Desrochers, A. Mnemonic techniques in second-language learning. *Journal of Educational Psychology,* 1981, *73,* 780–795.

Pressley, M., & Levin, J. R. The keyword method and recall of vocabulary words from definitions. *Journal of Experimental Psychology: Human Learning and Memory,* 1981, *7,* 72–76.

Pressley, M., Levin, J. R., & Delaney, H. D. The mnemonic keyword method. *Review of Educational Research,* 1982, *52,* 61–91.

Pressley, M., Levin, J. R., Kuiper, N. A., Bryant, S. L., & Michener, S. Mnemonic versus nonmnemonic vocabulary-learning strategies: Additional comparisons. *Journal of Educational Psychology,* 1982, *74,* 693–707.

Pressley, M., Levin, J. R., & Miller, G. E. How does the keyword method affect vocabulary comprehension and usage? *Reading Research Quarterly,* 1981, *16,* 213–226. (a)

Pressley, M., Levin, J. R., & Miller, G. E. The keyword method and children's learning of vocabulary with abstract meanings. *Canadian Journal of Psychology,* 1981, *34,* 283–287. (b)

Pressley, M., Levin, J. R., & Miller, G. E. The keyword method compared to alternative vocabulary-learning strategies. *Contemporary Educational Psychology,* 1982, *7,* 50–60.

Raugh, M. R., & Atkinson, R. C. A mnemonic method for learning a second-language vocabulary. *Journal of Educational Psychology,* 1975, *67,* 1–16.

Rubin, D. C. The effectiveness of context, before, after, and around a missing word. *Perception and Psychophysics,* 1976, *19,* 214–216.

Sternberg, R. J. *How to prepare for the Miller Analogies Test.* Woodbury, New York: Barron's Educational Series, 1974.

Sternberg, R. J., & Powell, J. S. Comprehending verbal comprehension. *American Psychologist,* in press.

Sternberg, R. J., Powell, J. S., & Kaye, D. B. The nature of verbal comprehension. *Poetics,* 1982, *11,* 155–187.

Tulving, E. Subjective organization in free recall of "unrelated words." *Psychological Review,* 1962, *69,* 344–354.

Tulving, E. Subjective organization and effects of repetition in multitrial free-recall learning. *Journal of Verbal Learning and Verbal Behavior,* 1966, *5,* 193–197.

Tulving, E., & Pearlstone, Z. Availability versus accessibility of information in memory for words. *Journal of Verbal Learning and Verbal Behavior,* 1966, *5,* 381–391.

Werner, H., & Kaplan, E. The acquisition of word meanings: A developmental study. *Monographs of the Society for Research in Child Development,* 1952, No. *51.*

8

Reading, Vocabulary, and Writing: Implications for Computer-Based Instruction

Charles A. Perfetti

INTRODUCTION

In this chapter I raise some general issues concerning verbal processes and instruction. These issues are drawn from implications of cognitive theory and research, especially in reading and vocabulary. Though detailed examples of computer-based instruction are not provided, there will be some hypothetical illustrations of the kinds of computer-based instruction in reading, vocabulary, and writing that are implied by theory and research. The first section raises some of the general instructional issues for the case of reading. Later sections deal with vocabulary and, finally, writing.

READING PROCESSES AND READING INSTRUCTION

One dilemma of reading instruction, including computer-based instruction, is to choose between the basic-but-dull and the complex-but-engaging. A familiar form of this dilemma is the choice between "decoding" and "comprehension." It is especially tempting to choose the latter. Not only is comprehension a more complex cognitive ability than decoding, but it is more interesting to design tasks for comprehension. Further, the promotional potential of comprehension games on the computer may well be greater than the promotional potential of decoding games.

On the other hand, there can be little doubt that facility in verbal coding is important in allowing comprehension. There is ample evidence that speed of decoding and comprehension are highly correlated (Perfetti & Lesgold, 1979). There is also reason to believe that context-independent word coding is that which distinguishes skilled from less-skilled readers, rather than use of context (Perfetti & Roth, 1981; Stanovich, 1981). Furthermore, there is now slightly stronger reason to conclude that the correlation between decoding speed and comprehension reflects an underlying causal relationship, at least among beginning readers (Lesgold, this volume; Lesgold & Resnick, 1982). Lesgold and Resnick, in a longitudinal study of beginning readers, found time-lag correlations to suggest that gains in decoding speed tend to precede, rather than follow, gains in oral reading performance.

Higher cognitive abilities are at least as important as decoding for skilled performance in reading and other verbal tasks. However, it is possible to doubt whether higher cognitive abilities are fundamental in limiting performance in the way lower-level verbal abilities are. For example, the knowledge of text structures in comprehension is critical to describing how comprehension works. However, it is likely that the use of some text structures and other schemata are, relative to decoding and vocabulary knowledge, more universally acquired and less dependent on schooling. Some demonstrations of this possibility are beginning to appear. Graesser, Hoffman, and Clark (1980) predicted sentence-reading times of adults according to variables reflecting both lower-level and higher-level text structure. They found that higher-level factors, especially the narrativity of the passage, predicted more reading time variance than lower-level variables. However, when they examined fast and slow readers separately, they found that the most important factors differentiating reading rates of the two groups were lower-level factors such as the number of words and number of propositions. Thus, the use of narrative structure, which was important to describe overall reading performance, was not important in describing individual differences. Narrative schemata may be more universally acquired than vocabulary and decoding.

A second example of this principle comes from a study by Weaver and Dickinson (in press) of learning-disabled subjects. They report that in recalling a story, normal and learning-disabled students were not different in the extent to which they used categories of story grammar (Stein & Glenn, 1979). Rather, differences between the two groups of students were mainly in recall of detail and exact wording. Again, the suggestion is that narrative structures are critical in comprehension but they are less likely to produce ability differences.

This is not to suggest that those structures more specialized than the structure of simple stories are acquired by all students. Certainly, by definition, sensitivity to special text types and knowledge of special content domains cannot be expected to be universal. The real question is whether special instruction is implicated. Particle physics, the text forms of sonnets, and decoding are all unlikely to be learned without specific instruction. The structure of culturally salient story forms *is* likely to be so learned.

These assumptions do not imply that instruction can ignore comprehension tasks. They do imply that lower-level skills should get some attention if there is evidence that they are not well learned. Recent proposals for computer-based instruction have emphasized reading comprehension instruction based on models from artificial intelligence (Collins & Smith, in press). The Collins and Smith proposal especially urges instruction in comprehension monitoring and active hypothesis testing during reading. Such programs are doubtless useful and they certainly reflect interesting issues in cognition. It is perhaps reasonable to hope that the creative applications of cognitive science to computer instruction will not be confined to just those cases high in cognitive visibility. The advantages of computer-based instruction and the creative application of cognitive science apply also to instruction in fundamentals, as some chapters in this book point out. The capabilities of the computer for control and sequencing of materials and for providing feedback and keeping records have been known for years. The creative game potential of computers has also become obvious and should be exploited as well. The dilemma between the dull-but-basic and the engaging-but-complex is solved by making decoding engaging and comprehension basic.

In making connections between reading processes and instruction, I assume that reading comprehension involves an interplay among three classes of competence—*word coding, conceptual knowledge,* and *comprehension strategies.* In terms of general information processing, these competencies correspond to pattern recognition, semantic memory, and control processes, respectively. In addition to this three-way division of competencies, there is a two-fold division of instructional events: those that represent new *learning* and those that represent *practice* based on previous learning. Proposals for instruction can be directed at any of the six combinations of target competencies and instruction type.

I suppose it is possible that strong opinions exist concerning where computer instruction ought to be focused within this framework. However, I see no defense for a claim that payoff for computer instruction will be higher, for example, in practice than in learning, or in comprehension than decoding.

Nevertheless, there may be adequate reason to suggest that practice is especially important from the student's point of view. If the verbal efficiency hypothesis is correct (Perfetti & Lesgold, 1979) then simply being accurate at word recognition is not sufficient to enable fluent comprehension. Instead, a student needs to increase word-coding skills to a high level of efficiency. It may not be quite correct to characterize the required level as attention-free or truly automatic. However, it is, at minimum, a level of skill characterized by reduced allocation of processing resources.

The instructionally relevant fact is that this level of skill is not universally acquired in classroom instruction. Indeed, there is evidence that decoding speed and accuracy differences, related to general verbal skill, exist even among adults (Curtis, 1981). It may be that factors limiting adult verbal abilities are different than those limiting children's reading ability (see Perfetti, 1983). However, it is clear that speed and efficiency are characteristic of skilled verbal performance at all ages. Practice in the elementary grades may be useful for increasing the verbal efficiency of students who do not reach high efficiency otherwise.

A major assumption I wish to make is that the three competencies are strictly separable. *Word coding* is the activation of a word form in memory given a linguistic input—a grapheme string, in the case of reading. The semantic knowledge stored with the word has no consequence, in principle, for this coding. In fact, I believe that word coding should be thought of as an *autonomous* processing level. The force of this assumption is that, in skilled performance, word coding is a process that occurs independently of meaning context. It is affected by frequency, orthographic structure, length, and perhaps phonetic properties—but not meaning, at least for the skilled reader (Hogaboam & Perfetti, 1978).

Conceptual knowledge is stored, by assumption, in an organized and interconnected manner. Thus, while coding is autonomous, interpretation of word meanings is dependent on conceptual knowledge. However, although interpretation of meanings depends on context, there is a sense in which semantic processes are autonomous, somewhat like word coding. For example, whereas context does determine the interpretation of an ambiguous word, there is evidence that more than one of the word's meanings are always activated, regardless of context (Swinney, 1979). This activation is short-lived, so it has no effect on comprehension. It is, however, a further example of an autonomous low-level process. The semantic knowledge itself is a matter of interconnections among words and among semantic attributes, and this is usually what vocabulary instruction is trying to affect.

It is possible that both access to meaning and the structure of meaning can be objects of instruction.

In this framework, *comprehension strategies* apply, in part, to processes that can be autonomous. Such activities as monitoring for contradictions and answering questions during reading all presuppose some lower levels of comprehension. There is every reason to suppose that such activities reflect skillful, active processing and constitute important objectives for instruction.

In summary, I assume that though computer instruction can be designed to strengthen numerous information-processing components, instruction aimed at practice is an important objective. This is not because of intrinsic potentials of the computer, but because practice can strengthen skills that may suffer the most from not being exercised. Coding, conceptual knowledge, and comprehension strategies can all benefit from practice as well as learning. The potentially autonomous nature of coding processes, and some meaning processes, make them especially suitable for practice.

CODING PRACTICE

Given the foregoing discussion, there is a case to be made for designing practice tasks for coding. For such tasks, let us assume we have students in grades two through five. The students have had beginning-reading instruction and they are receiving classroom instruction on reading-related tasks. If they have had a phonetically-based program of instruction, so much the better. If not, we can hope it does not matter too much. We assume they have "learned to read." The objective is to provide practice at efficient word coding.

The reading of texts is a good way to practice reading, and this includes reading books, cereal boxes, virtually anything with print. The computer advantage in this is to provide control of materials based on what needs to be practiced and to provide some incentive value. Reading practice can be disguised in the form of clever games to make it more palatable (see Lesgold, this volume). Moreover, even more mundane tasks that lack creative play components are probably more engaging on the computer. However, this is a situation that should change as computers become increasingly commonplace in schools. As the novelty wears off, a greater burden must be carried by the intelligence of the courseware. For now, the engaging principle is that a dull task on the computer terminal will engage students' attention better than a dull task at their desks.

Of course, a more fundamental advantage is the monitoring and record-keeping work of the computer. It allows a teacher to know more about how much time was spent on the task and how good performance was. Some of the properties used in tutorial systems can be applied to this problem. Especially important is to have records of students' strengths and weaknesses on diagnostic coding skills that are used both in selecting what needs to be practiced and the standards of performance to be sought.

What should coding tasks include? What needs to be practiced? A reasonable possibility is to be guided by theories and research concerning skilled performance. In reading, skilled performance seems to be based on effective context-independent word recognition. Besides general accuracy and speed, skilled performance is characterized by use of orthographic information, use of phonemic information, and independence of context. The empirical bases for these claims include the marked advantage of skilled readers in reading pseudowords (Hogaboam and Perfetti, 1978), the tendency for skilled readers to show phonemic confusions in short-term memory for visually presented material (Liberman, Shankweiler, Liberman, Fowler, & Fischer, 1977), and the small effect of word predictability on identification latencies of skilled readers (Perfetti & Roth, 1981; Stanovich, 1981). These specific skill characteristics need to be more firmly established and understood. Meanwhile, however, they provide a reasonable groundwork for computer-assisted practice. They are not an arbitrary list of things skilled readers have that less-skilled readers do not. Rather, they are those aspects of skilled decoding that may be instrumental in reading skill. Orthographic knowledge provides the data to enable rapid word identification. It makes the reader less dependent on holistic pattern recognition and more able to demonstrate generalized recognition processes. These generalized processes are the heart of reading an alphabetic language, even one lacking a transparent orthography. Reading pseudowords, rather than words, is an especially appropriate test of these generalized orthographic processes.

As for phonemic information, its status is less clear. Perfetti and McCutchen (1982) have suggested that activation of phonemic information stored with words and letters might be an automatic (passive) part of word reading. Further, we suggested that the activation plays a role in comprehension. To take seriously the idea of automatic activation is to doubt the feasibility of including it in instruction. However, there does seem to be at least some evidence that phonemic processes are especially characteristic of the skilled reader and not so characteristic of the less-skilled reader (Byrne & Shea, 1979; Liberman et al., 1977). It may be worthwhile to assure that phonemic processing is promoted in instruction.

Finally, the context-independent nature of decoding is a consequence of finely honed decoding skills, not a cause of it. This independence from context is probably the hallmark of skilled performance in any area. Think of motor skills or physics problem-solving. In driving a car, for example, applying the responses appropriate for steering, clutching, and gear shifting, with a minimum influence of differences among cars, is characteristic of skilled performance. In physics problem-solving, recognizing the underlying principles regardless of the verbal context of the problem is one of the characteristics of expert performance (Larkin, McDermott, Simon, & Simon, 1980). In reading, recognizing *hill* when it follows *There is a chicken on the* . . . as easily as when it follows *Jack and Jill went up the* . . . is also characteristic of skilled performance. The implication is that context-independent identification performance can be used as an instructional objective, if not an instructional task. For example, a criterion for context- independent identification can be set, such that, for a given set of words, there is no more than a 10% difference between the time needed to recognize the words in context and the time needed to identify them in isolation.

Because phonemic and orthographic processes are intricately intertwined in reading, tasks can easily be designed to practice both. Indeed, it would take special perverse effort to separate them. For example, a task which practices both orthographic patterns and phonemic processes would be the Rhyme Find Task. The student is asked, preferably by audio, to make a keyboard response every time a display contains a word that rhymes with a target. Display words vary in orthographic patterns, for example, a word to rhyme with *beet: neat, Pete, feet,* etc. Three patterns are represented and a fundamental fact of orthography is drilled. The fact that the task is solved only by sound assures attention to phonemic patterns. It should be simple enough to add game components—beat the clock, etc. (see Lesgold, this volume). Feedback could be arranged in the form of comparisons between the student's mean for previous sessions and a block of trials from the current sessions. Diagnosis and performance standards are important parts of the record-keeping. For example, a more difficult version of the task is achieved by adding pseudowords.

WORD CONCEPTS

A case can be made that vocabulary knowledge is one of the most important factors in verbal ability. Vocabulary test scores are highly correlated with general measures of verbal ability and academic success among adults and children. Indeed, a large and precise vocabulary can be considered the public test of the educated person.

Vocabulary knowledge has at least two components: the size of the vocabulary and the quality of the semantic knowledge. The number of word entries in semantic memory and the distinctive semantic features stored with each entry are both part of vocabulary knowledge. These components are referred to, respectively, as the breadth and depth of vocabulary (Anderson & Freebody, 1979).

A recent study by Curtis (1981) demonstrates that these are two different aspects of vocabulary knowledge. On the basis of their scores on a multiple-choice vocabulary test, Curtis classified subjects as high or low in vocabulary knowledge. The items from the multiple-choice test were then sorted into groups, based on their difficulty and discriminability. Of special interest are those words that were highly discriminating between high- and low-knowledge subjects. In individual testing, the subjects were asked to define these words or to provide synonyms. They were also asked to provide any association they could to any unknown word. Low-knowledge subjects not only failed to give accurate definitions and synonyms to these words, but they also typically failed to give even vaguely related associations. High-knowledge subjects typically did produce such associations, e.g., "*desist* is like *cease and desist.*" Low-knowledge subjects often gave these associations to the easy, nondiscriminating words but not to the moderately difficult discriminating words. These data suggest, as Curtis (1981) concluded, that the difference between high and low vocabulary knowledge, as measured by multiple-choice tests, is not due only to differences in the sort of precise semantic knowledge that enables a discrimination among choices. It extends to the number of words with which people have any familiarity at all. Of course, Curtis also found that the high- and low-knowledge subjects were differentiated by the precision of their semantic knowledge, that is, high-knowledge subjects did produce more correct definitions and synonyms, controlling for the total number of associations of any kind. This is not surprising. It directly reflects what multiple-choice vocabulary tests seem to measure. More interesting is that differences in scores on such tests reflect differences in minimal familiarity with the words.

Interestingly, Curtis found that her low-vocabulary subjects also made "decoding" errors on the discriminating group of words. That is, when they were asked to read aloud the printed word, 25% of the time they failed to read it correctly. Such errors were nearly nonexistent for high-vocabulary subjects, even for words they did not know. This finding parallels one of the results of the Perfetti and Hogaboam (1975) study of the relationship among reading comprehension, word identification, and vocabulary knowledge. In that study, third- and fifth-grade children who scored high in comprehension showed little relationship between word decoding speed and vocabulary knowledge. By contrast, low-skilled readers were much faster at words they had got correct on a vocabulary test than on words they had got incorrect. Thus, in both elementary school and college, some lower-achieving students seem to have an interdependence between word recognition and semantic knowledge that is not characteristic of higher-achieving students. This probably reflects a genuine autonomy of word-identification processes for the higher-achieving students, for example, greater knowledge of orthographic rules. However, it is also likely that it reflects their greater superficial familiarity with words.

In any case, students with low vocabulary knowledge seem to have a characteristic with interesting implications for instruction. They are both unfamiliar with and unable to read (decode) large numbers of words. It is not just that their knowledge is less precise; rather, it is lacking even a single feature in semantic memory. That decoding continues to be a problem for some college students when words are unfamiliar should cast doubt on the assumption that elementary decoding abilities are universally acquired. The suggestion I would make from all this is that practice on word forms is a useful exercise. If many students are able to get through elementary and secondary school with little learning of word forms and word meanings, then an instructional environment which increases appropriate verbal exposures throughout elementary school years may be called for.

An issue to raise, aside from particular proposals to implement vocabulary instruction, is whether vocabulary is best learned in organized semantic domains. It is likely that there is something of a trade-off between the amount of practice required and the organization of the semantic domain. Learning words from an organized semantic domain could promote depth, while learning from a less organized domain might promote breadth. However, whether breadth or depth are learned may depend more on the criterion of learning, rather than on the organization of the domain. No matter how word concepts are selected for instruction, a goal of breadth can be promoted by extensive but more superficial verbal encounters, whereas depth can be encouraged by more discriminating encounters with fewer concepts. The point for computer-based instruction is that a goal of superficial breadth perhaps should be taken seriously as an instructional goal.

Imagine, for example, a sorting task that presents the student with three categories and a list of words. The third category is "not a word" and the other two are semantic domains that change from time to time and can be hierarchial. Examples are "human emotions" and "things to eat" (to demonstrate how different the domains could be). A later sequence could demand finer distinctions within previously presented categories, for example, "happy feelings" and "sad feelings." Feedback could include the number of correctly classified words and a simple definition for incorrectly classified words. Why use nonwords? In order to emphasize the usefulness of practice on word forms and the role of word *familiarity*. Thus, even in the absence of more precise knowledge about its meaning, the student can see that *ecstasy* is more similar to *joy* than to *sadness,* and that a legitimate letter string, such as *shatspy,* is unrelated to either, although it could be. Task examples with these properties are easily developed and tasks can combine to organize around the semantic domain, for example, sorting tasks, reading tasks, and simple production tasks. For example, to encourage context sensitivity, word-choice tasks can require student selection of the right word (e.g., *ecstasy* or *determination*?) in a given text. The computer, of course, keeps a record of individual student performance and also a dictionary record. Frequently missed words can be defined or exemplified.

Note that record-keeping is one of the critical values of computer practice. Records of accuracy and speed can be kept for individual words. At any given session at the terminal, words are selected for instruction according to performance. The idea of practice is that words would be encountered even when they are already partly known. Words less well known, however, should get more practice. I would envision a central dictionary record that serves for all tasks. Words mastered at advanced levels of the sorting task, for example, would get less practice in other tasks.

A central dictionary can have several important features. One is that it has a rich lexical component as well as a record-keeping component. Its centrality derives from the usability of its lexical component in all reading and vocabulary tasks. The dictionary should be accessible by a simple keyboard response, no matter what particular task a child is engaged in. The computer eases the primary pain of book dictionaries, which is search. It is likely that for most children and adults, searching a dictionary for an unfamiliar word is too much trouble and too disruptive of the reading which has initiated the need for a search. It is fortunate, indeed, that word meanings can be inferred from context (see Sternberg, this volume), because learning from dictionaries is an achievement of only the most determined and the most linguistically curious. The computer dictionary, by contrast, gives instant access to word meanings without search and with minimum disruption of the reading task. However, another feature of the central dictionary is that it should allow "disruption" when the student wants it. This is accomplished by continually allowing the student the choice between more information about the word he has looked up and returning to his reading task. Thus, the dictionary is always accessed by typing in the word. The word and a brief definition are printed on the display screen. If there is text already present because of a computer reading task, the first step would be for the word to be located in the text. The text is separated at the line below the word to keep the word's context available while its meaning is printed just below. After the definition has been printed, the child chooses between more information about the word and going back to the reading task. For example, the next printing would display examples of the word's primary uses. The next choice for more information could produce words from the same semantic category. A next choice could list some near semantic opposites from within the category. The basic idea is to allow in-depth examination of the word's semantic field, when the student wants it, and to allow quick access and exit back to the current program when that is what is desired.

WORD KNOWLEDGE AND EFFICIENCY

Because efficiency in decoding seems to be desirable beyond accuracy, what about efficiency in semantic access? Of course, semantic access is the objective of word reading and fast access is characteristic of skilled performance. However, is there reason to believe that speeded semantic access is characteristic of performance beyond efficient decoding or recognition? The available evidence on this is not conclusive. However, at least one study (summarized in Perfetti, 1983) suggests that skilled readers are faster than less-skilled readers at accessing semantic category information, even when the time for word recognition is controlled. In a search task, the skill difference was larger when a familiar category instance was the target, than when a particular word was the target. However, compared with research at the level of coding, the conclusion concerning speed of semantic access is less well established. It is possible that, holding constant knowledge of a word's meaning, most of semantic access is accounted for by name-level access (decoding).

In any case, rapid access to semantic information stored with a word is helpful in comprehension. If so, instruction in vocabulary could affect comprehension both by establishing word meanings and by facilitating rapid access to them. Evidence on whether vocabulary training does facilitate comprehension is rather mixed, with some studies reporting effects (e.g., Draper & Moeller, 1971) and others reporting no effects (e.g., Jenkins, Pany, & Schreck, 1978). This should serve as a warning that relationships between vocabulary knowledge and comprehension are not necessarily straightforward (see also Anderson & Freebody, 1979). In particular, though word knowledge does enable comprehension, the sort of word knowledge that makes a difference may not be the sort that can be learned in brief instructional experiments. A recent study reported in Beck, Perfetti, and McKeown (1982) puts this issue in focus. Our assumption was that instruction had to be extensive to have an impact on comprehension. To establish word meanings so that they are readily accessible is the key objective. This objective is not likely to be met by one or a few encounters.

Accordingly, the strategy of Beck *et al.* (1982) was to provide long-term vocabulary instruction for an entire fourth-grade classroom. Vocabulary instruction was part of daily classroom activity over the course of the school year for 104 words. A set of comparably difficult uninstructed words was used as controls. Prior to instruction, these words were all unknown for these students as well as for a control classroom. Each week, some 8–10 words were introduced and taught in various ways for that week. By having review sessions for some words at various times following the week of instruction for a set of words, it was possible to vary the amount of practice for the words. Those words that were subsequently reviewed formed a class of words receiving *more practice* than those words not reviewed. Thus, in addition to about 2½ hours per week for a set of 8–10 words, some words had additional practice. Our hypothesis was that the extra practice could make a difference in the level of accessible knowledge acquired, especially in speed of processing.

Beck *et al.* (1982) tested the effects of the instructional program on several measures. In addition to vocabulary knowledge measured by a multiple-choice test, there were tasks requiring speeded semantic decisions of single words and verification of simple sentences (e.g., *Stern people are serious*). The effect of instruction on story recall was also tested. Stories were written to include key instructed and uninstructed words, at a rate of about 1 key word per 11 words of text. This density was sufficiently low so that some comprehension of the passage was possible even without knowledge of the key words. It was also possible to infer meanings from context, at least in some cases. However, our assumption was that such inferences are something of a burden and that recall of the story would reflect the advantage of having been taught word meanings.

The results showed gains in all tasks. Thus, vocabulary instruction affected not only performance on a vocabulary test, but it led to faster semantic decisions (controlling for accuracy) for both single words and simple sentences. And it resulted in better meaning-preserving recall of stories containing instructed words. A particularly telling fact is that students gained enough control over the words to *produce* them in their story recalls. Thus, speed of semantic access and comprehension are affected by vocabulary instruction, provided the instruction is sufficient.

What is "sufficient"? All words were involved in at least 5 days of instruction. Those that received additional practice appear to have been learned to a slightly higher level. There was at least partial support (in the speeded tasks) for the prediction that extra practice words would be processed more quickly. However, their advantage was slight relative to the gain produced by instructed words over control words. Apparently, more instruction and more practice are slightly better. On the other hand, it may be more impressive, from a practical standpoint, that performance was so good following a week of instruction.

In the context of computer-assisted practice, I take these results to demonstrate the general usefulness of vocabulary training for comprehension. Though speeded access is not necessarily an instructional objective, it can be taken as an indication that semantic information is easily accessible. It is this accessibility that may determine whether the instructional effects will be reflected in comprehension. Certainly, the specific instructional tasks are important. The tasks used in the Beck *et al.* study, described in detail in Beck, McCaslin, and McKeown (1980), were a very diverse lot. They included a wide variety of exercises, speeded tests, and games, only some of which were pencil-and-paper tasks. However, one general point about the instruction seems clear. Beck *et al.* (1982) did not use well-defined and well-structured semantic domains. The words were chosen from the target vocabulary of a basal reading program and organized into ill-defined semantic classes. It is quite possible that success would have been even greater for more coherent semantic domains. However, it seems clear that instruction can be successful in less coherent semantic domains, provided instruction is reasonably thorough.

Consider again breadth and depth as dimensions of vocabulary learning. It seems that both are characteristic of skilled verbal performance. However, the instructional implication is not necessarily that instructional tasks should be designed separately for each dimension. Instead, I assume that instruction with depth as an overall objective will achieve breadth as a by-product of incomplete mastery. At the same time, at least some of the instructional tasks may be superficial. This seems to describe the vocabulary instruction experiment of Beck *et al.* (1982). It included depth tasks that required fairly precise knowledge by the child, and breadth tasks that required mainly evidence of familiarity. Thus, the general objective is for the student to acquire word meanings to some depth. In support of this objective, those tasks that are primary learning tasks involve at least some depth of meaning. However, there are benefits of more superficial processing in tasks that strengthen and practice the accessibility of the semantic information.

COMPREHENSION AND TEXT STRATEGIES

In addition to word processes, there are critical contributions of higher-level strategies to comprehension. Instruction in these strategies is both possible and worthwhile, as others have pointed out (e.g., Collins & Smith, in press). As an example of a comprehension strategy, consider writing. My perspective on the issues raised in writing is complementary to other discussions of writing instruction (see chapters by Rubin, and by Levin, Boruta, & Vasconcellos, this volume). It emphasizes the local text-driven component of writing, rather than its planning or story-telling components.

There are several reasons for discussing writing as a comprehension strategy. One is that the distinction between *active* and *passive* processing (which sometimes seems to differentiate comprehension and decoding) is more clearly and usefully made between writing and reading. Compared with writing, comprehension is a rather passive process. A second reason for considering writing is that writing implies comprehension. A student who is learning to write is also practicing his comprehension skills. Finally, writing has an interesting property that it shares with decoding, but not with comprehension. It does not seem to come naturally to most students without help. I am not claiming that comprehension instruction is pointless. I am suggesting that a level of comprehension especially worth teaching is that level implicated by writing.

The operative principle is that instruction is needed for skills that do not develop easily without instruction. This principle must be applied to skills whose mastery are important for other achievements. Decoding is an example of such a skill. For higher-level skills, the principle also applies. Some skills, even complex ones, develop without much direct instruction, while others do not. Writing at a level of minimal competence may need instruction, whereas comprehension of stories may not.

Consider an analogy between a student's acquisition of verbal skill and an American soprano's mastery of Italian opera. For the soprano, reading and singing Italian are, like decoding, fundamental and not likely to happen naturally. We grant her a great voice, but some direct instruction in the language is necessary. Of course, just as decoding is not what reading is ultimately about, being able to read *sempre libera* and render it in perfect Italian diction is not what operatic singing is all about. There is a lot to learn about performing. To perform as Violetta in *La Traviata,* for example, some tutoring on how to express coquettishness, love, and fatal illness, while singing, would be helpful. Less helpful is coaching on how to recognize these emotions in other people. Such recognition is in fact probably a prerequisite for a convincing performance. But instruction is superfluous because she will have ample opportunity to develop these social and emotional comprehensions. To produce them on cue is what needs instruction. At an oversimplified level, this is also the problem of the student in need of verbal instruction. The student may have less need for instruction in strategies to comprehend text than in strategies to produce text.

What are the kinds of writing activities that are most appropriate? I suggest tasks that have some control over what the student has to attend to. Tasks that give global objectives, for example, writing a story, are not likely to help students as much as tasks which are modest enough to allow some control over text features. Tasks involving the detection and correction of gaps within a text or the production of a few corrected sentences exemplify useful tasks.

Children seem to have trouble noticing, or at least verbalizing, contradictions in text content (Markman, 1979). What is more surprising, perhaps, is the extent to which even college students fail to notice inconsistencies in texts (Wilkinson, Epstein, Glenberg, & Morse, 1980). The chances are they produce them in writing as well. In general, there are several possibilities for such lapses of logic. One is that logical thinking does not develop universally. Another is that reading (and writing?) do not promote attention to coherence. Tasks which force attention to inconsistencies may help at least the attentiveness part of the problem. The following text exemplifies this idea:

Johnny had two brothers but no sisters.

He often liked to ride his bike.

One day he asked his sister to ride with him.

The faster he went the more he liked it.

After an initial text display long enough to be read, the text can be repeated a phrase at a time with the student required to delete a phrase and correct it. The computer provides text rewrites and pointers when required. Production demands should be minimized by, for example, use of a simple deletion command which strips away a word or an entire line with a single response. This may be one place where graphic displays could help. For example, an arrow pointing from the inconsistent to the antecedent sentence would help direct attention to the part of the text to be deleted.

Notice that even though writing demands are minimal, comprehension is required. The basic suggestion is that those processes that are *active* in writing are good candidates for comprehension instruction as well.

A second example of this principle derives from recent research by Mc-Cutchen and Perfetti (in press). The issue in this research is the development of local text coherence in children's writing. Local coherence is essentially the degree to which a given sentence honors the semantic commitments made by the previous sentence. For example, Sentences (1) and (2) below show local coherence because the commitment of Sentence (1) is met by Sentence (2).

1. The President promised to veto any new appropriations bills.
2. Congress was not eager to do battle.

There are no explicit lexical ties between these two sentences. However, they show coherence because the semantic commitments of Sentence 1, that is, to follow up with something about the budget, is met by Sentence 2. Of course, some inference, what Clark and Haviland (1977) call *bridging,* is required to make the connection. Coherent writing, in fact, is usually marked by lexical ties between sentences. This example simply illustrates that such ties are not necessary.

Neither are such ties sufficient for coherence. This can be seen easily enough by substituting a new Sentence (2) in the previous example.

1. The President promised to veto any new appropriations bills.
2. The President was especially pleased to receive a new saddle from Roy Rogers.

Despite an explicit lexical tie these sentences fail to show coherence at the semantic level.

The point of these examples is to provide a framework for summarizing the writing data of McCutchen and Perfetti (in press). Obviously, these sentences were not written by young children. However, they exemplify important patterns observed in their writing. Children in the second and fourth grades were much less likely to write locally coherent sentences than children in the sixth and eighth grades. Instead, younger writers (and some older writers as well) produced sentences that were semantically unconnected. The writing of these children could be characterized as a list structure. There was a unified global theme and each sentence connected back to the theme. However, a given sentence often failed to connect with the previous sentence.

This summary of the data, although a bit oversimplified, suggests the following general conclusion. Children master some global constraints on their writing, for example, topic relevance, before acquiring control of local coherence. Of course, this is partly a question of grammatical devices to help mark coherence and there are developmental differences in the use of those devices (McCutchen & Perfetti, in press). However, beyond specific grammatical devices, it is clear that sensitivity to local semantic commitments undergoes development. Many younger children write either as if they are unaware that sentences should be connected or as if they do not attend to the semantic implications of a given sentence.

In either case, the suggestion I make here is that writing tasks that promote attention to local coherence might be useful. These could easily be tasks which promote comprehension monitoring and minimize actual production, as in the bike-riding example provided earlier in this section. Of course, children's writing is an area in which cognitive research has been fairly recent (Bereiter & Scardamalia, 1981), and instructional possibilities at this point are more constrained by creativity than data. However, specific local production problems of the sort mentioned above, which arise from the demands of simultaneously meeting many cognitive and text constraints, will be good candidates for instruction. That this sort of suggestion looks a bit like comprehension, and not a lot like writing, is part of the point. An emphasis is placed on control of local text processes as opposed to global text structures. It assumes that a reader and a writer construct a model of text (Collins, Brown, & Larkin, 1980) as they are processing it. Making a fit between local text parts and the text model is a critical part of both processes.

SUMMARY

Choices between more fundamental and more engaging instructional content can be made easier by making the fundamental more engaging and vice versa. My view of the evidence suggests that lower-level skills of *decoding* and *word knowledge* are critical in verbal functioning. They are also teachable. Both accuracy and speed of processing can be taken as instructional objectives. Though there are many ways to teach *word knowledge,* there is evidence that even loosely organized semantic content can be learned to a highly generalized degree, affecting comprehension, for example. There is enough evidence to guide computer instruction. Comprehension strategies have a less obvious rationale for instruction, although they are doubtless important. Active attention to local text features may be useful for instruction in writing and comprehension.

REFERENCES

Anderson, R. C., & Freebody, P. *Vocabulary knowledge* (Tech. Rep. No. 136). Urbana, Illinois: University of Illinois, Center for the Study of Reading, August, 1979.

Beck, I. L., McCaslin, E. S., & McKeown, M. G. *The rationale and design of a program to teach vocabulary to fourth-grade students.* Pittsburgh: University of Pittsburgh, Learning Research and Development Center, 1980.

Beck, I. L., Perfetti, C. A., & McKeown, M. G. The effects of long-term vocabulary instruction on lexical access and reading comprehension. *Journal of Educational Psychology,* 1982, 74, 506–521.

Bereiter, C., & Scardamalia, M. From conversation to composition: The role of instruction in a developmental process. In R. Glaser (Ed.), *Advances in instuctional psychology,* Vol. 2. Hillsdale, N.J.: Erlbaum, 1981.

Byrne, B., & Shea, P. Semantic and phonetic memory codes in beginning readers. *Memory & Cognition,* 1979, 7, 333–338.

Clark, H. H., & Haviland, S. E. Comprehension and the given-new contract. In R. O. Freedle (Ed.), *Discourse production and comprehension.* Norwood, N. J.: Ablex, 1977.

Collins, A., Brown, J. S., & Larkin, K. M. Inference in text understanding. In R. J. Spiro, B. C. Bruce & W. F. Brewer (Eds.), *Theoretical issues in reading comprehension.* Hillsdale, New Jersey: Erlbaum, 1980.

Collins, A., & Smith, E. E. Teaching the process of reading comprehension. In D. K. Detterman & R. J. Sternberg (Eds.), *How much and how can intelligence be increased?* Norwood, New Jersey: Ablex, in press.

Curtis, M. E. *Word knowledge and verbal aptitude.* Unpublished manuscript, University of Pittsburgh, Learning Research and Development Center, 1981.

Draper, A. G., & Moeller, G. H. We think with words (therefore, to improve thinking, teach vocabulary). (ERIC Document Reproduction Service No. ED 036 207). *Phi Delta Kappan,* 1971, 52, 482–484.

Graesser, A. C., Hoffman, N. L., & Clark, L. F. Structural components of reading time. *Journal of Verbal Learning and Verbal Behavior,* 1980, 19, 135–151.

Hogaboam, T., & Perfetti, C. A. Reading skill and the role of verbal experiences in decoding. *Journal of Educational Psychology,* 1978, 70, 717–729.

Jenkins, J. R., Pany, D., & Schreck, J. *Vocabulary and reading comprehension: Instructional effects* (Tech. Rep. 100). Urbana, Illinois: University of Illinois, Center for the Study of Reading, August, 1978.

Larkin, J. H., McDermott, J., Simon, D. P., & Simon, H. A. Expert and novice performance in solving physics problems. *Science,* 1980, 80, 1335–1342.

Lesgold, A. M., & Resnick, L. B. How reading disabilities develop: Perspectives from a longitudinal study. In J. P. Das, R. Mulcahy & A. E. Wall (Eds.), *Theory and research in learning disability.* New York: Plenum, 1982.

Liberman, I. Y., Shankweiler, D., Liberman, A. M., Fowler, C., & Fischer, F. W. Phonetic segmentation and recoding in the beginning reader. In A. S. Reber & D. L. Scarborough (Eds.), *Towards a psychology of reading.* (The proceedings of the CUNY conference.) New York: Wiley, 1977.

Markman, E. Realizing that you don't understand: Elementary school children's awareness of inconsistencies. *Child Development,* 1979, 50, 643–655.

McCutchen, D., & Perfetti, C. A. Coherence and connectedness in the development of discourse production. *Text,* in press.

Perfetti, C. A. Individual differences in verbal processes. In R. F. Dillon & R. R. Schmeck (Eds.), *Individual differences in cognition.* New York: Academic Press, 1983.

Perfetti, C. A., & Hogaboam, T. The relationship between single word decoding and reading comprehension skill. *Journal of Educational Psychology,* 1975, 67, 461–469.

Perfetti, C. A., & Lesgold, A. M. Coding and comprehension in skilled reading and implications for reading instruction. In L. B. Resnick & P. Weaver (Eds.), *Theory and practice of early reading* (Vol. 1). Hillsdale, New Jersey: Erlbaum, 1979.

Perfetti, C. A., & McCutchen, D. Speech processes in reading. In N. Lass (Ed.), *Speech and language: Advances in basic research and practice.* New York: Academic Press, 1982.

Perfetti, C. A., & Roth, S. F. Some of the interactive processes in reading and their role in reading skill. In A. M. Lesgold & C. A. Perfetti (Eds.), *Interactive processes in reading.* Hillsdale, New Jersey: Erlbaum, 1981.

Stanovich, K. E. Attentional and automatic context effects in reading. In A. M. Lesgold & C. A. Perfetti (Eds.), *Interactive processes in reading.* Hillsdale, New Jersey: Erlbaum, 1981.

Stein, N. L., & Glenn, C. G. An analysis of story comprehension in elementary school children. In R. O. Freedle (Ed.), *New directions in discourse processing.* Norwood, New Jersey: Ablex, 1979.

Swinney, D. A. Lexical access during sentence comprehension: (Re)consideration of context effects. *Journal of Verbal Learning and Verbal Behavior,* 1979, *18,* 645–660.

Weaver, P. A., & Dickinson, D. K. Scratching below the surface structure. Exploring the usefulness of story grammars. *Discourse Processes,* in press.

Wilkinson, A. C., Epstein, W., Glenberg, A. M., & Morse, E. *The illusion of knowing in studying texts.* Paper presented at the annual meeting of the Psychonomic Society, St. Louis, November, 1980.

PART III

Courseware for Classrooms

In contrast to the emphasis on theory in the previous section, the chapters of this section emphasize *applications* of theory. Each of the following chapters applies principles from cognitive science to the design of usable courseware.

Two chapters are concerned with courseware for the teaching of reading. Alan Lesgold discusses the design of instructional games for promoting reading skills. His suggestions for courseware are embedded in a theoretical perspective that squares with the analysis presented in the immediately preceding chapter by Perfetti. Echoing the major principles introduced by Lesgold and Perfetti, Alex Cherry Wilkinson examines research on eye movements and word recognition in reading. He goes on to describe how findings from this research guided the design of a program for promoting efficient methods of text selection and word recognition in young readers.

Two further chapters focus on computerized methods for teaching students to write. Andee Rubin describes courseware for writing stories, drawing on examples from two programs she and her collaborators designed. Her discussion nicely merges the perspectives of a teacher concerned with language arts and a courseware designer concerned with recent research on the rhetorical and discourse structure of narratives. James Levin, Marcia Boruta, and Mary Vasconcellos revive the distinction between novices and experts, using the distinction as a device for organizing their observations of children's use of a text-editing program. Their chapter presents evidence from projects that ranged from writing a story to collaborative production of a class newsletter.

In these concluding chapters, we return to issues raised in the introductory chapter by Wilkinson and Patterson. What the concluding chapters offer are attempts to integrate cognitive science and courseware design. They provide prototypes for the continuing dialogue between theory and practice.

9

A Rationale for Computer-Based Reading Instruction

Alan M. Lesgold

IMPLICATIONS FROM READING RESEARCH

Psychology has made contributions to reading instruction throughout its existence as a science. In the earlier part of the century, the primary contribution of psychology was to emphasize the interdependence of different levels of perception and understanding. It was shown that there is separate psychological structure at each of several levels of text: letters, words, and sentences. Also, there were demonstrations that sentence-level processes played a role in disambiguating words and that recognition of a word could sometimes occur faster than recognition of a single letter. This early work was important in shaping the basal reader that is the foundation of classroom reading instruction today. The small catechism-like books, which children had to memorize and read aloud, were replaced by the more substantial readers that contained instruction relevant to all levels of the reading process.

A second influence came with the behavioral period in psychology's history. This influence led designers of reading instruction to analyze the act of reading into its apparent components and to attempt to teach these components separately. It soon became clear that in order to perform such analyses, it was necessary to represent the act of reading as a process in which data flowed from one skill component to another. However, the tools for capturing the nature of the interactions between skill components and for verifying componential analyses have come only recently.

Overall, the recent contributions of psychology to a better understanding of the reading process have come from four areas: (1) research on the structure of texts at the level of discourse and on the sensitivity of the reading process to this level of structure; (2) variations in the process of reading and understanding as a function of the extent of the reader's prior knowledge of the topic addressed by the text; (3) understanding of the word recognition process and of word-related knowledge; and (4) analysis of the dynamics of the reading process and of the effects that high or low levels of component efficiency have on the overall process.

Discourse Processes

Work on discourse processes has been very prominent in recent years. We now partly understand how the structure of a discourse (text) influences how it is understood, which parts are remembered, and how the acquired information is organized in the reader's memory. This work has generated some practical consequences for the design of texts to facilitate comprehension. Because of such work, writers and editors can have a better sense today of how a text should be constructed so that it conveys the information the writer intends to convey.

However, research on discourse processing has had little influence on instructional practices (though it has influenced the design of texts). It would have been convenient if discourse research had revealed some specific rules of comprehension that poor readers were missing and could be taught. This was an important goal of discourse research, one which largely has not been met. A prevalent finding is that poor readers pick up the most important and most central information from a text but lag behind better readers in acquiring and remembering elaboration, complexity, and detail. Because main points have many different forms, the poorer readers must be able to understand quite a variety of textual types, so instruction aimed at teaching them the types of structures found in different texts will probably not be productive. It seems, so far, that poor readers need to have more efficient processes in general, rather than to be taught some special comprehension rules that they lack. At least, it would seem that general efficiency problems are the first we should attack.

Knowledge Effects

A somewhat different pattern of results has arisen in one subdomain of the study of comprehension that addresses the effects of prior knowledge on learning from discourse. Work by Voss (Bisanz & Voss, 1981; Voss, Vesonder, & Spilich, 1980) has shown a substantial effect of topic-specific knowledge on the qualitative and quantitative aspects of comprehension. Knowing a lot about the general domain to which a text is relevant makes the text easier to comprehend. When one reads a text, one attempts to relate its content to prior experience or prior knowledge. When a text refers to an area about which the reader has extensive prior knowledge, that text can be read more efficiently, and thus more completely.

These results concerning prior knowledge suggest that one way to improve reading ability is to improve general knowledge in the specific areas about which the student is likely to read in the future. Presumably, some components of reading skill can only operate in the enhanced environment that results when one has relevant prior knowledge. If so, then reading materials on subjects with which the student is already familiar should permit practice of skill components that could not otherwise be exercised.[1] Alternatively, practice in reading might be preceded by efforts to familiarize the children with basic knowledge of domains covered by the texts they will be reading.

One area of potential future work that has not been developed thus far is the interaction among knowledge of specific problem domains, the schemata and procedural skills that are needed to understand verbally stated problems, and the problem-solving skills themselves. For example, the boundary between reading comprehension and solving word problems in arithmetic is not clear-cut. One could develop approaches to helping students solve word problems that involve aspects of comprehension skill as well as problem-solving skill (Greeno & Kintsch, personal communication, 1982). This sort of comprehension training may be the way in which research on discourse comprehension finally influences instructional design.

Word Knowledge

A related consideration derives from work done by Beck, Perfetti, and McKeown (1982) and by Glaser and Curtis (personal communication, 1982).

---

[1]This phenomenon is common in many areas of skill. Sudnow (1978), for example, writes about whole new domains of skill in piano playing that only became accessible (practicable) when a particular musical style had been heavily practiced.

This work has shown the importance that developing extensive and speedy word knowledge has for the overall acquisition of reading skill. Glaser and Curtis have been studying the components of verbal aptitude. Because vocabulary is often tested in aptitude tests, they undertook the task of determining the specific vocabulary capabilities that distinguish the high-verbal person from the less-skilled. Their basic findings have been that the high-verbal person not only knows the definitions of more words, but also has more knowledge that relates to each known word. Thinking of human knowledge as a network of conceptual relationships, we can describe their results as showing that the persons high in verbal ability have more words tied into their networks and also have more links, on average, from any given word's encoding to other concepts they know.

Related work in the area of computer comprehension of natural language (Small, 1980) has also demonstrated that much of our power to understand complex or ambiguous texts rests in word-specific knowledge. This work has shown the power of language-understanding systems that have no general syntactic ability, but rather have all parsing generated by the specific words of the text as they are recognized. Such systems seem to resolve textual ambiguities that are otherwise not well handled by computers.

Classroom research by Beck et al. (1982) strongly suggests that reading ability can be improved by a vocabulary-training program that emphasizes the speed of access for word knowledge, as well as the richness of that knowledge. Fourth-grade children were taught approximately 100 words over a five-month period. Following instruction, the children performed tasks designed to require semantic processes ranging from single-word semantic decisions to simple sentence verification and memory for connected text. On all these tasks, instructed subjects performed at a significantly higher level than control subjects matched on measures of vocabulary and comprehension prior to instruction. Further, words for which more instruction was provided were processed more quickly by the subjects than words for which they had received less special intervention. Instructed subjects learned the word meanings taught by the program and used instructed words more efficiently in tasks involving comprehension. Indeed, they even showed gains on standardized reading comprehension tests that were greater than the gains of their uninstructed matched classmates.

Automaticity

The Beck et al. (1982) study derived from a considerable body of work that shows that good readers are able to recognize words faster than poor readers. Perfetti and Lesgold (1977, 1979; Lesgold & Perfetti, 1978) have written extensively on this matter. In addition, numerous other studies done elsewhere strongly suggest that word-recognition speed is a critical requirement for successful reading (e.g., Frederiksen, 1978; Jackson & McClelland, 1979; Perfetti & Hogaboam, 1975).

A good way to understand the importance of speedy and efficient word processing is to reflect on what it takes, in general, for an idea to arise in one's mind. Clearly, the several components of a new idea need to be present jointly in the person's consciousness (short-term memory) in order for that idea to form. However, one can only think about a certain limited amount at one time. If, during reading, part of the thinking capacity is given over to word recognition or word understanding, less is left as a meeting place for concepts that need to become interrelated in the reader's mind. By automating word recognition and understanding through extensive practice, the mental capacity consumed by those simple processes can be decreased (cf. Shiffrin & Schneider, 1977).

The core motivation for the ideas offered below is the belief that existing techniques for teaching reading do not guarantee that all children will receive adequate practice for automating their word-recognition ability. Further, some children may not have sufficient background knowledge (either general or related to specific wording) to handle successfully the reading-practice materials given to them by their teachers. In such cases, the practice time that is invested will not result in exercise of the intended skills.

THE AUTOMATICITY ARGUMENT

Because the ideas to be posed rest so heavily on the assertion that lack of word-processing efficiency is a major *cause* of poor reading comprehension, it is important to examine the evidence on that specific point with some care. Recent work by Lesgold and Resnick (1982) has begun to provide rather clear support for the automaticity argument. The support is of two types. It comes from a rather extensive longitudinal study of children in the primary grades, the period in which the primary skills of reading are taught. First, using structural equations modeling (Joreskog & Sorbom, 1978), they developed a causal model in which speed of word processing was assumed to determine subsequent reading comprehension performance. This model provided an adequate account of their longitudinal correlations. Second, it was shown that the specifics of instruction can affect the course of development of word processing speed. From the time children entered first grade, they were regularly given a battery of laboratory tasks that measured word processing skills and oral reading tasks that provided error and speed data. In addition, records were kept of the children's performances on the annual achievement tests given by the schools.

The method of structural equations modeling is rather complex, but the main conclusion is easily summarized. Lesgold and Resnick specified a model in which constructs representing word-processing speed at different points in the curriculum were estimated from measures of word-recognition speed and oral reading speed. The model also assumed a comprehension construct, which was measured by standardized tests. The best-fitting models of the correlational data showed larger predictive paths *from* word processing speed to *subsequent* comprehension than vice versa. For example, the average weighting for paths from speed to subsequent comprehension was as great as the average path from one year's comprehension to the next year's, while the average path from comprehension to subsequent speed measures was only one-tenth as large. Lesgold and Resnick concluded that during the first two years of schooling, word-processing speed is an essential precursor of comprehension success. Subsequent analyses of data over a longer time period are planned.

Another interesting finding in the Lesgold–Resnick study was that even though the curriculum used by the children offered substantial possibilities for students to progress at their own rates, there were children making normal progress through the curriculum who were neither acquiring word-processing speed nor succeeding on comprehension tests. Though there were only a few of these children in each cohort, they were indicative of a phenomenon that can be observed in other ways as well. Children's progress in reading is largely measured by *what* they can do, not by *how well* or *how quickly* they can do it. In contrast, I propose using the computer to provide levels of specific practice and measures of mastery that go beyond what schools normally provide. Activities that emphasize efficiency of performance can be added to the curriculum by implementing them on microcomputers. The data discussed above suggest that such activities would be a worthwhile experiment in instruction.

Although these data show the causal influence of word-processing speed on subsequent comprehension, they leave an important question unanswered. They do not tell whether word-processing speed, or the underlying capabilities on which it might depend, is modifiable in all children. There is no complete answer to that question, but there are data that speak to it. The data, also from Lesgold and Resnick (1982), have to do with differential patterns of skill acquisition in children who received instruction from different reading series.

There were data both from children who were taught with a standard basal reading series and from children taught with the New Reading System, usually referred to as NRS, that Isabel Beck created a few years ago. NRS is a program that emphasizes phonics, recognition of word components, as well as comprehension. In both groups of children, those who did better on reading comprehension tests were the ones who were faster on oral reading and on vocalizing individual words. However, there are differences in the pattern of change in word-processing speed in the two curricula.

In the basal curriculum, word-processing speed was remarkably constant over the first 2 years of instruction. That is, when tested on words recently introduced into their readers, the children read them at the same speed throughout the later part of first grade and all of second grade—they were at constant speed on progressively harder words. The NRS children showed a very different pattern. They started slower and ended faster than the basal group. One interpretation of this result is that, for at least some of the children, there is an initial cost of phonics-based instruction. Early reading is slower. However, eventually, the subword recognition skills acquired with phonics-based instruction lead to faster performance than would have been the case if whole-word instruction had been used exclusively.

Obviously, a finding such as this requires extensive investigation and replication. It is necessary to establish just what occurs, when, and with whom. Nonetheless, it is intriguing, and is a worthy basis for instructional experimentation.

HOW TO PROCEED

With microcomputers now readily available, it is tempting to consider using them for providing additional practice in word recognition. That is part of the rationale for this volume. It is important to note at the outset that small microcomputer systems, especially those most popular in schools, are not inherently well adapted to use for this purpose. We have some important engineering to do. Existing microcomputers in schools tend to have poor-quality screen characters; they tend to have no audio output capability; and they tend to depend on a typewriter keyboard for student input. Children who have trouble in reading may not easily be able to receive instructions from a poorly printed screen message—if they could read they would not need the machine. Because they cannot read well, sloppy fonts may be especially problematic for them. And, of course, if their skill is insufficient for reading instructions, it is also insufficient for a combination of reading and hunt-and-peck typing.

There are several solutions to this problem, including (1) touch screens, in which children respond by pointing to part of a display; (2) cheap audio output, even though it is of marginal quality; and (3) input devices, such as paddles or the mouse.[2] Even more important, once we are aware of the problem, we can sometimes engineer solutions that require no additional hardware, such as simple menus, introduction of the program by the teacher, and other approaches that eliminate the need for screen-based instructions. Useful materials can be created, though this will be easier with the newest microcomputers than with those that schools have already bought.

Given that the situation looks hopeful, the important question is: What shall we use the computer for? Basically, I see two important uses for the classroom microcomputer: for providing practice in word recognition and providing better diagnostic data on children's progress. As a practice device, the computer is ideal, since it can embed practice in a variety of game formats and otherwise keep children's attention. Teachers derive little satisfaction from such activity, so they are willing to consign it to a machine. As a diagnostic device, the computer adds the possibility for detailed timing of children's reading performance, leading to the possibility of expressing reading achievement in terms of how efficiently children can read, as well as what they can recognize.

Practice Opportunities

I see a primary role for microcomputers in providing pleasant opportunities for children to practice recognizing words and component parts of words, to practice making decisions about the meanings of words quickly, and even to practice higher-level reading activities—but always with the emphasis on practice to improve efficiency, not on initial learning. We understand practice better than we understand the process of providing new conceptual knowledge. Therefore, we are more likely to be able to consign the task to a machine. Further, recent studies show that the extent of time children are actually engaged in reading activities varies widely from school to school, from classroom to classroom, and from child to child.

---

[2]A *paddle* is an input device with a rotating knob and one or more buttons. Thus, it can convey left-right information or up-down information. Ordinarily, a cursor moves on the screen as the knob is turned. When the cursor is where the user wants it to be, he pushes the button. A *mouse* is a device, developed at Xerox Palo Alto Research Center, for conveying two-dimensional information. When the mouse is pushed in a specific direction on a table top, a cursor makes corresponding movements on the screen. Again, the buttons can be used for confirmation of user choices. In both cases, the utility of the device depends not only upon the hardware itself, but also upon the software for tying user movements to cursor movements, for tolerating small displacement errors, and accepting confirmation in a straightforward manner.

The approach to this problem that seems the most promising is to create games that provide the desired practice. In any area of skill, practice can be tedious. Reading is no exception. Just as we create special ways to motivate ourselves to acquire practice in other skills, we will have to do this for reading practice. Surely, the best way to practice reading is to read for some purpose. Having children read books to find out things that they want to know is an obvious way to provide extra reading practice. However, it has some shortcomings. The available materials in domains the child is interested in pursuing may not be at the right level of difficulty. Also, though teachers or designers may choose materials because of their potential for certain types of practice, there is always the possibility that children may use the materials in ways that do not in fact provide practice in optimal forms. The best way to have control over what the child is doing is to control the text and the specifics of the activity in which the child is to engage. This control is most easily achieved with games.

One type of game, with which Isabel Beck has been experimenting, has a *Beat the Clock* format. Children are asked to find specific words or subword components in a displayed array. A manipulable time limit can be imposed, a clock can tick, and other inducements can be provided to emphasize speeded performance. The format can be extended to include a wide variety of exercises involving the specifics of either the meaning or structure of words (or both), subword groupings, sentences, and even larger units.

ADAPTING TO DIFFERENT STUDENT LEARNING
AND PLAYING STYLES

Another approach involves the use of game formats such as *Adventure* or *Dungeons & Dragons.* In such games, the text that is displayed or the activity required to move ahead successfully in the game can be manipulated to produce a wide variety of practice opportunities. Students might even be allowed to create portions of the game to suit their own desires. Systems or *kits* (in the sense of Goldberg, 1979) for student-created games will require careful design. The problem is to allow the student to invent variations on a game while constraining the choices to exactly those that will provide a specific form of practice. Further, the constraints should not appear arbitrary to the student, who should never be in the position of having specified a game only to be told, after doing all the work, that the game was unacceptable.

These possibilities can be better understood via an example. Suppose we wanted to allow students to build their choice of a variety of board games that were more or less like *Monopoly.* That is, they would have a board (a region on a screen) on which could be placed a game track. The student might be able to specify the structure of such a track by either drawing it or describing it. For example, the board might be a square with 12 spaces on a side or a set of interconnected cells sketched with a light pen. It would then be necessary to provide some sort of label for each cell (square).

At this point, we have a game *shell* into which specific practice opportunities can be inserted. This shell consists of a set of displayed or implicit gameboard locations on which the player can be located, a move structure for getting from one location to one or more others, and additional events, like *Chance* cards in *Monopoly,* which can occur in specific locations. Many games have a move structure of the following sort: when it is your move, you (1) roll the dice, (2) move forward the number of squares indicated, and (3) possibly execute some process to find out if something else will happen. The system should be able to move a piece forward as a function of a dice roll, though the student may want to change the nature of the dice, spinner, or other move generator. What is more important is to provide a means of allowing the student to specify what the consequences of landing on any given square might be. It is here that attention to the practice goals of the game needs to be considered.

To the shell can be added both a story line, the adventure being undertaken by the game player, and a curriculum, the specific performances that must be made by the child in order to advance in the game. For example, one could have almost any sort of performances required by the *Chance* cards in a *Monopoly*-type game. Or, one could have various questions that must be answered to determine a next move in an *Adventure* game. Such questions might require reading a specific piece of text from the screen and using the information it contains.

Standard programming techniques are very compatible with this approach of decoupling the structure of the shell or game board, the story line, and the performances required to advance. Within limited game types, it should be possible for the system to take the student's specifications and modestly alter them to maximize practice. For example, the text that a student must read to know what to do at a given point could contain target vocabulary. Alternatively, the student could be given a standardized frame to edit. For example, the student might want a treasure clue to be revealed at a given square. The student could request that a clue be given, leaving it to the system to put the clue into a code. Someone landing on the square in question would then have to break the code to get the clue.[3]

---

[3]A reviewer inquired whether children might not get so wrapped up in designing games that they would not spend enough time playing them and getting the drill the games are supposed to provide. One easy answer to this sort of problem is to make the chance to redesign the game be a reward for completing a certain amount of practice.

This sort of flexible adaptation to different personalities ought to be a basic feature of the games we develop. A side benefit of divorcing reading goals from game structure is that it will make it easier for a game to explain its purpose to a teacher or parent. Once an explicit representation of the instructional goals for a game exists, having an object that interacts with another person to explain what the game is designed to teach, and even what it just taught a specific student, will be much more straightforward.

ADAPTING TO DIFFERENT TEACHER PREFERENCES

Similar approaches permit adaptation to differences in teaching styles. Teachers may hold strong feelings about the types of games they want in their classrooms, even about whether a game format is acceptable at all. Though we want to shape their opinions, it will also be useful to allow the teachers some flexibility in selecting which game shells will be available to the student. Presumably, a nongame shell that offered direct practice would also be quite possible, and some teachers may prefer to use that option some of the time.

These considerations lead to the following approach to game tailoring: A set of shells, including games, nongame practice, and a user kit for designing new shells, should be available to the teacher, who can then specify a menu of specific shell alternatives from which the student can choose. In the absence of this teacher intervention, all options, including the possibility of creating a new version, should be available to the student.

Diagnostic Opportunities

When a child is reading a lot of information from a computer screen and using it to make various decisions, considerable timing data are available. Such data can be the basis for a variety of diagnostic processes. For example, one could design situations in which the child must press a key to see each new sentence and then record the average reading time per syllable for each sentence. Over several hours of reading, enough data might accumulate to allow computing of stable averages on a word-by-word basis. If the presence of certain words in a sentence made that sentence take longer to read, this information could be summarized and could guide the teacher in selecting vocabulary for subsequent exercises.

Going one step further, a similar approach might be used to produce an achievement test that directly measured processing speed at a microscopic level as well as processing competence or accuracy. The data so far in the

Lesgold–Resnick longitudinal study support the utility of this form of data for predicting success in standard reading curriculum settings. Thus, one could look at processing speed for a selected pool of words, at average reading time per sentence, or other indices of word-recognition efficiency. In addition, by using multiple tasks and story lines, one might be able to determine whether the child was universally inefficient in information-processing speed, inefficient on specific vocabulary, or inefficient with respect to specific knowledge domains.

Comprehension Skills

I have avoided suggestions for computer-based development of comprehension skills for several reasons. First, such instruction will require more powerful computer resources than schools have today (although the needed resources will be available soon). Second, it is not yet clear that generic comprehension instruction is a worthwhile activity, except perhaps in the area of vocabulary development. My suspicion is that what we might hope for in comprehension instruction will more properly be part of computer-based math and social science instruction than a separate component. As I suggested above, the skills needed to interpret arithmetic word problems include some of the very skills of conscious analysis that we might otherwise want to teach as "reading."

For example, one could imagine tutorial systems that lead students through problem texts sentence by sentence. For each sentence, a variety of levels of assistance might be available, including animated enactment of the sentence's meaning, Socratic probe questions, and abstract symbolic representation of sentence meaning. Considerable research will be needed to develop a theory of problem understanding that can drive modeling of the child's comprehension skills for word problems; such work is underway in several laboratories and should result in the tools needed to provide comprehension-related coaching systems for problem solving. Another possibility is development of similar capabilities in less structured domains, such as history or political science. Efforts by Collins and his associates (e.g., Collins & Stevens, 1982) seem to be a step in this direction.

THE NEED FOR INTELLIGENCE

Some of the possibilities I have suggested can be implemented even on simple microprocessor systems. The programs could even be written in BASIC.

However, the use of techniques that result from research in artificial intelligence will add substantially to the richness and utility of such systems and will be essential to the development of serious tutorial capabilities. Thus, it is important that the computer systems acquired by schools be of sufficient power to permit exploitation of intelligent tutorial programs. At the very least, hardware acquisition plans should bear in mind the future importance of machines of greater power.

In addition to tutorial capabilities, there are some uses that become possible only when more powerful resources are available. Three ways in which intelligence would be useful in computer-based reading practice systems are intelligent tutoring, intelligent prescription, and intelligent explanation of games to parents and teachers. All three possibilities assume a system with multiple intelligent entities, each of which can monitor, and make decisions on the basis of, the actions of the others. Such systems require a style of programming called *object-oriented design,* best typified by languages such as Smalltalk. They also require a construct from artificial intelligence called the *blackboard.* By object-oriented design is meant a system consisting of entities that receive messages from other entities and act in specified ways on the basis of those messages. The entities are called *objects.* Objects that have been activated by the receipt of a message may operate sequentially or in parallel. When the messages between objects are placed in a central location that all objects monitor, we call the location a *blackboard.* Blackboards allow objects to be aware of the patterns of communication in the system and to act on the basis of those patterns.

The Prescriber

One object of some interest is the prescriber. The prescriber I envision would monitor the student's interactions with a game and watch for signs of specific classes of problems. When specific problems were noted, the prescriber might send a message to the teacher, advise the student to try something different, or advise the game-playing object to change the specific words it was using or to modify the time limits for responding. The prescriber might also use the interaction patterns between the game object and the student as the basis for updating a diagnostic profile of the child. If done continually, this updating would eliminate periodic standardized testing. Whenever test scores were wanted, the current profile could be printed.

The Research Assistant

Once the concept of continual monitoring of the child's performance by an independent part of the system is established, it is possible to generalize it. The diagnostic profile need not be limited to what the teacher or school staff want. It can also include evaluative information for the system designer, including usage data on various game options and game-playing patterns. A research-assistant object in an instructional system would, in principle, be more useful than a human research assistant, if only because it would always be paying attention to the child using the system. As we become concerned with specifying the details of instructional games systems, better data gathering and intelligent data reduction will be required.

Explaining Games to Parents

A final use of intelligent monitoring objects is to explain to parents what is going on when a child plays a reading game. In many communities, electronic games do not have a positive reputation. Further, all fun-looking games, electronic or otherwise, are suspect to some teachers and parents. It would be ideal to have an intelligent object that was specifically designed to look at the updated diagnostic profiles for children and at the games they had just played and then tell parents or the teacher what skills each child practiced.

Experience in other domains, such as medical diagnosis systems, suggests that a system is more likely to be accepted if it has an ability to explain why it is doing what it is doing. In medicine, everyone agrees that diagnosis is important. In schools, there is not universal agreement that games have a role. Thus, the need for explanatory components in computer-based practice games will be particularly great.

REFERENCES

Beck, I. L., Perfetti, C. A., & McKeown, M. G. The effects of long-term vocabulary instruction on lexical access and reading comprehension. *Journal of Educational Psychology,* 1982, *74,* 506–521.

Bisanz, G. L., & Voss, J. F. Sources of knowledge in reading comprehension: Cognitive development and expertise in a content domain. In A. Lesgold & C. Perfetti (Eds.), *Interactive processes in reading.* Hillsdale, New Jersey: Erlbaum, 1981.

Collins, A., & Stevens, A. L. Goals and strategies of inquiry teachers. In R. Glaser (Ed.), *Advances in instructional psychology* (Vol. 2). Hillsdale, New Jersey: Erlbaum, 1982.

Frederiksen, J. R. Assessment of perceptual, decoding, and lexical skills and their relation to reading proficiency, In A. M. Lesgold, J. W. Pellegrino, S. D. Fokkema, & R. Glaser (Eds.), *Cognitive psychology and instruction.* New York: Plenum, 1978.

Goldberg, A. Educational uses of a Dynabook. *Changes in education* (Vol. 3). London: Pergamon, 1979.

Jackson, M. D., & McClelland, J. J. Processing determinants of reading speed. *Journal of Experimental Psychology: General,* 1979, *70,* 717–729.

Joreskog, K. G., & Sorbom, D. *LISREL: Analysis of linear structural relationships by the method of maximum likelihood* (Users guide, Version IV, Release 2). Chicago: International Education Services, 1978.

Lesgold, A. M., & Perfetti, C. A. Interactive processes in reading comprehension. *Discourse Processes,* 1978, *1,* 323–336.

Lesgold, A. M., & Resnick, L. B. How reading disabilities develop: Perspectives from a longitudinal study. In J. P. Das, R. Mulcahy, & A. E. Wall (Eds.), *Theory and research in learning disability,* New York: Plenum, 1982.

Perfetti, C. A., & Hogaboam, T. W. The relationship between single word decoding and reading comprehension skill. *Journal of Educational Psychology,* 1975, *67,* 461–469.

Perfetti, C. A., & Lesgold, A. M. Discourse processing and sources of individual differences. In P. Carpenter & M. Just (Eds.), *Cognitive processes in comprehension,* Hillsdale, New Jersey: Erlbaum, 1977.

Perfetti, C. A., & Lesgold, A. M. Coding and comprehension in skilled reading. In L. B. Resnick & P. Weaver (Eds.), *Theory and practice of early reading.* Hillsdale, New Jersey: Erlbaum, 1979.

Shiffrin, R. M., & Schneider, W. Controlled and automatic human information processing (Vol. 2). Perceptual learning, automatic attending, and a general theory. *Psychological Review,* 1977, *84,* 127–190.

Small, S. *Word expert parsing: A theory of distributed word-based natural language understanding.* (Technical Report TR–954 NSG-7253). College Park, Maryland: University of Maryland, Department of Computer Science, September, 1980.

Sudnow, D. *Ways of the hand: The organization of improvised conduct.* Cambridge, Massachussetts: Harvard University Press, 1978.

Voss, J. F., Vesonder, G. T., & Spilich, G. J. Text generation and recall by high-knowledge and low-knowledge individuals. *Journal of Verbal Learning and Verbal Behavior,* 1980, *19,* 651–667.

10

Learning to Read in Real Time*

Alex Cherry Wilkinson

INTRODUCTION

In 1980, Huey wrote a classic book on reading and gave it a revealing title: *The Psychology and Pedagogy of Reading*. The twin goals of Huey's book, as announced by its title, were the two concerns that have, for virtually a century now, promoted a continuing dialogue between educators and psychologists, practitioners and theorists, teachers and researchers. These two concerns are to formulate scientific accounts of the mental processes by which people read, and to devise effective methods for teaching reading. Today, the two traditional goals are joined by a third, whose sig-

*READINTIME was designed and written by Alex Cherry Wilkinson with assistance from Chuck Bilow. Development of READINTIME was supported by grants from the Royalty Fund of the Wisconsin Center for Education Research, and from The Foundation for the Advancement of Computer-Guided Education. Preparation of the chapter was supported by grant NIE-G-81-0009 from the National Institute of Education to the Wisconsin Center for Education Research. Any opinions, findings, and conclusions or recommendations in the chapter are the author's and do not necessarily reflect the views of the Institute or the Department of Education. Correspondence should be addressed to Alex Cherry Wilkinson, Psychology Department, University of Wisconsin, 1202 West Johnson St., Madison, WI 53706.

nificance we have only begun to appreciate. Were Huey's treatise to be rewritten today, it would properly be titled *The Psychology, Pedagogy, and Technology of Reading.* With the advent of computer-based instruction in reading, we may well experience a reorientation of both theory and practice that represents a change more fundamental than merely an improvement in scientific or instructional method. The questions that scientists think to ask about the psychology of reading and the goals that teachers specify as pedagogical objectives will, I think, change qualitatively as they become linked to computer technology.

Describing this qualitative change is a major goal of this chapter. My principal concern is to examine how computer technology will affect both scientific inquiry and educational practice. The chapter begins by defining some ways in which reading on a computer is, or at least can be, different qualitatively from reading on a printed page. Next comes an analysis of two aspects of reading that are important in both research and instruction, particularly in computerized instruction. These two aspects of reading are word recognition and text selection. Finally, a concluding section provides a theoretical and programmatic summary. Throughout the chapter, examples are provided from a working computer program called READIN-TIME.

TWO MODES OF READING: COMPUTER AND PAGE

In the special case of a text being presented on the screen of the computer exactly as it would appear on a page of paper, reading on the computer is likely to be no different than reading on the page. There may be a significant difference between computer and page, however, if the text is presented in any of several ways that use the special talents of the computer. Ways in which a text may be displayed by a computer vary on three important dimensions: framing, pacing, and allocation of control. Framing concerns how much text is available to be read at any moment in time and where the available text is placed in the reader's visual field. Pacing is the speed of reading a framed portion of the text. Allocation of control concerns whether and how the reader determines the framing and pacing of the text.

Framing

On a printed page, the frame of the available text corresponds to the physical boundaries of the page. On a computer, many frames are possible.

The frame can be a screenful of text, a paragraph, a line, a sentence, a phrase, a word, even—perish the thought—a single letter. The program READINTIME can display any text with any of these frames.

Does it matter which frame is used? If the frame is such that one and only one letter is visible at any moment, the text would be rendered unreadable (Kolers & Katzman, 1966; Newman, 1966). Research on eye movements has shown convincingly that at a given instant in time, a skilled reader has a visual span of about 15–25 characters, which is approximately 2–4 words (Rayner & McConkie, 1977). In addition, when skilled readers are reading unfamiliar, expository material of the sort usually found in textbooks, they fixate almost every word individually (Just & Carpenter, 1980). One might suspect, therefore, that an appropriate frame, for good readers at least, may be a line or a phrase.

Importantly, different frames might be appropriate for different purposes. For example, teaching students about the paragraph as a level of textual organization may be aided by having the students read with paragraphs framed. On the other hand, there may be circumstances in which it would be desirable to force the reader to proceed word by word. For example, a skill that novice and poor readers may need to perfect is identification of a word independently of its context (Perfetti, this volume; Stanovich, 1980). Having to read with the word as the frame might well encourage students to polish this skill.

Plainly, the many frames that may be used when reading on a computer raise new questions for research and new possibilities for instruction. It will be many years before we know the answers to these questions. Whatever we find, I suspect that readers of the future will view the printed page as an inflexible and ill-framed anachronism.

Pacing

On a printed page, a reader's normal pacing is systematic but irregular. Skilled readers spend more time reading some words than others. The reader's time of fixating a word increases if the word occurs with low frequency in the language, has many letters or syllables, has certain grammatical functions, or marks the end of a sentence or paragraph (Just & Carpenter, 1980). We do not know whether these factors associated with the reader's pacing correspond to psychological processes that are essential for effective reading. Empirically, the correlations are well established. Like all correlations, however, they are vulnerable to the charge of being coincidental rather than causal. A skeptic might protest that these factors, which allegedly control the reader's pacing, could be dispensible by-products of a style of reading that happens to suit the printed page. The skeptic's position has some support in research conducted by Juola, Ward, and McNamara (1982).

Styles of reading that are possible on a computer may help us to determine which of the factors are psychologically important for moderating a reader's pacing and which are not. For example, a style of reading called RSVP—an acronym for rapid serial visual presentation—involves using a frame of one word, with successive words all presented in the same location at the center of the computer's screen. Typically, the time for each word is the same, although it is possible to vary the time according to factors such as word frequency, number of letters, and grammatical function. READINTIME can present any text in this manner.

Allocation of Control

Control of the printed page rests wholly in the reader, who can decide freely what part of the page to read, when, and how fast. On a computer, too, full control may be vested in the reader; however, it may also be vested partly or wholly in the machine. Although it seems unlikely that one would ever want to wrest all control from the reader, there are a number of circumstances in which it might prove to be valuable to steal some of it. For example, there are occasions when a teacher would consider it desirable to spur on a reader who is going too slow, or to rein in one who is going too fast. Another example is control of decisions to reread a misunderstood portion of a text or to skip portions of minor significance. Readers of the printed page routinely make these decisions. Regrettably, we know little about how a choice to reread or to skip is made. A possibility considered in a later section of this chapter is that by allocating some of the decision making to the computer, we can subject the process to controlled experimental study, and perhaps learn how to teach students to make their own decisions more wisely.

PRIORITIES FOR COMPUTERIZED READING

As a device for displaying text, the computer can supply virtually any desired combination of framing, pacing, and allocation of control. The great appeal of the device is its marvelous potential. Texts can be presented, timed, and controlled by computer in ways that were unimaginable only a decade ago. As a result, we face the pleasantly perplexing problem that confronts anyone who has unexpectedly inherited great wealth: How can we wisely invest what we suddenly have in abundance but are poorly prepared to manage?

Criteria for Setting Priorities

We need criteria for determining which methods of computerized reading should be the first to be programmed, used in research, and implemented in teaching. I suggest that this determination should be guided by three criteria. The three criteria represent the viewpoints of the three contemporary contributors to our understanding of reading: psychology, pedagogy, and technology.

Perhaps the simplest and least controversial criterion is the technological one. Methods of displaying text that are unique to the computer should have higher priority than methods that essentially copy the printed page. The cost of developing software argues forcibly against doing on a computer anything that could be done similarly, at far less expense, in ordinary print. For reference, call this the criterion of technological novelty.

Second, although the method of display should be novel, it should be founded, nonetheless, on principles known to govern reading of the printed page. For example, evidence concerning readers' eye movements suggests that a moving frame of text in a computer-controlled display should move syllable-by-syllable or word-by-word. It should not move letter-by-letter, for the simple reason that readers do not move their eyes in such small steps. In essence, this criterion specifies that the display should be designed with appropriate consideration of relevant psychological research; it is a criterion of sound psychological design.

Finally, preference should be given to methods of display that promote skills known to be educationally problematic. In short, we should use the computer to teach what most needs to be taught. Thus, the third criterion is pedagogical importance.

Overview of READINTIME

A program developed with these criteria in mind is READINTIME. The program is written in UCSD-Pascal for microcomputers. For a student, READINTIME currently provides two classes of activity. There are games designed to promote fluency in recognizing single words. In addition, a meaningful text can be read in several ways that vary in framing, pacing, and allocation of control.

For a person designated by READINTIME as the manager, who could be either the teacher or a researcher, extensive records can be kept. These records specify the games or readings assigned to students and report data on the students' performance of their assignments. Optionally, students can be permitted by the manager to select their own games or readings, in which case records are kept concerning what the students selected and how they performed. Once a student has completed a set of assigned or selected readings, the student will not be able to proceed until the manager has inspected and cleared the student's record. To ease the manager's burden, simple facilities are provided for inspecting students' records rapidly and for making group assignments. Although the records are not quite as detailed as those that might be kept in a laboratory experiment, they are more than adequate for investigating a variety of scientifically important questions. Records of this sort are vitally important for developing and revising the software, too.

Important as these record-keeping capabilities may be, they are not the major concern of this chapter. Instead, I shall review the current and prospective capabilities of READINTIME as a tool for instruction and research. The review will analyze READINTIME with respect to the three criteria of technological novelty, psychological design, and pedagogical importance.

WORD RECOGNITION

One approach to computerized instruction in reading emphasizes teaching students to be fluent in recognizing individual words. This section illustrates this approach with games for word recognition that are incorporated in READINTIME, and gives the technological, psychological, and pedagogical rationale for these games.

Word Games in READINTIME

Two games in READINTIME were designed to promote rapidity of word recognition. In their current states these games are running programs that can be used with any set of words that a teacher or a researcher might select. The games allow wide variation in the ability of the game-player and are meant to accomodate readers at almost any level of reading ability.

The easier of the two games is called STOPPER. Its purpose is to introduce new words to a student in a way that forces the student to attend to the word's spelling or orthographic structure. In STOPPER, a word appears gradually in the center of the screen. At the option of the teacher or researcher, the word may appear letter-by-letter, syllable-by-syllable, in groups of letters that correspond to orthographic or spelling units, or in fact in any piecemeal manner that proceeds from left to right. All previously presented constituents of a word remain visible as each new constituent is added. The student is instructed to press the spacebar as soon as the last constituent of a word appears.

In effect, the student's task is to "stop" the computer exactly at the end of the word. If the student responds before the final constituent has appeared or after a deadline time following completion of the word, an error message gives feedback that the response was too fast or too slow. If the student successfully responds between the moment of completing the word and the deadline time, a congratulatory message is given. All the words in a set are presented in this manner and the student is then given the option to repeat the set. The student also has the option to reset the rate at which constituents are added to a word during its gradual presentation. A future version of the game may have the computer continually monitor the student's performance and calibrate the rate to keep it challenging. Presently, the rate may vary from 100 to 900 msec for each constituent. The response deadline is automatically set to vary with the presentation rate, over a range from 500 to 950 msec.

The more difficult game is LOOKFOR. This game is an adaptation of a detection task often used in psychological research. Its purpose is to teach rapid perceptual recognition of words. In LOOKFOR, a target word is shown briefly near the top of the screen. Then several words are presented successively at a single location near the center of the screen. Each word is visible for a brief time, is obliterated with a ●00-msec mask of Os overwritten with slashes, and is followed by a brief period in which the screen is blank. One of the words presented in the center of the screen is the previously shown target. The student's task is to press the spacebar as soon as the word currently visible at the center of the screen is the target word. The student's response must occur after the target word has been presented but before the next word appears. Feedback is given to tell whether the student's response was too fast, was successfully timed to hit the target, or was too slow. Following this feedback, a new target word is shown and the same list of words is presented again in the center of the screen in a new, randomized order. The game continues until each word in the list has been the target once. Then the student is given the option to repeat the list and to reset the length of time between the time a word is presented and when it gets obliterated by the mask. This time may vary from 50 to 450 msec.

As with STOPPER, a future version of LOOKFOR may have the computer monitor the student's performance and calibrate the pace of the game to make it optimally challenging.

Technological Novelty

First, we must evaluate STOPPER and LOOKFOR on grounds of technological novelty. Clearly, the piecemeal appearance of a word in STOPPER and the masking of words in LOOKFOR would be impossible on paper. Equally important, both games capitalize on the capability of the computer to vary pacing and to allocate control. The pace of presentation can be tailored to the individual student, and can be made gradually more rapid. In this way, the games have the potential to promote rapidity of word recognition with a task designed to be challenging for the individual while avoiding the twin deficiencies of being either frustratingly too hard or boringly too easy. Control of the game is allocated partly to the computer and partly to the student. If the pace is uncomfortably fast or slow, the student can change it. At the same time, once a set of words has been initiated, the student must accomodate to a pace of presentation that is wholly under the control of the computer.

Psychological Design

How well do these games satisfy the criterion of psychological design? For illustration, I will mention one feature of each game that was deliberately incorporated into its design according to a principle drawn from psychological research.

The design of STOPPER was based on a task analysis of the sort that is common in experimental research on cognitive processes. The task analysis specified that the game should require the student to pay careful attention to every constituent of a word. It was assumed that the word would be new to the student, and that the instructional goal would be to have the student learn the constituent structure of the word. Seeing the constituents one-by-one and having to know which is the final constituent makes STOPPER a plausible method for teaching constituent structure.

In designing LOOKFOR, each word in the centered list was obliterated by a mask because it is well established from research on human vision that the mask permits precise control of the word's psychological duration (e.g., Massaro, 1975, pp. 358–370). Without the mask, the psychological duration of the word would be longer than its actual physical duration. In effect, the mask disrupts information concerning the identity of the word that would otherwise persist in the visual system of the game-player for a short, possibly variable period of time after the word had physically disappeared.

Pedagogical Importance

A significant body of research indicates that rapid recognition of words is critical for effective reading. Notice that this statement concerns the rapidity of word recognition, not its accuracy. The same point is explicated well by Lesgold and Perfetti (this volume), and I will therefore cover it quickly. If children are asked to read a short list of words, all of which they can read accurately, their speed of completing the list increases dramatically over the first several years of schooling but begins to level off after about 6 years of education (Doehring, 1976). The speed with which children scan a printed text to locate a target word shows the same pattern of improvement over the same age range (Doehring, 1976; Friedrich, Schadler, & Juola, 1979). Among children, poor readers seem particularly penalized by slowness in vocalizing the name of a printed word (Perfetti, Finger, & Hogaboam, 1978; Stanovich, 1981). Among adults, a poor reader is slower than a good reader in deciding that two printed symbols have the same name, even though the two readers make the naming decision with comparable accuracy and are equally fast in making simpler decisions (Jackson, 1980; Jackson & McClelland, 1975, 1979).

Training in rapid recognition of words can be done better by computer than on the printed page. We must be clear, however, about what can be expected to result from such training. Undoubtedly, novice and poor readers can learn to recognize words more rapidly. But there is no assurance that the difference between good and poor readers will vanish as a result. In fact, some evidence suggests that good and poor readers differ in naming-speed for printed symbols they have barely learned, as well as for ones they have known and practiced at length (Hogaboam & Perfetti, 1978; Jackson, 1980). Nor is there any assurance that other aspects of reading, most notably comprehension, will improve as a side effect of faster word recognition. Evidence reported by Fleisher, Jenkins, and Pany (1979) showed no carry-over from faster word recognition to better comprehension. However, the data of Fleisher et al. indicated that when poor readers were trained to recognize isolated words more rapidly, they also learned, without direct training, to read meaningful texts more rapidly and, interestingly, with no loss of comprehension.

We can conclude that software for training rapid word recognition is well justified on grounds of pedagogical importance. The likelihood of a valuable educational payoff seems high. There should be no illusion, however, that rapidity of word recognition is a panacea for all the ills of inefficient readers, nor that it has any unique status as the single most important goal for computerized instruction in reading.

Possible Extensions

An obvious limitation of READINTIME in its present state of development is that its word games promote speedy recognition of words by methods that emphasize perceptual identification and ignore semantic knowledge. For the reasons explained by Perfetti (this volume) and by Sternberg, Powell, and Kaye (this volume), it seems likely that a more effective instructional program would promote three aspects of reading vocabulary: rapidity of perceptually recognizing a word, richness of the reader's semantic knowledge concerning the meanings of a word, and rapidity in gaining access to this semantic knowledge while reading. One way of revising READINTIME to promote richness of semantic knowledge and rapidity in accessing word meanings would be to add a game called FIND-LIKE. In this new game, as in the existing game LOOKFOR, the student's task would be to find a target word in a rapidly presented list. Unlike LOOKFOR, however, in which the target word itself is identified before presentation of the list, in FINDLIKE, only a semantic clue would be given in advance. The clue could be a synonym of the target word, or perhaps its etymological root.

TEXT SELECTION

The reader of a printed page has full control over selecting parts of the text to be read, reread, or skipped. In computerized reading, selecting a part of the text can be controlled fully by the reader, fully by the computer, or partly by each. The following section describes how control of text selection can be allocated in READINTIME, explains how text selection can be combined with framing and pacing, and judges the various combinations by technological, psychological, and pedagogical criteria.

Reading Text with READINTIME

READINTIME permits a text to be read with any of three kinds of framing. First, in a holding mode, a portion of a text is held still on the screen until the reader has finished reading it. Second, in a moving mode, only a portion of the text that resides inside a moving window is visible on the screen. The window moves across each line of text in a manner that mimics the eye movements of a normal reader. Outside the window, peripheral information about the layout of the text is provided by a dash at each physical location representing the position of a letter in the text. Finally, in the RSVP mode, the text appears one word at a time in the center of the screen.

In any of these modes, the text can be framed with or without pauses. The pauses can be put anywhere the teacher or researcher wants them, but would ordinarily be put at the ends of sentences or paragraphs. For example, if pauses were placed at the ends of sentences in the moving mode, the window of visible text would advance until its right or leading edge reached the end of a sentence. Then the leading edge would stop moving while the left or trailing edge continued moving until it, too, reached the end of the sentence. At this point, no text would be visible, and the reader would be obliged to pause.

Control of what happens during a pause depends on the mode. In the two dynamic modes, moving and RSVP, the student may or may not have an option, at the discretion of the teacher or researcher. Without an option, the student must simply pause for a fixed but brief time; after the pause, presentation of the text will resume. With an option, the student may elect to continue reading ahead or may retreat to the point of the previous pause and reread from there. In the holding mode, the student always has the option to go forward from a pausing point or to retreat to the previous pause.

Control of pacing also depends on the mode. In the moving and RSVP modes, the pace of reading is controlled by the computer. The rate can be as fast as 900 words per minute or as slow as 30. Pacing is under the control of the reader, however, in the holding mode, much as it would be if the text were on a printed page.

Technological Novelty

These modes of reading are virtually unique to computerized reading. Except for the holding mode without pauses, none of the foregoing combinations of framing, pacing, and allocation of control would be possible on the printed page.

Psychological Design

On grounds of psychological design, READINTIME is strong in some respects but weak in others. There are certain respects, however, in which the psychology of reading a text with READINTIME is largely a mystery. In these respects, goodness of psychological design is not an evaluative criterion; it is a matter for research.

A strong point in the design of READINTIME is that the moving mode of displaying a text is compatible with the scientific literature on readers' eye movements. It has been known for decades (Huey, 1908) that a reader's eyes move in jerks called *saccades* (which, never mind its esoteric sound, is merely the French translation of *jerks)*. More recent data (Just & Carpenter, 1980; Rayner & McConkie, 1977) have shown that readers fixate almost every word in a text of unfamiliar expository prose, and that successive saccades generally take the reader's eyes from one word to the next. Some noteworthy modulations of this largely word-by-word movement of the eyes are, first, that often only one fixation occurs for a pair of adjacent short words and, second, that a very long word may receive a longer-than-usual fixation.

Consistent with these data on eye movements, the window of visible text in the moving mode of READINTIME advances in sectors that correspond to a word in most cases, with two noteworthy exceptions. First, if there are adjacent short words on the same line of text, they are merged into a single sector. Second, a word longer than eight characters is divided at syllable boundaries into two or more sectors. Additional ways in which the moving window of text mimics the moving eye are that the words visible in the window at any instant are all on the same line and that at the beginning of a new line an automatic delay of 200 msec makes allowance for the long saccade from the end of the previous line. Thanks to these properties of the moving window, readers seem to adapt to it in short order.

A weak point of READINTIME, as currently designed, is that when students are allowed to control the selection of text, they do not have as much control as they should. On a printed page, the student could choose to retreat and reread, to advance normally, or to skip ahead. In READINTIME, no skipping is allowed, and a retreat must go exactly as far as the previous pausing point, which may be either too far or not far enough. This deficiency of READINTIME is correctable, of course. One way to correct it would be to have the computer continuously monitor the keys marked with directional arrows on the keyboard. Whenever the student presses one of these keys, the text displayed on the screen could move at high speed in the designated direction until the key is no longer being pressed.

Some aspects of reading a text with READINTIME cannot be adequately evaluated for goodness of psychological design with the scientific data that are currently available. Most notable in this regard is the word-by-word presentation of the RSVP mode. Where the necessary data are lacking, a teacher might be displeased, because the merits or faults of READINTIME as an instructional tool are unknown. A researcher, however, may be delighted, because interesting questions are raised that beg to be subjected to experimental study. One important question, for example, is whether in the RSVP mode a reader would comprehend a text better when the time for each word varies with the word's length or frequency than when all words are presented for the same time.

Pedagogical Importance

An obvious use of READINTIME as an educational tool would be to encourage slow readers to read faster. Although speed of reading is a desirable goal, provided that it is not achieved at the expense of comprehension, there is, I think, a more important pedagogical objective. More fundamental than teaching students to read rapidly is training them to be wise in selecting parts of a text to be read, reread, or skipped. By the same token, an important objective for research should be to advance our deplorably sparse knowledge of factors that govern readers' decisions to retreat, read on, or skim.

We know that all readers make regressive eye movements, although less-skilled readers make them more often (Gibson & Levin, 1975). There is also recent evidence that some regressive eye movements occur when readers find their initial interpretation of a sentence to be wrong (Carpenter & Daneman, 1981). Presumably, regression to an earlier point in the sentence allows the reader to repair the misunderstanding. There is no direct evidence, to my knowledge, that tells whether regressions ordinarily do occur when a misunderstanding is in fact in need of repair, or whether they sometimes occur without good reason when there is no misinterpretation to correct.

Data on skipping portions of a text, like the data on regressions, are sparse and leave many questions unanswered. Evidence from research on target detection shows that adult readers can scan a text at a surprisingly high speed to find a target word (Neisser, 1967), and that children become more efficient in such scanning as they progress through the first several years of school (Doehring, 1976; Friedrich et al., 1979). It seems likely that readers scan in much the same way when they decide to skip a portion of a text and try to locate a place in the text where they will resume reading in earnest. Whether readers do skip when they should, do not skip when they should not, and skip neither too much nor too little, are questions that none of the extant data address.

These unanswered questions concern a process that has lately been given the ungainly name of comprehension monitoring. It appears that young readers have minimal awareness of how to monitor their comprehension (Myers & Paris, 1978) and use erratic strategies for studying texts (Brown & Smiley, 1978). Both children and adults are often blind to inconsistencies and contradictions in a text that they would readily detect if they carefully monitored their understanding of the text (Glenberg, Wilkinson, & Epstein, 1982; Markman, 1979). Pedagogically, it might therefore be of considerable value to teach readers methods of monitoring their comprehension. One such method might be taught by training readers to make deliberate and thoughtful decisions about what parts of a text to select for rereading or skipping.

Needed Extensions

On grounds of both psychological design and pedagogical importance, a needed extension of READINTIME is a capability to allocate to the reader greater control of text selection. This capability alone, however, is not enough. There should be two additional extensions. First, some records should be kept concerning where in a text readers decide to skip or retreat, and how much they skip or how far they retreat. Second, a flexible capability should be added for interrupting the reader at any point and testing the reader's comprehension and memory of the text.

With these extensions, READINTIME would be a marvelous tool for both instruction and research. Consider, for example, three possibilities. First, it would be possible to collect extensive data on skipping and retreating for readers of any age. Few such data are presently available. Second, it would be possible to ascertain whether readers of various ages and ability levels become increasingly likely to skip as the importance of the currently visible text declines. Third, and perhaps most interestingly, it would be possible to assess systematically the degree to which a reader's decisions concerning text selection are founded on accurate monitoring of comprehension. In part, this assessment would be performed by providing an immediate test when a reader presses the key to initiate a retreat. The test would assess the reader's understanding of the material that preceded the pressing of the key. In this way, one could judge whether the reader's decisions to retreat tend to occur, as they should, when the text is poorly understood. Similar tests given when the reader chooses to advance in the text could assess whether the decisions to read ahead tend to occur, in contrast, when the text is well understood. An objective index of the reader's efficiency in monitoring comprehension could then be constructed by calculating the degree to which decisions to read on or retreat match up with good or poor comprehension, respectively.

CONCLUSIONS

To conclude, it may be productive to review the major theses of the chapter from two somewhat different perspectives. One perspective is theoretical; the other, programmatic.

Time and Context in Reading

An important variable for any theory of reading is time. Of critical importance is how readers distribute and coordinate in real time the cognitive processes of attending, perceptually identifying, comprehending, and remembering. The time required for recognizing the identity and meaning of a word may be especially important, and the games in READINTIME are designed to make this time more rapid. Setting aside time to decide whether to advance or reread is equally vital for effective reading; we need computerized tools to study these decisions and to help readers make them more wisely.

Real time, of course, is continuous. An adequate theory of reading must consider, therefore, the flow of events over time. What a reader does at a given instant while reading a text surely depends, in some respect, on what has transpired over a preceding span of time. The present moment occurs psychologically in the context of the recent past, and readers are cognizant of this context. Importantly, there is reason to suspect that readers of different ability use context in different ways. Novices and poor readers appear to rely heavily on the meaning and syntax of what they have already read as an aid in identifying a word they are currently trying to read (Lesgold, this volume; Perfetti, this volume; Stanovich, 1980). For them, word recognition is context guided, whereas for skilled readers it is largely context free. Can we conclude that skilled readers ignore context? I think not. Rather, they may use context to guide their decisions to read on, skim, or retreat. Perhaps unskilled readers, because they must use context for word recognition, are unable to use it effectively for text selection.

If these observations are correct, learning to read may be considered to be a process in which there is a gradual shift in how context guides cognitive processes occurring in real time. Contextual guidance of word recognition dominates the reading of the inexperienced and the unskilled. For the skilled reader, in contrast, freedom from a need to rely on context for word recognition enables contextual guidance of text selection.

Instructive Research

The foregoing theoretical perspective is founded, in part, on scientific data, but is also partly speculative. It provides a rationale for the two classes of instructional activity available in READINTIME: games that promote rapid recognition of words, and methods of reading a text under various combinations of framing, pacing, and allocation of control. There is no certainty, however, that the theory is correct, nor that the educational benefits of the program will be all the theory promises. Realistically, READINTIME must be viewed as a tool for both scientific research and instructional innovation. As such, READINTIME is an example of a programmatic orientation that may be called instructive research (see Resnick & Beck, 1976, for another example).

There is a debate, among psychologists, about the value of research that is based on efforts to train the unskilled in cognitive skills (Kuhn, 1974; Sternberg, 1981). The definitive premise of such research is that we can discover what cognitive skills people lack by investigating what skills can be trained for. The premise of instructive research, however, is somewhat different. Instructional applications are important, not because they test a theory of cognitive deficit, but because they provide a criterion of pedagogical importance for identifying issues to which research ought to be directed. Research motivated by this criterion is likely to have an instructional payoff for students and to be instructive for scientists as well.

REFERENCES

Brown, A. L., & Smiley, S. S. The development of strategies for studying texts. *Child Development,* 1978, *49,* 1076–1088.

Carpenter, P. A., & Daneman, M. Lexical retrieval and error recovery in reading: A model based on eye fixations. *Journal of Verbal Learning and Verbal Behavior,* 1981, *20,* 137–160.

Doehring, D. G. Acquisition of rapid reading responses. *Monographs of the Society for Research in Child Development,* 1976, *41*(2, Serial No. 165).

Fleisher, L. S., Jenkins, J. S., & Pany, D. Effects on poor readers' comprehension of training in rapid decoding. *Reading Research Quarterly,* 1979, *15,* 30–48.

Friedrich, F. J., Schadler, M., & Juola, J. F. Developmental changes in units of processing in reading. *Journal of Experimental Child Psychology,* 1979, *28,* 344-358.

Gibson, E. J., & Levin, H. *The psychology of reading.* Cambridge, Massachusetts: MIT Press, 1975.

Glenberg, A. M., Wilkinson, A. C., & Epstein, W. The illusion of knowing: Failure in the self-assessment of comprehension. *Memory & Cognition,* 1982, *10,* 597-602.

Hogaboam, T. W., & Perfetti, C. A. Reading skill and the role of verbal experience in decoding. *Journal of Educational Psychology,* 1978, *70,* 717-729.

Huey, E. B. *The psychology and pedagogy of reading.* Cambridge, Massachusetts: MIT Press, 1968. (Originally published, 1908.)

Jackson, M. D. Further evidence for a relationship between memory access and reading ability. *Journal of Verbal Learning and Verbal Behavior,* 1980, *19,* 683-694.

Jackson, M. D., & McClelland, J. Sensory and cognitive determinants of reading speed. *Journal of Verbal Learning and Verbal Behavior,* 1975, *14,* 565-574.

Jackson, M. D., & McClelland, J. Processing determinants of reading speed. *Journal of Experimental Psychology: General,* 1979, *108,* 151-181.

Juola, J. F., Ward, N. J., & McNamara, T. Visual search and reading of rapid serial presentations of letter strings, words, and text. *Journal of Experimental Psychology: General,* 1982, *111,* 208-227.

Just, M. A., & Carpenter, P. A. A theory of reading: From eye fixations to comprehension. *Psychological Review,* 1980, *87,* 329-354.

Kolers, P. A., & Katzman, M. T. Naming sequentially presented letters and words. *Language and Speech,* 1966, *9,* 84-95.

Kuhn, D. Inducing development experimentally: Comments on a research paradigm. *Developmental Psychology,* 1974, *10,* 590-600.

Markman, E. Realizing that you don't understand: Elementary school children's awareness of inconsistencies. *Child Development,* 1979, *50,* 643-655.

Massaro, D. W. *Experimental psychology and information processing.* New York: Rand-McNally, 1975.

Myers, M., & Paris, S. G. Children's metacognitive knowledge about reading. *Journal of Educational Psychology,* 1978, *70,* 680-690.

Neisser, U. *Cognitive Psychology.* New York: Appleton-Century-Crofts, 1967.

Newman, E. B. Speed of reading when the span of letters is restricted. *American Journal of Psychology,* 1966, *79,* 272-278.

Perfetti, C. A., Finger, E., & Hogaboam, T. Sources of vocalization latency differences between skilled and less skilled young readers. *Journal of Educational Psychology,* 1978, *70,* 730-739.

Resnick, L. B., & Beck, I. L. Designing instruction in reading: Interaction of theory and practice. In J. T. Guthrie (Ed.), *Aspects of reading acquisition.* Baltimore: Johns Hopkins University Press, 1976.

Rayner, K., & McConkie, G. W. Perceptual processes in reading: The perceptual spans. In A. S. Reber & D. L. Scarborough (Eds.), *Toward a psychology of reading.* Hillsdale, New Jersey: Erlbaum, 1977.

Stanovich, K. E. Toward an interactive-compensatory model of individual differences in the development of reading fluency. *Reading Research Quarterly,* 1980, *16,* 32-71.

Stanovich, K. E. Relationships between word decoding speed, general name-retrieval ability, and reading progress in first-grade children. *Journal of Educational Psychology,* 1981, *73,* 809-815.

Sternberg, R. J. Intelligence and nonentrenchment. *Journal of Educational Psychology,* 1981, *73,* 1-16

11

The Computer Confronts Language Arts: Cans and Shoulds for Education*

Andee Rubin

ELEPHANT AND LEOPARD, SCHOOL AND COMPUTER

Analyzing the impact of computers on education is like trying to predict the outcome of a confrontation between a lumbering old elephant and a supple young leopard. The educational elephant is both wise and wizened, bolstered by a long history, and laden with venerable—though often tired—traditions. Computer technology, on the other hand, has a short, explosive past and like the leopard, it often appears to change its spots. The possibilities arising from their meeting are legion, the principles of inter- action, unclear.

Formal education, like the elephant, has accumulated wisdom with age. It has slowed its pace to a cautious creep; the status quo weighs heavily on its steady feet. And like the proverbial elephant under the hands of several blind men, education is different things to different people. To some critics,

*The preparation of this paper was supported by the National Institute of Education under Contract No. HEW-NIE- C-400-81-0030 and the Department of Education under Contract No. 3008100314.

201

our current educational system has not fulfilled its charge of teaching the most basic skills. To others, creativity and a sense of open enthusiasm are sacrificed in the pursuit of more easily testable goals. Some see a pressing need for competency tests, while others fear their overuse and misapplication. With all these conflicting perceptions and pressures, it is no surprise that education moves slowly and cautiously.

Computer technology is the relative newcomer. Like the leopard, it changes appearance and direction and resists being pinned down. Hardware, software, and even software concepts can become obsolete overnight. Now there are even programs that claim to make programmers obsolete by programming computers themselves. Dissatisfaction with the state of the art in computers is often met with a variation of a comment originally made by Mark Twain about the New England weather, "If you don't like the way things are, come back in a month." Soon, the story goes, it will be possible to store more information, do calculations more quickly, print fancier documents, and perform more sophisticated tasks with available computers. The computer leopard moves swiftly, unpredictably and, at times, foolishly. From where it is now, it is hard to predict where it will be next or how stable its new resting place will be.

In the interaction between these two complex creatures, there is the possibility of either one dominating the other. Educational institutions have a tendency to drag their feet, taking slowly and often only temporarily to change. Use of audio-visual technology is commonly cited as a model for what the "computer revolution" might become—school closets are full of neglected audio-visual equipment. Will education fail to take advantage of the potential of computers? Will computer literacy, like modern math, peak as a fad and fade away?

The younger, more vociferous challenger might also dominate, forcing its own particular perspective on the educational status quo. Rightly or wrongly, computers are often seen by those who design instructional software as valuable primarily for drill and classroom management, a way to occupy students with "individualized instruction." Will these views be accepted unquestioningly by educators? Will the introduction of computers into schools compel classroom teachers to relinquish their initiative and control to a machine?

These two scenarios, of course, do not represent the only, or even the most likely, outcomes of the elephant-and-leopard encounter. A large range of compromises and negotiations is possible. And most exciting is the chance that a creative approach will emerge, modifying education in unpredicted ways, unleashing the potential of computers as sophisticated tools and establishing them as an exciting component of a powerful learning environment.

Against the general backdrop of the confrontation of computers and education, this chapter will discuss the role of computers specifically in language-arts education. It is organized around four issues which arise in the development of language-arts software:

1. the level of text on which the program focuses

2. the role of feedback

3. the possibility of providing an opportunity for learning by doing

4. the social environment the software supports

Examples of programs currently available or being designed are included in this chapter to illustrate each of the issues. The educational philosophy that emerges from these discussions emphasizes children's roles as active individuals who learn most effectively when they have some control over their educational environment and when the tasks presented to them are meaningful and motivating.

COMPUTERS AND LANGUAGE ARTS

Language arts are probably the most problematic area of education in which to assess the impact of computers. Though it is more immediately possible to envision the role of computers in teaching mathematics, many characteristics of language arts and computers do not at first glance seem to match. Computers are often viewed as number manipulators; language is made of letters, words, and sentences. Language arts require, at the core, creativity; computers require predominantly fixed, prescribed responses. Yet language arts may well be the area in which computers can have the most dramatic impact. All of the issues most frequently discussed in literature on the computer/education interaction (Fisher, 1982; Levin & Kareev, 1980; Naiman, 1982; Olds, Schwartz, & Willie, 1980; Papert, 1980) appear as well in the more narrow discussion of the computer's role in language arts.

The issues raised in this chapter arose during the development of language-arts software by my colleagues and myself at Bolt Beranek and Newman. We are currently working on QUILL, a microcomputer-based writing curriculum for upper elementary students under a contract from the Department of Education. For the past five years, we have also developed reading and writing software as part of the Center for the Study of Reading, sponsored by the National Institute of Education. The issues discussed here cover many of the decisions we made in designing our programs. I have attempted to state each of them neutrally, by asking, "What can be?" But I have also taken the liberty to express an opinion by asking, "What should be?"

AT WHAT LEVELS OF TEXT CAN/SHOULD LANGUAGE-ARTS SOFTWARE CONCENTRATE?

Designers of language-arts programs are subject to two strong influences which can profoundly affect the level of text dealt with by the program. First, workbook pages are both obvious and relatively simple ideas for programs, and workbooks focus primarily on word choice, spelling, and grammar. Second, the image of the computer as a mechanistic, detail-oriented tool pushes people toward activities focusing on the aspects of language that are most clear-cut and unambiguous. So, although texts can be analyzed and described at several levels (letters, words, sentences, paragraphs, themes), the vast majority of language-arts software currently available focuses on one of the first three: letters, words, or sentences. In fact, of 317 language arts programs listed in a Spring, 1982, catalogue published by Dresden Associates (1982), twenty-four required the student to manipulate text at the letter level (e.g., racing with the computer to type the next letter in the alphabet); one hundred seventy required the student to work with isolated words (e.g., choosing the correct synonym for a given word from a list of alternatives); eighty-two required the student to deal with phrases or sentences (e.g., choosing the correct verb for a given subject or dividing a group of words into two sentences).

Only twenty-one programs presented students with a whole text and asked them to read it, comprehend it, or even correct it. But programs largely limited to drill with letters, words, or phrases are not the inevitable outcome of using computers in language-arts education.

The Story Maker program, one of the programs our group developed, illustrates a different approach. From the beginning, one of our primary goals was to encourage children to focus on those aspects of text most often ignored by educational software (and, sometimes, by traditional textbooks)—text characteristics such as the logical flow of a narrative, the role of examples in an explanation, and the communication of characters' plans in a story. We were influenced by research in cognitive psychology investigating children's writing and reading. Research results indicate that children tend to "downslide" into concentrating on lower-level processes such as decoding (in reading) or spelling and handwriting (in writing) when the task becomes too complex for them to handle successfully at all levels

(Bruce, Collins, Rubin, & Gentner, 1982; Collins & Gentner, 1980). Our goal was to devise educational software to free children's attention from these details so they could concentrate on higher-level aspects of the text.

The first program we implemented is called Story Maker (Rubin, 1980; Rubin & Gentner, 1979). It is a tool that allows children to create stories by choosing options from a set of already-written story segments. After making a series of choices, a child has a completed story which he or she can read and show to fellow students and the teacher. If the computer has a printer, the child can get a copy of the completed story to save, illustrate, or take home. These choices are structured as a *tree,* similar to the kind of tree most frequently used for family trees, for diagrams of sentences in linguistics, and to represent the structure of the plant and animal kingdoms. Such a tree has its root at the top and its branches extending downward (see Figure 1).

The beginning of a story tree in Figure 1 illustrates the basic structure of a Story Maker activity. The tree is made up of a group of stories about a Haunted House; each story segment is contained in a box. Each story begins with "Lace opened the front door and . . . . " One possible story a child might construct within this story tree would start out: "Lace opened the front door and slipped into what looked like a bowl of spaghetti. Frankenstein was cooking it for his dinner."

The computer's role in the storymaking process is to present the structured options to children, keep track of their choices, and display or print the completed story at the end. The Story Maker program also displays a graph mirroring the structure of the story tree. Story segments are represented as boxes and the possible pathways between them as lines. On a color screen, the segments already chosen appear in a different color, while the current set of choices blinks.

The child's role in putting together the story is to make choices among directions the story can take. Because of the way the tree is structured, a choice a child makes early in the process will limit the continuations and endings the story may have. Thus, a child's decisions have consequences. In the story tree for "The Haunted House," for example, choosing "stepped on a mouse" at the beginning severely limits the stories that may follow; none of them, for one thing, involves Frankenstein.

In using Story Maker, children never get stuck worrying about punctuation, spelling or sentence structure since those details are resolved by the program. Children from kindergarten through sixth grade have used the program successfully. Because there are no right or wrong answers with Story Maker, we cannot make statements about the percentage of right answers children achieved or their grade-level equivalents. What we *can* say is that most children enjoy both the storymaking process and the end pro-

THE HAUNTED HOUSE

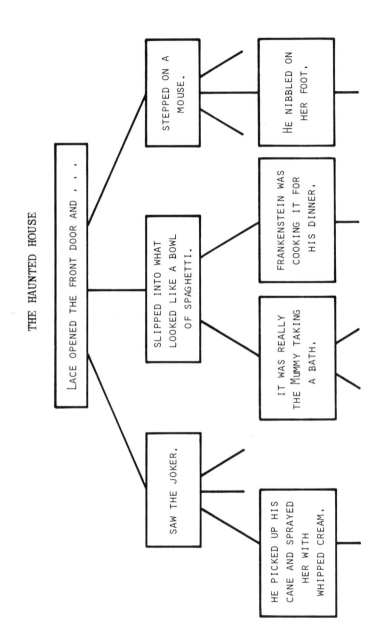

Fig. 1. The beginning of a story tree.

Never Go To Mcdonalds

Lace opened the front door and
slipped into what looked like a
bowl of spaghetti. Frankenstein was
cooking it for his dinner. Before
Frankenstein got too angry, Lace
suggested that they go to McDonalds.
When Lace and Frankenstein walked up
to the counter Frankenstein ordered
twenty-five quarter-pounders with
cheese, six gallons of coke, and
twelve large fries. The waitress was
too scared to ask him for the money.
After they carried all the food back
to the Haunted House, Frank ate every
bit of it and then...he ate Lace for
dessert!

Fig. 2. One child's illustrated Story Maker story.

duct. One fifth-grade boy spent an hour constructing a book of several different Haunted House stories for his younger sister, titled and illustrated each one (see Figure 2), drew a cover, and stapled them into a single volume.

Another particularly successful experience took place in a K–2 open classroom in which only some of the children could read. Two children who could read made a story from a science fiction story tree, reading their choices and the final product aloud to the nonreaders standing behind them. As the story progressed, the nonreaders even contributed some of their own choices. Without our consciously planning to do so, we had created a situation in which nonreaders could appreciate how reading and composing could be fun.

On the question of text level, then, it seems clear (by example) that it is possible for computers to offer language experiences which allow students to manipulate large pieces of text and to focus on the conceptual content of the passage. Given the overwhelming presence of programs that dwell on letters, words, and sentences, designers of educational software should make programs with a more sophisticated view of language a high priority.

The issue of conceptual level generalizes beyond language arts. In mathematics, arithmetic drill and practice programs are most common, but fail to exploit the potential of the machine. A more conceptually rich program, LOGO (Feurzeig & Papert, 1968; Papert, Watt, diSessa, & Weir, 1979), for example, gives students the opportunity to explore mathematical concepts by writing their own procedures to generate geometric figures. The excitement generated by children creating their own squares, circles and spirals far exceeds the motivation which comes from repetitive drill and practice. Mathematics software could move even further along the conceptual dimension by integrating reading and mathematics or by creating an environment in which math "experiments" could be carried out.

WHAT ROLE CAN/SHOULD FEEDBACK PLAY IN USING COMPUTERS IN THE LANGUAGE ARTS?

One of the most frequently heard arguments for using computers in education is their ability to provide immediate feedback on students' answers. Waiting several days or even several hours to find out whether a response is correct destroys the feedback cycle considered so central to learning; using a computer, a child can know whether the answer is right or wrong as fast or even faster than any person could respond. The unfortunate flip side of the coin is that judgments a computer can make are limited, in many cases, to preset alternatives, and the student's response is simply "right" or "wrong." There is little explanation of *why* one answer may be better than another.

In language arts, the problem is compounded by the fact that it is extremely difficult for computers to analyze free-form text. Thus, the possibility of a meaningful response in a situation less constrained than multiple-choice is quite unlikely. The computer cannot "evaluate" an English phrase in the same straightforward way it can evaluate an expression such as $(3 \times 4) + 52$, so it is difficult to come up with an appropriate response unless it has been explicitly included in the program.

An analysis of the potential role of computer feedback in education, then, is quite complex. One important distinction to draw is that between *feedback* and *response*. The Story Maker program described above does respond, because each time a student makes a choice, a new piece of text is added to the story and new choices are displayed. It provides no feedback, however, stated in terms of right and wrong. A program such as LOGO responds even more actively by carrying out instructions that are typed by the student. The program makes no assessment of correctness, but it does allow the child to make his or her own judgment as to whether the action taken by the computer was what the child intended.

In developing our own language-arts software, we have attempted to include some means of giving students a tangible measure of their progress without compromising our focus on the higher organizational levels of text. In Story Maker, one solution took the form of providing a goal for a child at the beginning of each story that describes something about the story to be generated—an event to take place, a particular structure to be included, or a certain rhetorical effect to be produced. A set of event-oriented goals for the Haunted House story tree is given here:

> Write a story in which . . .
> 1. Lace marries the Mummy.
> 2. Lace dies of rat bites.
> 3. Michelle helps Lace escape from the Vampire.
> 4. Lace gets eaten.
> 5. Lace meets the skeletons.

The computer also knows what paths through the tree satisfy each of the goals and can therefore compare a child's chosen path with the expected one and comment on whether they coincide. In a case where the two did not match, the program might say:

> Well, Andee, you didn't quite end up with the story I expected. It looks like all your choices were correct until choice #2. Remember, your goal was to write a story in which *a green tomato gets devoured by a monster.*

For choice #2 you picked *I feel terribly ripe today. "Dead ripe" it's called in tomato talk.*

A better choice would have been

I'm still a kid. It's easy to tell the grown-ups apart from the kids with us tomatoes because the kids are still a bit green like me.

In a moment, I will give you a chance to try this story again.

For some students, the goal feature provided additional motivation and focus to their Story Maker activities; others still preferred the more exploratory mode.

We investigated the issue of feedback further by designing Textman, another reading/writing program for upper elementary students (Zacchei, 1982). Textman is a variant of the familiar Hangman game, but instead of putting together letters to form words, players put sentences together to form texts. Players receive a list of sentences from which they are to choose and order the correct subset. They are also given a description of the text they are to construct. For example, they could choose a conversation between Alice-in-Wonderland and the Cheshire cat (see Appendix), a thank-you letter from a girl to her grandmother, a fable illustrating the theme that greed leads to bad consequences, or a paragraph from a suspense story. In this format, the author, intended audience, and purpose of the selection may be specified, as well as a few paragraphs that either precede or follow the text in question. All of the selections we used were taken from real texts, rather than being written explicitly for Textman. For each turn, the child designates a sentence and the position in the paragraph it should occupy; the program responds (1) that both choices are correct; (2) that the sentence does not belong in the paragraph; or (3) that it does belong in the paragraph, but in a different place.

Fifth-grade students in Lexington, Massachusetts, used the Textman program for 6 weeks. The game-like format of the activity seemed to increase their attention to the task. They were particularly careful about their guesses when they were about to hang the man; one child almost refused to make a final guess for fear of completing the figure and losing the game. We were not surprised by their enthusiasm for the program, but we were less prepared for the fact that they worked out some of the examples (which were reproduced in a notebook) at home, then checked them on the computer.

The feedback Textman supplies is quite limited at this point. One possible extension would be to provide some explanation to children for particular errors they make, for example, "Sentence 1 cannot go directly after sentence 3 because the speaker in sentence 3 hasn't been introduced into the story yet." Part of our research has been an attempt to identify the most common errors children make in the current set of Textman texts so that we can include explanatory responses in the program.

The issues surrounding the idea of feedback, then, are not yet completely defined. Children often respond to a program that judges that their answer is right or wrong—possibly because this is the model many school activities provide. On the other hand, requiring such feedback places significant constraints on the kind of responses a child can make. Alternate notions of feedback—in which, for example, students respond to each other using the computer—need to be explored.

HOW CAN/SHOULD COMPUTERS PROVIDE OPPORTUNITIES FOR LEARNING BY DOING?

The most limited view of computers' role in language-arts education provides children little opportunity for operating as initiating agents. Learning to read is often equated with learning to decode individual words (both on and off the computer); when reading comprehension is considered, selections on the computer are of necessity relatively short and questions are in multiple-choice format. When we consider writing, the gap is even larger. Some programs that purport to teach writing are actually drills concentrating on punctuation, capitalization, or usage. Real writing requires initiative and action on the part of the author; there is no substitute for *writing* in learning to write (Graves, 1977). Unfortunately, the traditional notions of computer-aided instruction (CAI) do not leave room for children to express themselves freely in writing.

This apparent impasse is fairly easily resolved, though, when we step outside the bounds of traditional CAI. By providing tools that facilitate writing and revising, and by creating communication environments that naturally encourage writing, computers may actually be able to offer new opportunities for learning by doing that are not available in noncomputer classrooms. Creating these situations is one of the goals of QUILL, the writing curriculum we are developing. The following examples are drawn from our plans for this curriculum.

The most obvious computer tool to provide to any writer—novice or expert—is a text editor. By facilitating revisions and thereby alleviating a writer's concern for getting a piece of writing letter-perfect the first time around, a text editor can help writers get started and keep going. A writer need not ask whether a revision is worth the trouble of recopying the page. Making a large change, such as rearranging paragraphs, is as simple to accomplish with a text editor as changing a few words. Thus, students are encouraged to regard a text constantly as a work in progress. Although research on the effect of using a text editor on children's writing is only in its preliminary stages, one of the most consistent results is that children do write *more* using a text editor than they do with pencil and paper (Levin, Boruta, & Vasconcellos, this volume; Daiute & Taylor, 1981).

Another kind of program that makes writing easier is one that offers formatting aids. These programs range from fairly standard tools for centering, indenting, and justifying text, to more sophisticated programs for producing tables of contents, title pages, and indexes for books or columns, and headlines for newspapers. For many children, producing attractive finished products with regular margins and evenly-indented paragraphs is an exciting possibility because it encourages them to view their writing with respect. Given a suitable classroom environment, these formatting tools give children the opportunity to publish their written work—that is, to polish it and make it available to an audience of classmates, friends, teachers, and parents. A classroom newspaper activity, for example, might include the choosing of an editorial board responsible for the paper's layout, submission of articles to the editors of various departments (news, features, sports, food), and finally, construction of the newspaper, including headlines, bylines, graphics and a listing of editorial board members. An alternate activity might be less structured, allowing students to write, read, and even comment on articles whenever they wish as the newspaper grows. In both cases, the most important feature is that the newspaper articles are written to be read, not to be turned in as a composition and forgotten.

Producing expository text is another area where computers can help provide a meaningful context for learning by doing. Although students in the upper elementary grades are occasionally asked to write informational pieces, these do not often serve to inform anyone of anything; the teacher, often the only person who reads a student's work, usually knows the information already. In an attempt to change this pattern, we intend to include in our writing curriculum an information exchange system that allows students to enter questions about topics in which they are interested. Other students can then answer the questions from their own knowledge or reading. One question may receive several answers or a composite response started by one student and amended by others. Here again, students are learning to write by writing—and in a situation where the product is being written for and read by a real audience.

Integral to each of these potential uses of computers in language arts is the principle that the student remain in control of the computer–person interaction (Olds *et al.,* 1980). The student decides what to write and when to write it, using the computer's collection of tools to make the job easier.

Because learning to write is critically dependent on initiative, computer-based writing activities need to be especially cautious about undermining students' sense of control over their task.

WHAT KIND OF SOCIAL ENVIRONMENT
CAN/SHOULD THE COMPUTER SUPPORT?

As in the foregoing discussion of learning by doing, the traditional CAI image provides only a limited answer to the question. The predominant image of children using computers is of a single child sitting alone in front of a terminal for a prescribed period of time several days a week. The computer keeps track of his or her performance and progress, and produces periodic records for the teacher. Students are not aware of each other's experiences or problems with the machine; in fact, the lack of opportunity for competition is often noted as a positive characteristic of CAI. Unfortunately, it also reduces the opportunity for fruitful communication among students.

But computers do not have to restrict or isolate students to be used effectively. In fact, because language-arts education has as a primary goal the development of effective communication skills, an overabundance of non-communicative activities would be counterproductive. In terms of language-arts education, "communicating with a computer" should be taken as only one of its two possible interpretations: communicating with other people using a computer as an environment and tool.

The descriptions of formatting aids and an information exchange illustrate some ways in which students can communicate using the computer. In addition, we plan to include in our curriculum the most basic communication tool on a computer: a message system. Such systems have been used to increase communicative potential in areas as different as the computer-science research community (Rude, Malone, & Mooers, 1979) and a school for the deaf (Rubinstein & Rollins, 1978). In the deaf school, a message system was only one of several programs provided for the students, yet it accounted for well over its share of computer use. A computer-based message system has some advantages over other methods of communicating because it allows messages to be left at any time (in contrast to the telephone), it provides a permanent copy of the message which can be reread (in contrast to oral messages) or even printed several times (in contrast to letters). In addition, copies of the same message can be sent to several people simultaneously and, with the appropriate hardware, messages can be sent over long distances. This last possibility is currently being realized in

a connection between microcomputers in Oceanside, California, and Atha-
pascan schools outside of Fairbanks, Alaska (Kleiman & Humphrey, 1982).

Not only does a message system enhance communication possibilities for
students, it can also catalyze the formation of social groups in a classroom
or school. Clubs can form around topics of common interest such as di-
nosaurs, punk rock groups, jokes, or book reviews. Relevant messages can
then be automatically sent to all members of the club. Becoming a "computer pal" with a child in another classroom can lead to social interactions
that would not have occurred otherwise.

All of the components of the writing curriculum I have described so far
emphasize the idea of audience, but have not explored the possibility of
group authorship. An extension to Story Maker makes collaboration on a
story relatively simple. The basic idea is that, after exploring a story tree
and creating several stories from it, many children want to add their own
segment. A second program, Story Maker Maker, makes it possible for
students to add their own segment or sequence of segments, or to continue
a branch of the story rather than letting it end. Not only does this method
provide a natural audience for the story pieces children write (as classmates
use the tree, they read each other's contributions), but the end product is
a group story—or, more accurately, a group of group stories. The Haunted
House story tree was actually composed by several third graders who gradually added their own ideas to the existing tree.

Recent experience using text editors and related programs in upper elementary classrooms has demonstrated that there are advantages to two children working at a terminal together. Often one will remember the technical
details (such as when to type RETURN) if the other one forgets. If two
children work well together, they can enhance each other's writing process
and help avoid writer's block. However, there is an inevitable conflict here
between fostering collaborative writing and giving children the opportunity
to develop their own personal writing "voice" (Graves, 1977). One partial
solution is to encourage one child to dictate while the other transcribes; this
preserves a single child's authorship while still making it possible for one
to help the other through difficult spots. Another approach is simply to
mix individual and collaborative writing experiences throughout the curriculum.

Similar possibilities exist when computers are introduced into other subject areas. Writing LOGO procedures—another form of composition—has
been successfully accomplished by individual students and students working
in pairs. The SEARCH series, developed by Snyder in Cambridge over the
past several years, requires students to work in groups because it displays
complex information for only a short time. Groups of four or five students

learn that the only way to complete the activity successfully is to divide up the responsibility for reading information off the screen (Jabs, 1981).

The possibilities for social structures instigated by computers in education are much more complex than the choice between keeping the machine in the classroom and removing it to a resource room. Computers can either encourage or discourage communication among students; they can either isolate or integrate their reading and writing experiences. Much of the choice depends on the teacher, the already established structure of the classroom (Amarel, this volume), and the possibilities the software makes available.

CONCLUSION

In the context of the meeting between the elephant of education and the computerized leopard, the issues surrounding the uses of computers in language arts are not only significant but far-reaching in their implications. Each of the issues discussed above has its parallels in other subjects. Taken together, they represent important issues to consider in designing software, creating a curriculum, organizing a classroom, and training teachers. How much will we allow the current excitement surrounding computers to influence education? To invade it? How much will we tame that excitement? Behind these decisions lie fundamental questions about educational philosophy and the role of schools. How they will be played out in the computer arena is one of the more interesting questions about education today.

ACKNOWLEDGMENTS

I would like to thank Chip Bruce and Kathleen Starr for help in overcoming writer's block; Allan Collins, Andy Fox, Jim Levin and Denis Newman for helpful comments; and Cindy Hunt for putting it all together. Requests for reprints should be sent to Andee Rubin, Bolt Beranek and Newman Inc., 50 Moulton Street, Cambridge, Massachusetts 02238.

REFERENCES

Bruce, B. C., Collins, A., Rubin, A. D., & Gentner, D. Three perspectives on writing. *Educational Psychologist,* 1982, *17,* 131–145.

Carroll, L. *Alice in Wonderland.* New York: Washington Square Press, 1951. (Original publication: 1865.)

Collins, A., & Gentner, D. A framework for a cognitive theory of writing. In Lee Gregg & E. Steinberg (Eds.), *Processes in writing.* Hillsdale, New Jersey: Erlbaum, 1980.

Daiute, C., & Taylor, R. Computers and improvement of writing. Submitted to ACM Conference, 1981. (Reprints from Dr. Colette Daiute, Box 23, Teachers' College, Columbia University, New York, New York 10027.)

Dresden Associates, *School Microware,* Spring, 1982. (Copies from Dresden Associates, P.O. Box 246, Dresden, Maine 04342.)

Feurzeig, W., & Papert, S. A programming language as a conceptual framework for teaching mathematics. In *Proceedings of the NATO Science Conference on Computers and Learning,* Nice, France, 1968.

Fisher, F. *Computer-assisted education: What's not hcppening?* Unpublished manuscript, 1982. (Reprints from Dr. Francis Fisher, Haverford College, Haverford, Pennsylvania 19041.)

Graves, D. H. A writing process evaluation. *Language Arts,* 1977, *54,* 817–823.

Jabs, C. Game playing allowed. *Electronic learning,* November/December, 1981, Vol. 1, No. 2, 62–65.

Kleiman, G., & Humphrey, M. Word processing in the classroom. *Compute!,* March, 1982.

Levin, J. A., & Kareev, Y. *Personal computers and education: The challenge to schools.* Center for Human Information Processing Report 98, University of California, San Diego, 1980. (Reprints from Dr. James A. Levin, Laboratory for Comparative Human Cognition, University of California at San Diego, La Jolla, California 92093.)

Naiman, A. *Microcomputers in education: An introduction.* Cambridge, Massachusetts: Technical Education Research Center, Inc. and Northeast Regional Exchange, 1982. (Copies from Adeline Naiman, Technical Education Research Centers, 8 Eliot Street, Cambridge, Massachusetts 02138.)

Olds, H. F., Schwartz, J. L., & Willie, N. A. *People and Computers: Who teaches whom?* Newton, Massachusetts Education Development Center, 1980. (Copies from Dr. Judah Schwartz, Education Development Center Inc., 55 Chapel Street, Newton, Massachusetts 02160.)

Papert, S. *Mindstorms: Children, computers, and powerful ideas.* Brighton, England: Harvester, 1980.

Papert, S., Watt, D., diSessa, A., & Weir, S. Final Report of the Brookline LOGO Project, Artificial Intelligence Memo No. 545, Artificial Intelligence Laboratory, Massachusetts Institute of Technology, September 1979. (Copies from Dr. Seymour Papert, Division of Study and Research in Education, Massachusetts Institute of Technology, Cambridge, Massachusetts 02139.)

Rubin, A. D. Making stories, making sense. *Language Arts,* March, 1980, 285–298.

Rubin, A. D., & Gentner, D. An educational technique to encourage practice with high-level aspects of texts. Paper presented at the National Reading Conference, San Antonio, December, 1979. (Reprints from Andee Rubin, Bolt Beranek and Newman, 50 Moulton Street, Cambridge, Massachusetts 02238.)

Rubinstein, R., & Rollins, A. *Demonstration of use of computer-aided instruction with handicapped children.* Cambridge, Massachusetts: Bolt Beranek and Newman, Report No. 4049, 1978. (Copies from Charlotte Mooers, Bolt Beranek and Newman Inc., 50 Moulton Street, Cambridge, Massachusetts 02238.)

Rude, R. V., Malone, D. L., & Mooers, C. D. *The Hermes message system.* Cambridge, Massachusetts: Bolt Beranek and Newman, 1979. (Copies from Charlotte Mooers, Bolt Beranek and Newman, 50 Moulton Street, Cambridge, Massachusetts 02238.)

Zacchei, D. The Adventures and Exploits of the Dynamic Story Maker and Textman. *Classroom Computer News,* May/June, 1982, Vol. 5, No. 2, 28–30, 76–77.

APPENDIX: A SAMPLE TEXTMAN ACTIVITY:
Alice and the Cheshire Cat

The Cat only grinned when it saw Alice. It looked good-natured, she thought: still it had very long claws and a great many teeth, so she felt that it ought to be treated with respect.

"Cheshire-Puss," she began, rather timidly, as she did not at all know whether it would like the name: however, it only grinned a little wider. "Come, it's pleased so far," thought Alice, and she went on. "Would you tell me, please, which way I ought to go from here?"

___	___	___	___	___
A	B	C	D	E

1. "—so long as I get somewhere," Alice added as an explanation.
2. "Oh, you can't help that," said the Cat, "we're all mad here. I'm mad. You're mad."
3. "Digging for apples, indeed!" said the Rabbit angrily. "Here! Come and help me out of this!"
4. "That depends a good deal on where you want to get to," said the Cat.
5. "Oh, you're sure to do that," said the Cat, "if you only walk long enough."
6. "Talking of axes," said the Duchess, "chop off her head!"
7. "How do you know I'm mad?" said Alice.
8. "I don't much care where—" said Alice.
9. "Then it doesn't matter! which way you go," said the Cat.
(Carroll, 1951).

12

Microcomputer-Based Environments for Writing: A Writer's Assistant

James A. Levin
Marcia J. Boruta
Mary T. Vasconcellos

INTRODUCTION

How does one become an expert writer? Recent work on problem solving (Chi, Feltovich, & Glaser, 1981; Larkin, McDermott, Simon, & Simon, 1980) has shown that expert solvers of physics problems bring several different organizations to bear on these tasks, initially applying more global qualitative analyses, then moving toward more detailed quantitative expressions. The qualitative conceptual organizations of the task guide experts through the details of the local quantitative analysis, allowing them to solve the problem quickly. Novices, on the other hand, only have the more local level of analysis, and start writing equations, getting lost in the details because they lack the overall organization.

---

*The Spencer Foundation and The Sloan Foundation provided financial support for this work. Send request for reprints to J. A. Levin, LCHC (D-003), UCSD, La Jolla, CA 92093.

This difference between novices and experts has a direct analogy in the writing domain: experts appear to the uninitiated to start by writing words, yet novices who do so quickly get lost in the details, producing muddled text. An expert writer differs from a novice by operating at several different levels, both global and local, while a novice writer, like the novice physics problem solvers, can operate only at a few local levels.

We have been conducting research into the nature of writing expertise and its acquisition. Our approach has drawn upon the cognitive science framework for writing developed by Bruce, Collins, Rubin, and Gentner (1982). Within this framework, writing is a communicative action that results from multiple cognitive processes that operate simultaneously, producing text through their interaction. For example, there are processes that draw a letter on paper, those that select words and order them in sentences, and those that generate, select, and organize ideas. While an expert writer can operate competently on these many levels, a novice tends to become locked into the more local levels, a phenomena called *downsliding* by Bruce *et al.*

The concept of dynamic support for writing is central to our work. We have been constructing microcomputer-based environments for writing that provide tools that assist at different levels in the writing process. These environments serve both as powerful research settings for investigating the multiple processes of writing, and as teaching techniques for helping novice writers acquire expertise. One of these environments is a word processor program that people can use to generate and modify their own text, which we call a Writer's Assistant.[1] The writer types the text into a microcomputer and the text is displayed on a video screen. When the computer is attached to a printer, the writer can easily produce a printed copy. This system is simple enough that elementary school children have quickly learned to use it to create and modify text of different sorts.

The Writer's Assistant is a powerful tool for research on the writing processes. It serves as a data collection device, since it keeps a detailed "trace" of the keystroke actions taken by a writer in generating and changing the text. We have been using these trace data to study the processes involved in writing. For example, two boys, Gerry and James, used the Writer's Assistant to create a story they named "Dragon Tamer." We have used their data to analyze relatively low-level processes, such as spelling or typing correction. For example, in one case, Gerry and James changes sour to sor¢¢¢r to sorcery.

---

[1]The Writer's Assistant program has been written in UCSD-Pascal by Jose Vasconcellos. It is based on an early version of the UCSD-Pascal Screen Editor. Thanks to Dr. Kenneth Bowles and the members of the UCSD-Pascal Project for their assistance.

Data from the Writer's Assistant also show indications of higher-level, more global actions. The Writer's Assistant keeps track of large-scale deletion of previously entered text, as well as insertion of new text. For example, in the story described above, the title of the story initially was "Dragon Slayer." At the very end of their writing process, the boys deleted that title, and replaced it with "Dragon Tamer." This title change reflects a major thematic modification that the boys made halfway through their story. They had described the king's promise as "whoever slayed the dragon would get his daughter's hand in marrige, and riches beyond imagination." They then went back and inserted after "slayed" the phrase "or tamed." From this, we can infer that they had decided at this point to end the story with the hero taming the dragon and claiming his reward rather than the conventional, more violent ending.

To complement these keystroke data, we have conducted detailed field observations of children using this system in the classroom. The keystroke data files tell what was typed in what order; the field notes tell who did the typing and what interactions occurred during the course of the writing. With this information we have begun to look at the progression to expertise in writing.

A second major function of the Writer's Assistant for our research is to allow us to provide differing amounts of support in different areas to novice writers. By observing their writing actions, given selected kinds of support, we can start to disentangle the complex interactions among the multiple processes that constitute writing. This use of microcomputer-based writing environments is similar to an approach to educational evaluation called "dynamic assessment" (Brown & Ferrara, 1982; Feuerstein, 1979), which measures ability or knowledge in terms of the amount of help needed by the subject in order to solve a problem successfully.

DYNAMIC SUPPORT FOR WRITING

Support is provided by any resources external to a person that contribute to the accomplishment of a task. Dynamic support is support that allows a novice to accomplish a task, but which is progressively withdrawn as the person acquires expertise. In the domain of writing, our aim has been to provide sufficient support to allow novices to accomplish writing tasks that serve the novices' own goals. For novices, much of the effort of writing is distributed externally, both over other people in the setting and over inanimate resources, such as print and computers. As the novice writer becomes an expert, this external support becomes less necessary, as more of the cognitive processing can be done by the writer. Our goal in designing microcomputer-based environments for writing has been to create settings in which the support provided by the environment can be reduced dynamically as the writer progresses to expertise.

A Classroom Electronic Newspaper

In our work with a third–fourth grade classroom during the spring of 1981, we focused the writing activities of the children by using an Apple II computer to create classroom newspapers. The newspaper text file was structured into different sections (news, sports, TV reviews, cookbook, jokes, etc.). The students worked on each issue of the newspaper over the course of a month, adding new stories and modifying existing ones. Then the paper was printed out and distributed. We provided dynamic support within this writing environment in several ways. Some sections of the newspaper provided considerable structure, requiring only that the children fill in the blanks, in a sort of computerized "mad-lib." For example, one story form was:

ONCE A ##### WAS ##### IN A #####.
HE TRIED TO GET ##### THROUGH THE #####.
HE ##### WITH ##### AND #####, BUT HE #####.

One child filled in these blanks to produce the following little "story":

ONCE A FROG WAS IN A POND .HE
WANTED TO SEE THE WORLD . HE TRIED TO
GET THROUGH THE CAGE . HE TRIED
WITH ALL HIS MIGHT , BUT HE CHOULDN'T.

A pair of children, Taffy and Edwin, filled in the blanks in the first sentence, then finished the story in a completely different way. This writing environment, unlike paper and pencil worksheets, allows them easily to go beyond the support provided.

ONCE AN APPLE WAS COMPUTER IN A
CLASSROOM. SHE HELPED TEACH CHILDREN
HOW TO SAY SOMETHING. ONE DAY THE
COMPUTER BROKE DOWN BECAUSE SHE HAD
NO CHILDREN TO TEACH. THE CHILDREN
CAME BACK AND PUT A BANDAGE ON HER

SCREEN. THE COMPUTER FELT BETTER AND
BEGIN TEACHING AGAIN. THE CLASS LIVED
HAPPILY EVER AFTER.

Other sections provided partial support: A story was started but left for students to finish, or a question was posed and students inserted their own replies. For instance, in a "Letters to the Editor" section, the question was posed, "How is writing with the computer different from writing with pencil and paper?" Various groups of students supplied various answers: "Because its funner and easier than writing with pencil and paper. Also it does not hurt your hand." responded Jane and Mary.

In some sections, just the section header was supplied ("Weather") and students started new stories with this minimal support. Even in these cases, there quickly arose social/computer support in the form of other students' articles in these sections. One weather report started "Today is May 9, 1981. It is really nice out. The sky is clear, and there are very few clouds. . . . " The next article, by Taffy and Alice, went: "Today is June 5, 1981. It's cloudy today . The temperture is 72 deegres. The grass is dewy . It might rain. One reason I think so is because a class did an Indian rain dance."

The newspaper file thus contained sections that varied in the amount of support they provided to writers, from substantial support to minimal support. The children were allowed to select which section to work on during their writing time, and most of the children worked on several different sections during the school year. Some children moved beyond even the minimal level of support provided by the "section header" support, creating totally new text files that started with a blank screen.

The Writer's Assistant

The Writer's Assistant itself provided substantial support for writing. It is a "screen" editor, and thus follows the general principle of "what you see (on the screen) is what you get (when you print it out)." When changes in the text are made, the text on the screen is correct. There are no erasure marks, no crossed out sections, no squashed insertions. The cost of correcting errors or making changes is lowered so that students easily can create "perfect" text. Papert, Watt, diSessa, and Weir (1979) describe a "learning-disabled" girl who had great difficulty writing with paper and pencil. She was able to write much more fluently when given the opportunity to create error-free text. Whenever she did make an error with the "line" editor she was using, she pushed the RETURN key until the error scrolled off the screen. The ability to create perfect text was cited by our novice writers as a great advantage over pencil and paper. In the "Letters to the Editor" section of the class newspaper, the question was posed, "How is writing with the computer different from writing with pencil and paper?" One response entered by two fourth-graders went, "You can write faster and better. You also don't need to erase." Another pair of writers concurred: "Because you can go faster on the computer. Also you don,t have to use pencil and paper and you don,t have to erase mistakes you make."

The Writer's Assistant, like many computer editors or word processors, has two ways of deleting text. One way is with a "Drop" command, which allows text to be deleted anywhere in the text. The other way is with a single character erase key, which can be used while entering new text. This "local" deletion is most often used to erase a single character just typed, because to delete previous characters requires also deleting all the intervening ones as well.

The Writer's Assistant also provides a set of other commands, some standard for computer text editors and others specially tailored for helping elementary school children enter and modify text. As with most other text editors, the Writer's Assistant provides ways to move through the text, either letter by letter, line by line, or screenful by screenful. The Writer's Assistant also provides ways to find a particular pattern of characters in a text, to replace systematically specified characters with others, and to move blocks of text.

We provided the children with some special commands to help them write. These included a command to carry out spelling verification of a selected word, a command to rearrange text by putting it into either paragraph format or individual sentence format, and a command to allow writers to try out combinations of words or phrases systematically. Because the Writer's Assistant was designed especially for the beginning writer, a "Help" command was added to the program, which provided information about how to use the commands.

The special command that was used most frequently by the students was the spelling verification command. To use this command, the writer moves the cursor over a word and asks for verification. The Writer's Assistant searches a spelling file, attempting to make a phonetic match. If a match is found, the word is presented to the writer, along with a short definition. If the writer doesn't accept the suggested word, then the search continues, until the spelling file is exhausted. With this approach to spelling correction, the writer has first to make a guess at the correct spelling of a word, then immediately receives feedback about that guess.

Social Support for Writing

Social support for writing was provided in several important ways. The use of the computer in the classroom we worked in went very smoothly, largely because the class was organized into "centers" among which pairs of students rotated, during three days each week. This same classroom was run on a "whole class" basis two days a week, so we were able to see repeatedly that the uses of microcomputers described here were much more compatible with a "center" organization than with a "whole class" organization. The other advantage of the "center" organization is that it provided a natural way to allocate turns on the one computer in the classroom to students, in a way that each student could understand and anticipate. Also, it made computer use an integral part of the classroom curriculum.

It was crucially important that pairs of children used the computer at a given time. From the point of view of the teacher, the demand upon his resources was substantially reduced, as most of the problems that arose for one student could almost immediately be handled by the other student. Quinsaat (1981) describes in detail the advantages of having pairs of children use the computer in a classroom. In contrast to the stereotype that computer use leads to isolation of students from their peers, this paired student use generates substantially increased interaction between peers, compared with other classroom activities. The interactions are most often cooperative interactions, with mutual benefit to both students in dividing up the task at hand. For research purposes, having pairs of children use the computer generates ecologically valid "protocols" of the children's writing processes, as each child explains to the other what actions to take and reasons for those actions when there is a conflict.

Because many of the trivial problems could be handled by the students themselves, the teacher was able to allocate his time to the computer writing center in a more fruitful way, providing different kinds of support tailored to the needs of the students. For some relatively expert students, he assigned them to the center without further involvement on his part. For other students, he would suggest a writing task to work on at the beginning, allowing them to work on this task by themselves. For more novice writers, he would spend his time with the pair, providing overall direction, while leaving the details to be worked out by the students. For total novices, he would actively elicit the contents of the newspaper stories, and sometimes even type the stories in. Thus, he was providing very dynamic support, in exactly the way that teachers have always provided such support to the extent allowed by the organizational limitations of their classrooms.

Dynamic support was also provided by the sequence in which the teacher introduced the computer and the Writer's Assistant. In our work with a classroom in the spring of 1981, the teacher introduced the children to the computer through the use of a Typing Tutor program, which helped them to learn the location of the letters on the keyboard. Next, they used a Story Maker program (Rubin, 1980) to generate and print out a number of stories. The Writer's Assistant was then introduced, with the children given simple "fill-in-the-blank" exercises that only required using the basic commands. Finally, the children learned to carry out the full range of text generation and manipulation, as new commands were introduced in the context of less-structured exercises within the class newspaper activity.

The same teacher ran two summer school classes, each of which only extended over 2 weeks. In these classes, the teacher bypassed using the typing tutor, starting immediately with the storymaker program and the Writer's Assistant. There was a wider range of ages in these classes, with the older children quickly mastering the Writer's Assistant and entering completely new stories, younger children working .within the more supportive frame of the newspaper file, and the youngest children continuing to work with the Story Maker program.

EXPLORATORY ANALYSIS OF WRITING PROCESSES

We present here some preliminary analyses of pilot data collected in the initial stages of our study of problem solving while writing, using the microcomputer-based environments described above during the spring of 1981. Our work in this area is ongoing; we worked with the same teacher during the fall of 1981, and continued the study through the winter and spring of 1982, collecting data of the use of these writing tools during a full school year. Our preliminary data are presented here to illustrate some of the ways we have tried to integrate keystroke data with field observation in order to shed light on the multiple interacting processes involved in writing.

Analysis of Problem-Solving Episodes

By using both keystroke data and field observation notes, we have been able to analyze episodes in which writers have encountered and solved problems in writing. In this context, a problem is defined as a situation in which people are unable to reach some goal after repeated attempts (Hutchins & Levin, 1981). Writers can be "blocked" at any of the multiple levels of processing involved in writing.

The "block" to writing may occur at relatively low levels. For example, two boys, Howie and Sam, were entering into the class newspaper a review of a book called "Charlie and the Chocolate Factory." They were just finishing the first part of the review: ". . . Then the mother said who is going to take Cahharlie to the chocolate factory." Howie started the next sentence: gGranpa gGorge said Il/will". Looking around for the apostrophe key, so he could type *I'll,* he pressed *7,* the key, which when shifted, gives the apostrophe. They erased that and tried holding down the CTRL key and typing *7,* then holding down the ESC and 7 keys. After repeated attempts to solve this low-level problem, they selected an alternative action, perhaps less satisfactory on its own merits, but "satisficing" in that they could proceed with the overall task. Finally, Sam said, "Just type *I will.*" Howie typed, "I will take him."

This episode illustrates the benefits of having pairs of children use a computer together, both for research and for learning. Often, when one child encounters a block in writing, the other child, bringing a different point of view, can solve the problem by suggesting an alternative approach. The first child not only benefits from having the immediate problem solved, but is exposed to alternative ways to think about the task. Taking a different "point of view" can often lead to breaking through a problem-solving block (Hutchins & Levin, 1981).

The interaction in this "apostrophe" episode was characteristic of the ways these boys interacted while writing, and was also common among other pairs of children we observed. These boys did not strictly divide the task into components at the same level, a division of labor which we observed in other kinds of computer use (Levin & Kareev, 1980). We have seen two kinds of peer-level division of labor: some children divide the task into long alternating turns with little participation when it is not their turn; other children alternate at much shorter time intervals (for example, sharing the typing of a single word). These two boys participated simultaneously but at different levels. One took prime responsibility for entering text, and the other participated at a more global level, suggesting what to say. The "typer," however, took an active role in the composition process, as he didn't always follow suggestions, but instead would type something different or would stop to discuss what should be said.

By combining both keystroke data and field observation notes, we have been able to identify some of the ways that children can deal with "blocks" to writing. Although the keystroke data show precisely what actions were ultimately taken, the field observations add rich detail of who took those actions, what discussion and nonverbal interaction preceeded the actions, and the manner in which the actions were taken.

Analysis of Deletion Episodes

We have analyzed the keystroke data of children's work with the Writer's Assistant to produce a classification of the episodes of deletions. Most of the deletions occur during "local editing." This is the use of the single character delete key while entering new text.

Most of the local deletion episodes are singlets: 56% of the 141 episodes in the Dragon Tamer story, for instance, were isolated, single-letter deletions. The remaining multiple, adjacent deletions followed one of the following patterns: total replacement (*in* → at), partial replacement (*in* → on), and overdeletion (*in* → if). We classified the cases of local deletion made during an insertion into the following categories: (1) capitalization (a letter is replaced by the same letter of the opposite case); (2) correction of spelling or typing errors (one or more letters in a word are changed, while other letters are retained); (3) punctuation and spacing (adding or deleting periods or spaces, changing periods to commas, adding commas); (4) correcting verb tense (ending of verb deleted, different ending added); (5) word choice (all the letters of a word are deleted and another word is entered); and (6) adding omitted words (words are deleted, a word added, then the deleted words reentered).

Major structural changes were carried out by using the separate deletion command. By comparing what is deleted and what is then inserted, we have evidence of the level of text organization the writer is concentrating on at that moment. For example, the data can provide an indication that the writer is "downsliding" at that point, focusing on the local details of word selection and spelling, and ignoring the large-scale organizational issues (Collins & Gentner, 1979).

Global Evaluation of Impact

At the beginning and at the end of the use of the Writer's Assistant during the spring of 1981, children in the experimental class and in a control class wrote on a topic using paper and pencil. The students generated these pre- and post-computer-use writing samples under instruction to do the best they could in the time given. No other help was given by the teacher. We have analyzed these samples with respect to two measures: (1) length of samples, in number of words, and (2) overall quality of the samples, using a holistic rating on a four-point scale. Our analysis of these data indicates a significant change in the writing of the children in the experimental class.

We found an increase of 64% in the number of words in the prompted writing of the experimental class after working for 4 months with the microcomputer writing environments, increasing from an average length of 45.1 words per sample to 74.1 words per sample. The control classrooms showed no increase in average length in their prompted writing samples (pre = 44.6; post = 46.4).

The quality rating was based on a four-point scale, with the judge blind to the classroom from which the samples belonged.[2] The judgments were "holistic," with adherence to topic and organization emphasized. The mechanics of spelling and punctuation were deemphasized. The qualitative score for the experimental class increased from 2.00 to 3.09 after the 4-month period in which they were using the Writer's Assistant. The control classrooms had a pre-experiment score of 2.27 and a post-experiment score of 2.24.

ONGOING WORK

Our computer-based environments for writing have been constructed to provide us with data on the cognitive processes involved at different points in the multilevel interacting complex that comprises writing. We are extending the current work in three main directions: (1) development of an interpreter of interactive text; (2) construction of an electronic message system; and (3) the implementation of various writing simulation games. Each of these directions will give us powerful new ways to collect data on writing processes at different levels.

Interactive Text

One new direction is developing environments in which writers can create and modify interactive text. This is text for which the writer builds in alternative choices that the reader can take. A reader interacts with a computer program that displays text and presents alternatives from which a reader can select. The text displayed after a reader makes a choice is an interactive product of the alternatives provided by the writer and the selection made by the reader. (The writer and the reader may be the same person at different times, or different people.)

This interactive text interpreter allows a writer to structure text in various ways for readers. For example, the writer can provide an initial table of

---

[2]Our thanks to Marilyn Quinsaat for performing the holistic scoring of the writing samples.

contents, where a choice takes the reader automatically to the selected section. Or the writer can create a "story world," within which the reader can explore creating his or her own particular story. The concept of interactive text was foreshadowed by the Story Maker programs developed by Rubin (1980; Chapter 11, this volume). A "Dungeon Master" in a *Dungeons & Dragons* game could use this interactive text mechanism as a sort of "Dungeon Master's Assistant," which presents the descriptions of the parts of the dungeon occupied by the players.

For research purposes, this interactive text interpreter will help us gather data on larger-scale text organization, as writers will be encouraged to build these units into their interactive texts. By observing detailed data on creation and modification of the various text units in an interactive text, we will have much richer data on the higher-level organization of writing.

Electronic Message Systems

One of the main foci of our research (and a second direction) has been on the role that external resources play in writing and in the acquisition of writing expertise. We have been working with Ron and Suzanne Scollon of the University of Alaska, Fairbanks, to develop a system using microcomputers in classrooms that will allow children in San Diego to send and receive electronic messages from children in Alaska. This exchange of messages gives us yet another way to bring social resources to the educational setting, broadening the range of peers available for children to draw upon for learning and problem solving. Microcomputer electronic message systems have tremendous implications for education, especially education in remote isolated areas, as they open up an immensely wider range of resources to previously limited educational settings.

Writing Game Worlds

A third direction is to develop various kinds of educational computer games that involve aspects of writing. "Adventure" worlds, in which the characters are words or letters, mystery games in which the secret lies buried in the "deep" structure of text, or action games for which the correct sequence of actions generates a message, are some examples we have been developing. For example, we have worked out the initial structure for a "word market" communication game (which would use the electronic message system described above). In this game, each player starts out owning certain words, and can communicate only using those words. However, a player can bargain with other players, trading surplus words for words needed to communicate.

SUMMARY

We started by constructing various kinds of dynamically supportive environments for writing, so that we could gather detailed data about the processes involved in writing, especially when writing problems occur. By using both keystroke data collected by the Writer's Assistant program and ethnographic notes collected by field observation, we have examined some aspects of writing expertise and the acquisition of these skills.

Many of the constructs of problem-solving research can be used to characterize expertise and problem-solving abilities in writing. Recent research on problem solving, especially in solving scientific problems, has focused on the multilevel representations that experts bring to bear in tackling problems. Other research on problem solving in everyday settings has pointed to the critical importance of external resources (Levin, 1981). The parallel between the Gestalt notion of "being blocked" in problem solving and the notion of "writer's block" is obvious. The power of the analogy is that it suggests using the construct of "conceptual reorganization" from the problem-solving domain for instructing writers on how to overcome writing blocks.

Our current efforts are focused on ways to construct writing environments that allow us to collect richer data on the writing processes. These data will, we hope, allow us to address more fully the issue of multiple levels of processing, the rich ways of using external resources, and the progressive acquisition of skills initially supplied by external resources in becoming an expert writer.

ACKNOWLEDGMENTS

Thanks to Allan Collins, Dedre Gentner, Marilyn Quinsaat, Bob Rowe, Andee Rubin, and Jose Vasconcellos for providing social resources for this project. Thanks to the Oceanside School District, especially the expert and novice writers in the C-2 classroom. Our thanks to Jean Lave, Bud Mehan, and Margaret Riel for comments on previous drafts.

REFERENCES

Brown, A. L., & Ferrara, R. A. Diagnosing zones of proximal development. In J. Wertsch (Ed.), *Culture, communication, and cognition: Vygotskian perspectives.* New York: Cambridge University Press, 1982.

Bruce, B., Collins, A., Rubin, A. D., & Gentner, D. Three perspectives on writing. *Educational Psychologist,* 1982, *17,* 131–145.

Chi, M. T. H., Feltovich, P. J., & Glaser, R. Categorization and representation of physics problems by experts and novices. *Cognitive Science,* 1981, *5,* 121–152.

Collins, A., & Gentner, D. A cognitive science framework for writing. In L. W. Gregg & E. Steinberg (Eds.), *Cognitive processes in writing: An interdisciplinary approach.* Hillsdale, New Jersey: Erlbaum, 1979.

Feuerstein, R. *The dynamic assessment of retarded performers: The learning potential assessment device, theory, instruments, and techniques.* Baltimore: University Park Press, 1979.

Hutchins, E. L., & Levin, J. A. Point of view in problem solving. *Proceedings of the Third Annual Conference of the Cognitive Science Society,* Berkeley, California, 1981.

Larkin, J. H., McDermott, J., Simon, D. P., & Simon, H. A. Expert and novice performance in solving physics problems. *Science,* 1980, *208,* 1335–1342.

Levin, J. A. Everyday problem solving. *Proceedings of The Third Annual Conference of the Cognitive Science Society,* Berkeley, California, 1981.

Levin, J. A., & Kareev, Y. Personal computers and education: The challenge to schools (CHIP Report 98). La Jolla, California: Center for Human Information Processing, 1980.

Papert, S., Watt, D., diSessa, A., & Weir, S. Final report of the Brookline LOGO Project. Pt. 2: Project summary and data analysis. (*LOGO Memo No.* 53) Cambridge, Massachusetts: Artificial Intelligence Laboratory, 1979.

Quinsaat, M. Q. *Implementing computer technology in classroom settings: An anecdotal report of long-term use.* Paper presented at the NIE Conference on implementing computer technology in classroom settings, Washington D. C., 1981.

Rubin, A. Making stories, making sense. *Language Arts,* 1980, 285–298.

Author Index

Numbers in italics show the page on which the complete reference is cited.

Subject Index

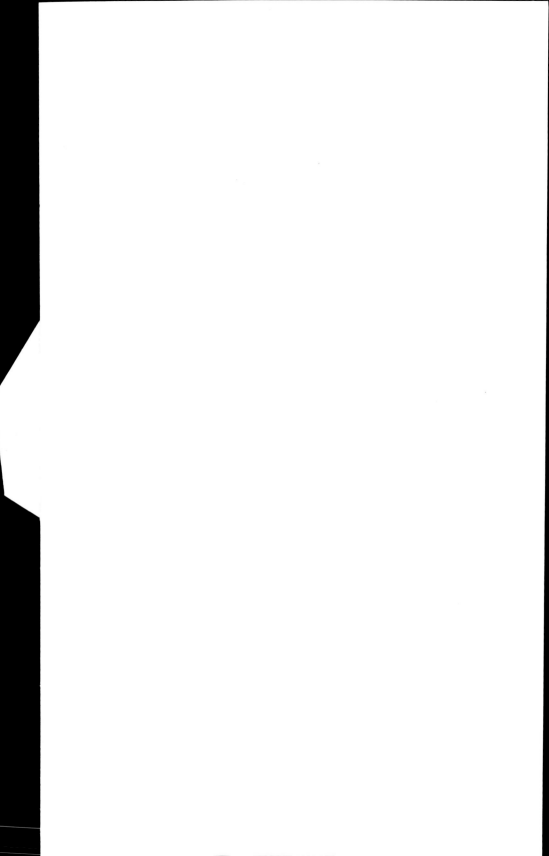

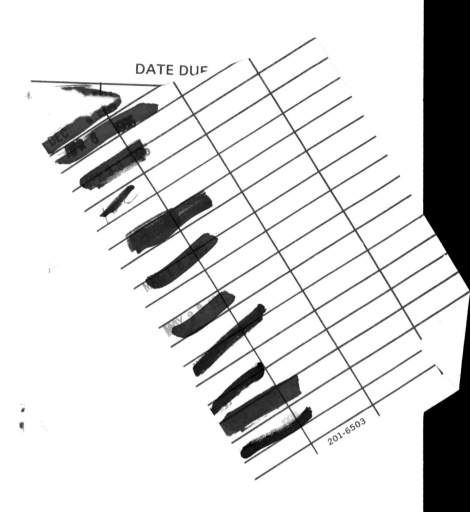

DATE DUE

201-6503